APPLIED LEISURE & TOURISM FOR GCSE

FOR ALL AWARD

FOR GCSE

ROB JONES

EDITED BY JACKIE DICKINSON

Acknowledgements

Page design: Caroline Waring Collins (Waring Collins Ltd)
Cover design: Tim Button (Waring Collins Ltd)
Graphic origination: John A Collins (Waring Collins Ltd)
Graphics: Kevin O'Brien (Waring Collins Ltd)
Consultancy and classroom testing: Claire Madeloso and students at Alsop High School
Special thanks: John A Collins

Picture credits

Andrew Allen 4 (tr), 7, 8 (br), 10 (tr and bl), 12 (bl), 13 (tr), 14 (tr), 16 (tl and br), 18 (tl and br), 19, 20 (mr), 22 (tr), 28 (br), 46, 52 (tr), 65 (mr and br), 66 (tr), 68 (br), 73 (mr), 76 (tl and br), 79 (l and r), 80 (br), 83, 93, 124 (bl), 140 (tr), 144 (bl), 145 (bl), 148 (br), 149 (ml), 152 (br), 153, 158 (tr and br), 161, 171, 205 (tr), 222; Blackpool Council 91; Camelot 37 (tr); Copthorne Hotel, Birmingham 71; Corel 8 (tl), 41 (br), 125 (bl); Eurocamp 88, 194 (br); Getty Images cover; Glynn Vivian Art Gallery 17 (bl); Grand Theatre, Swansea 199 (br); Greyhound pub 16 (tr); Heathcotes 124 (tr); JJB Sports 129 (br); Jackie Dickinson 53 (bl), 58 (m), 123, 202 (ml), 206 (mr), 213; John Collins 9 (br), 13 (br); Kate Haralambos 187; Madame Tussauds 20 (tr); Manchester Airport 126 (mr), 186 (br), 212 (bl); Metropolitan Borough of Wirral 15; PhotoDisc 8 (br), 12 (br), 47, 54 (br), 86 (tr), 166, 183, 14 (tr), 205 (tl), 212 (tl); Photofusion 9 (bl), 13 (tl and bl), 17 (tl), 48 (tl), 52 (br), 68 (mr), 96 (br), 116 (mr), 163, 174, 189, 206 (l), 212 (br); Plas y Brenin, the National Mountain Centre 23; Rex Features 10, 24, (bl), 28 (tr and bl), 32 (bl and br), 34 (br), 36 (l and r), 39, 43, 54 (tl), 61 (br), 62 (mr), 66 (bl), 80 (bl), 81 (b), 84 (tr), 96 (mr), 98 (br), 103, 107, 152 (mr), 175, 192 (ml and mr); Spirit Group 188 (tr); TopFoto 4 (br), 8 (tr), 12 (tr), 14 (mr), 16 (bl), 17 (tr), 20 (br), 21 (tr and br), 22 (mr and bl), 24 (tl, tr and bl), 25 (br), 26 (l and r), 27, 29 (tl, tr, bl and br), 30, 31, 33, 34 (bl), 35 (mr and br), 37 (bl), 38 (t and m), 40 (tl and br), 41 (tr and ml), 42 (tr and br), 44 (br), 48 (br), 49, 50, 53 (tl), 55, 58 (tr), 59, 60 (tl), 61 (tr and bl), 62 (bl), 64 (mr), 67, 68 (ml), 69 (br), 80 (tr), 81 (t), 84 (br), 85 (tl and br), 89, 98 (tr and mr), 132 (tl), 152 (ml), 154, 173 (tr), 184 (mr), 192 (br), 193, 199, 203, 215, 223.

Cartoons

The cartoons in this book have been specially drawn by Alan Fraser.

Every effort has been made to locate the copyright owners of material used in this book. Any omissions brought to the attention of the publisher are regretted and will be credited in subsequent printings.

British Library Cataloguing in Publication Data
A catalogue record for this book is available from the British Library.

ISBN 1 902 79687 X

Pearson Education
Edinburgh Gate, Harlow, Essex CM20 2JE

© Rob Jones

First impression 2005, Second impression 2007
Printed in China WC/02

Contents

What is the leisure industry?

Getting started...

When people are not at work or at school, they have time to themselves. Some of this time is spent sleeping, eating, shopping, washing and doing other essential everyday things. Any time left over after this is called leisure time. People can spend this time in a wide variety of ways. Look at the leisure activities below.

Watching TV

Eric Watson is fifteen. He spends three hours every evening watching television. Eric prefers indoor leisure activities because he likes to be at home.

Playing golf

Derek and Patricia Clark are both retired. They spend a lot of time together and their favourite leisure activity is golf. They enjoy golf because it keeps them fit and they like meeting other retired people at the golf club.

Watching football

Pauline Simmonds is sixteen and a keen football fan. She supports her local team, Stockport County, and goes to all the home matches. Pauline likes football because it is exciting and gives her a chance to be part of something.

Potholing

South Wales Caving Club

Eugene Adamowic is 27 and a software engineer. He works very hard, sometimes up to 50 hours a week. At the weekend, he enjoys the outdoor life. His favourite leisure activity is potholing which involves exploring caves and riverbeds that are deep underground.

(a) Name two other leisure activities that you think each of the people above might enjoy.
(b) Which of the people above have (i) the most (ii) the least, leisure time? Explain your answer.

The leisure industry

BUSINESSES	GOVERNMENT AND LOCAL AUTHORITIES	CLUBS AND SOCIETIES	NATURAL ENVIRONMENT

THE LEISURE INDUSTRY

PRODUCTS	FACILITIES	SERVICES	OPPORTUNITIES

The leisure industry provides products, facilities, services and opportunities for a wide range of different people. These are provided by various organisations or they exist because of the natural environment.

Businesses provide most of the things that people need to enjoy their leisure activities. For example, JJB Sports sells products that can be used to play sports such as football, cricket and golf. There are specialist shops that sell camping and skiing equipment, CDs, DVDs and computer games. Some businesses offer services such as restaurants, day trips, hotel accommodation and sun beds.

The government and local authorities provide a range of facilities and amenities that are available to everyone. Examples include leisure centres, swimming pools, parks, museums, galleries, libraries, community centres and sports halls. Some of these are provided free of charge.

Clubs and societies are set up by groups of people to provide opportunities and facilities for others to take up a particular leisure activity. For example, the Scout and Guide Associations provide opportunities for young people to enjoy activities such as camping and orienteering. Many communities set up sports clubs and enter teams into competitions and leagues. Any group of people can set up a club or society. This helps to share the costs and provides activities for other people.

The natural environment often provides the setting in which leisure activities are enjoyed. There are many different places of outstanding natural beauty in the UK which offer opportunities for outdoor activities such as camping, skiing, sailing, bird watching, swimming and climbing.

Growth in the leisure industry

Figure 1 *Total spending on recreation, culture, hotels and restaurants 1994-2002*

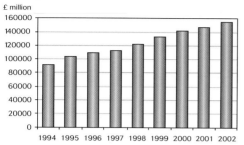

Figure 2 *Weekly earnings for men 1995-2003*

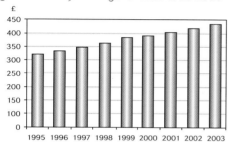

Figure 3 *Weekly earnings for women 1995-2003*

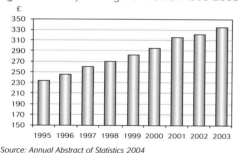

Source: Annual Abstract of Statistics 2004

Why has the leisure industry grown?

Figure 1 shows that spending on leisure has increased. The leisure industry has grown for a number of reasons.

○ People have more time to themselves because working hours have been reduced. The average working week has fallen from 45 hours in 1953 to around 37 hours in 2004.

○ People have more money to spend. Their incomes have increased and many living costs have fallen. Figures 2 and 3 show that weekly earnings for both men and women have increased in the period 1995 to 2003.

○ More people retire early. This means they do not have to work and can spend more time on leisure activities.

○ Technological advances in household equipment such as washing machines and dishwashers, have reduced the time spent on domestic chores.

○ More paid holidays allow people the time and money to spend on leisure.

How has the leisure industry changed over the last 20 years?

As well as huge growth in the leisure industry, there have been other changes too.

Developments in technology These have resulted in new leisure activities such as computer games, DVDs, surfing the Internet and texting on mobile phones. A home computer can be used to buy tickets for events, book holidays and arrange car hire.

Communications have improved More people now have cars, air travel reaches wider destinations and other transport systems have improved. This has given people greater access to leisure facilities.

Changes in tastes and fashion People change their tastes and follow new fashions all the time. Some new leisure activities include bungee jumping, skydiving and skateboarding. TV programmes have helped to make activities such as DIY, gardening and cooking increasingly popular.

Developments in business Businesses provide more leisure activities and have also created new ones – for example, out of town retail parks. There are more restaurants, fast food outlets, sports shops, fitness centres, garden centres, DIY stores, video shops and attractions than ever before. They use marketing and advertising to promote their products and services.

Some prices have fallen Many leisure activities are cheaper. For example, air travel, some sports equipment, computers, mobile phones and some restaurants. But some leisure costs are dearer such as Premier League football tickets and rail travel.

Quick quiz

1 **True or false?**

- ✪ Travelling to work is a leisure activity.
- ✪ A sports hall provided by the local council is a leisure facility.
- ✪ A private golf club that charges £2,000 for membership is not a leisure facility.

2 Which of these leisure activities might appeal most to a family with young children?

(a) Potholing **(b)** Paragliding **(c)** Trip to a safari park **(d)** White-water rafting

3 Which of these leisure activities is **not** likely to be provided by a club or society?

(a) Flower arranging **(b)** Chess **(c)** Holiday abroad **(d)** Rambling

4 Which of these are reasons for the growth in the leisure industry?

(a) More people work **(b)** Incomes have risen

(c) Paid holidays have increased **(d)** More people retire early

5 State two changes that have taken place in the leisure industry in the last 20 years.

Exam practice

The Jacobs Family

Mr and Mrs Jacobs have two children aged five and eight. A lot of their leisure time is spent together. On Saturday afternoons they often go to the cinema. On the way back, they go to a local pub that caters for children. They have a meal and some drinks.

On Saturday night when the children have gone to bed, Mr and Mrs Jacobs play Scrabble. Later in the evening they have an Indian take-away delivered. They also open a bottle of wine and usually watch a late-night film on the television.

On Sunday mornings, Mr Jacobs takes the two children swimming. Mrs Jacobs enjoys a couple of hours on her own, reading the newspaper.

1. (i) Look at Figure 4. Which age group pays most visits to the cinema? *(1 mark)*
   (ii) What does the graph tell you about the popularity of the cinema? *(1 mark)*
2. (i) State two ways in which pubs cater for children. *(2 marks)*
   (ii) Explain why pubs have started to cater for children in recent years. *(6 marks)*
3. Give examples of the organisations which might be providing the leisure activities enjoyed by the Jacobs family. *(7 marks)*

Figure 4 *Cinema visits by age*

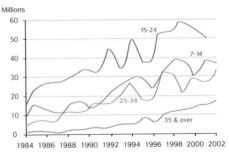

Children's play area

2 The key components of the leisure industry

Getting started...

The types of leisure activity that people enjoy fall into different categories. For example, people might enjoy DIY, cooking, gardening and reading. These are all home-based leisure activities. Look at the leisure activities below.

Enjoying history

Patti Smith is a student at Warwick University. She is studying history and loves the subject. In her leisure time, she enjoys visiting places of historical interest. Last month, she visited the Tower of London, Hadrian's Wall, and Warwick Castle.

The Tower of London

Eating and drinking

Jenny Thompson and her best friend Ellen Ramprakash both work for a travel agent in Cardiff. Every lunchtime they enjoy going to Caffè Nero for a coffee and a sandwich. On Friday and Saturday nights, they go out socialising in the local pubs, wine bars and nightclubs.

The theatre and music

Sourav Singh is a newspaper reporter. He lives in London and enjoys going to the theatre. His favourite play is *The Mousetrap* by Agatha Christie which he has seen seven times. Sourav also enjoys going to pop concerts. One of his favourite artists is Christina Aguilera.

Christina Aguilera at the MTV Music Awards

The outdoor life

Jim Collins is retired and lives on his own in Blackburn. He enjoys fly-fishing and visits a local trout fishery called The Stocks in the Forest of Bowland. He also likes walking and makes regular visits to the hills and moors in the surrounding area.

In which of the following categories would you place the above leisure activities?
- *Sport and physical recreation*
- *Visitor attractions* • *Arts and entertainment*
- *Countryside recreation* • *Catering*
- *Home-based leisure* • *Children's play activities*

Sport and physical recreation

Up to 30 million people in the UK take an active part in sport or physical recreation. The most popular activities for adults are walking and swimming and for children, swimming and cycling. The range of activities is huge. It includes badminton, bowling, croquet, fencing, fishing, golf, gymnastics, hockey, horse riding, netball, skating, squash, surfing, table tennis and windsurfing to name just a few.

Sport can be competitive, where teams or individuals play against each other to win, or it can be enjoyed as an activity in its own right. The advantages of sports and physical activities are that they:

✪ help to keep people fit and healthy
✪ help to build a person's character
✪ enable people to socialise
✪ enable people to take part in something such as a team.

Some people prefer to be spectators. They might go to venues and watch any of the sports mentioned above.

Arts and entertainment

The Government plays a big role in this area as it funds many of the UK's museums and art galleries. Examples of activities in this category include going to:

✪ the cinema to see a film
✪ a museum to see a historic display
✪ the theatre to see a play, concert, ballet, opera, or pantomime
✪ an art gallery to see an exhibition
✪ a nightclub or disco.

Table 1 below shows attendance at cultural events by the over 15 age group in 2002/03. The cinema is clearly the most popular.

Table 1 *Attendance at cultural events*

	Percentages
Cinema	61
Plays	24
Art galleries/exhibitions	24
Classical music	13
Ballet	7
Opera	7
Contemporary dance	5

Source: Office for National Statistics–adapted from Social Trends 34

Countryside recreation

Britain has a wide variety of rural landscapes and attractive countryside. Some examples include:

✪ The Scottish Highlands and Islands
✪ The Welsh Mountains
✪ The Lake District
✪ The Yorkshire Dales
✪ The New Forest.

The natural environment provides people with the opportunity to enjoy walking, rambling, cycling, climbing, potholing, orienteering, fell running, sailing, swimming, water-skiing, fishing, gliding and many other activities.

Fell walking

Home-based leisure

Everyone spends some of their leisure time at home. Watching television is the most popular activity. The development of cable, satellite and digital TV has increased the number of viewing channels that people can choose from. Playing computer games is the second most popular activity. Other activities include gardening, DIY, reading, entertaining friends, listening to the radio and to music, enjoying take-away meals and handicrafts.

Children's play activities

Children have a lot of leisure time and local authorities and organisations provide a wide range of activities to cater for them. These include public play areas where children can use swings, seesaws, slides and climbing frames. There are also adventure playgrounds, holiday play schemes, toddlers' clubs and crèches. Some large department stores and shopping malls provide supervised play areas where children can play in safety while their parents are shopping.

The advert below is for a drama school during the school holidays.

EASTER DRAMA SCHOOL
(IN PARTNERSHIP WITH EDGE HILL COLLEGE)

Monday – Wednesday : 10am – 4pm
Thursday : 1pm – 4pm

£35.00 for 1 person, £30.00 each for two or more people in the same immediate family

This year's Easter Drama School will be inspired by a performance of Andrew's Angry Words by M6 Theatre Company. The young people will also devise thier own piece of theatre, which they will perform for friends and family on the last day.

The Drama School will not just keep everyone busy for the week; it will also mean lots of fun, new friends and the acquisition of some nifty acting skills.

Suitable for 8 – 12 year olds

If you would like to book onto the Easter Drama School please call 01695 584480 and we will send you an application form.

Catering

Places to eat and drink are part of the catering industry. Nearly two million people are employed in this industry and it is worth around £50 billion per year. Businesses provide nearly all the pubs, bars, wine bars, restaurants, hotels, bistros, fast-food outlets and cafés where people eat and drink. Eating out has become a very popular leisure activity. The choice available is huge and still growing.

Visitor attractions

Visitor attractions provide opportunities for groups, families and individuals to enjoy a day out. They may be places of interest, places of outstanding natural beauty or a purpose built attraction such as a theme park. Some of them are free to visit, such as a museum, but many others charge an entrance fee. Other examples of visitor attractions include:

- cathedrals
- zoos
- castles
- leisure parks
- historic sites
- steam railways
- botanical gardens
- stately homes.

A stately home

Interrelation between components

Some of the leisure activities mentioned so far fall into more than one of the key components. Some examples are given below.

- Football is a sport which people play but others might just watch it on TV at home.
- Horse riding can be classed as both a sport and a countryside recreation activity.
- Gardening is home-based but it is also a physical activity.
- Ronnie Scott's is a famous jazz club in London but it also provides dining facilities.
- Alton Towers is a popular visitor attraction but also provides a range of catering facilities.
- A visitor attraction like the National Gallery is also a facility for enjoying the arts.

The provision of catering facilities is a common development in nearly all of the key leisure activities.

Quick quiz

1 **True or false?**

- ✪ The arts can be enjoyed at a museum.
- ✪ Dudley Zoo is a visitor attraction.
- ✪ Computer games would fall into the sport and physical recreation component.

2 Match these three activities with the key components (a) to (e).

- ✪ Tenpin bowling
- ✪ Camping in the Yorkshire Dales
- ✪ Watching a video

(a) Home-based leisure
(b) Sport and physical recreation
(c) Arts and entertainment
(d) Countryside recreation
(e) Catering

3 Give two examples of children's play activities

Exam practice

A Day Trip to London

Peter and Jenny Hoggard are twins. On their seventeenth birthday, they were given £60 each to spend on a day out in London.

They planned to visit the British Museum in the morning, take a flight on the London Eye at 1pm and then go to a football match at White Hart Lane, the home of Tottenham Hotspur, in the afternoon.

Entrance to the British Museum was free and the match tickets were £30 each.

After their flight on the London Eye, they had a light lunch at Costa Coffee.

Peter and Jenny each bought a hotdog at half-time from a vendor at the football match.

Talking about the trip on the way home, Jenny said, 'The Japanese Arts exhibition at the British Museum was seriously brilliant'. Peter thought the London Eye was cool. They could see for 25 miles and were able to spot Windsor Castle and the Palace of Westminster. Unfortunately, their team lost to Fulham in the afternoon so the day ended on a bit of a low note.

1. Approximately how many visitors did the most popular site shown in Figure 1 attract? *(2 marks)*
2. Which of the leisure activities enjoyed by Peter and Jenny falls into the following components?
   (i) Sport and physical recreation
   (ii) Visitor attractions *(2 marks)*
3. (i) How much did Jenny and Peter have to pay for their flight on the London Eye? *(1 mark)*
   (ii) Explain why you think admission to the museum was free. *(4 marks)*
4. Discuss which of the activities enjoyed by Peter and Jenny might be interrelated. *(7 marks)*

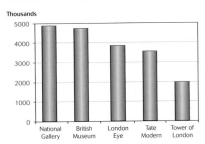

Figure 1 *Top five tourist attractions in London: number of visits 2001*

Source: Annual Abstract of Statistics 2004

The London Eye - 2004 Prices	
Adult	£11.50
*Senior (60 plus years)	£9.00
*Student (with valid NUS or ISIC card)	£9.00
Child (5-15 years)	£5.75
Must be accompanied by an adult aged 18 years or older	
Under fives	FREE
Fast Track	£25.00

Book online now to save 5%.
*Subject to conditions

3 Local leisure facilities 1

Getting started...

Some facilities provided by the leisure industry are local facilities such as health clubs, restaurants and cafés. This means that they are provided mainly for local communities. But there are also national leisure facilities which often attract very large numbers of visitors from all over the country, and sometimes the world. National facilities are often unique. Some examples include Alton Towers, Buckingham Palace and Legoland. Look at the facilities below.

The Eden Project

The Eden Project in Cornwall is a fairly new attraction. It is described as a living theatre of plants and people. It is built in a 50 metre crater and contains three climate zones, two of which are built in biomes (giant conservatories).

Humid Tropics Biome – has tropical plant life and rainforests from places such as Malaysia and West Africa.

Warm Temperate Biome – has plant life that can survive in droughts and poor soil such as olive trees and vines from the Mediterranean and South Africa.

The Outdoor Landscape – has a fabulous range of plants from India to Chile that rub shoulders alongside the native flora of Cornwall.

The aim of the Eden Project is to create a spectacular theatre in which to tell the story of human dependence on plants. In its first year it attracted 1.91 million visitors.

The Eden Project

The Oxford Arms

The Oxford Arms is a public house in Kirtlington, a small village near Oxford. It sells the usual range of wines, spirits, cask ales, lager and soft drinks. It also serves food and recently began to open in the mornings to provide breakfasts. Most of its trade is from regulars that live in the village but it also enjoy a bit of passing trade from traffic on the busy A4095.

A village pub

The Horwich Tennis Club

The Horwich Tennis Club has 130 members, all of whom live within a 6 mile radius. The club owns four grass and two clay courts. It is located on the outskirts of Horwich, a small town near Bolton. It is open every day in the summer but only at weekends in the winter. It has a bar but only serves a limited range of drinks and light snacks. Non-members cannot use the facility although members can sign in two guests.

Decide whether these facilities are local or national. Give reasons for your answer.

Leisure centres

Leisure centres are found in towns and cities. They are usually run by Local Authorities and they charge for their facilities. People can often become members and get discounts. One typical example is the Dudley Leisure Centre in the West Midlands. It caters for all age groups and has two swimming pools; a four court sports hall for badminton, basketball, volleyball, netball and other uses; five squash courts with a viewing gallery; multipurpose areas for martial arts, aerobics and meetings; a dome with an artificial pitch for five-a-side football and some sun beds.

Aerobics class in a leisure centre

Health clubs

Health clubs, or fitness clubs, are also found in towns and cities. They tend to be smaller than leisure centres and are usually run as businesses. Dragons Health Club, for example, owns 21 health clubs around the country. It provides facilities for swimming, squash, aerobics and gymnastics. There are also classes for yoga, step, stretch, aerobics and a bar area for socialising. Such clubs can be expensive. For example, the Bedford Dragons Health Club charges £48 per month for full membership. They also exclude children below the age of 16.

Dragons Health Club, Southport

Swimming pools

Swimming is the most popular leisure activity for children. Many of the country's swimming pools have been developed into full-scale leisure centres. However, many towns and cities still have local swimming pools. Pools can also be found in some schools and universities, although access to these is likely to be restricted to pupils and students. Swimming is a cheap leisure activity and is often available for less than £1.

Sports grounds

Local Authorities provide many of the facilities for playing outdoor sports such as football, rugby, cricket and hockey. Villages often have a plot of land set aside for a football pitch, which doubles as a cricket square in the summer. Cities usually have large plots of land set aside where there might be a dozen or more pitches. Changing rooms and other facilities tend to be fairly limited though.

Sports clubs

There are sports clubs in many communities which are often set up by local people. Over time, they develop their own facilities with money from subscriptions and fund-raising activities. They often enter teams in local leagues and provide training and coaching facilities for members. Some of the bigger clubs also have social facilities such as a bar, meeting rooms, dance floors and pool tables. Football, cricket, rugby league, rugby union, hockey, bowls and tennis often have their own clubs – sometimes with shared facilities.

A village cricket club

Local community centres

Community centres are set up all over the country. There are thousands of them providing meeting places and facilities for a wide range of people of all ages. Some are aimed at specific groups, such as youth clubs for teenagers. Others provide facilities for leisure classes in such things as cooking, learning a language or martial arts. They may be purpose built and provided cheaply by Local Authorities or based in public buildings such as schools and churches.

Parks

Many towns and cities have parks. Some are very spacious and might contain tennis courts, football pitches, cricket squares, pitch and putt and even a golf course. Others are much smaller and provide some open space and woodlands for walking, children's playgrounds and perhaps a lake or pond. Parks provide a place where city and town dwellers can enjoy some fresh air and open space.

A city park

Gardens

Some parks are very well kept and have garden areas where a range of lawns, plants and shrubs are grown. These are often quiet areas and offer seating facilities where people can sit and relax in the fresh air. Well-kept public gardens might also be found in towns and cities.

Country Parks

A Country Park is an area for people to visit and enjoy recreation in a countryside environment. It provides somewhere for people who do not necessarily want to go out into the wider countryside. Country Parks tend to be less formal than urban parks. Some have facilities, such as a car park, toilets, a café or kiosk, paths and trails, and information for visitors. Others have more, with museums, visitor centres, educational facilities, historic buildings and working farms. There are about 250 Country Parks in England and Wales.

Quick quiz

1. Which of the following is **not** likely to have a leisure centre?
   (a) City **(b)** Village **(c)** Town **(d)** Urban community

2. Which of the following is **not** likely to be provided by a city leisure centre?
   (a) 18-hole golf course **(b)** Badminton courts **(c)** Volleyball court
   (d) Five-a-side football pitch

3. Which of the following is **not** a local leisure facility?
   (a) Hesketh Park **(b)** Cannock Hockey Club **(c)** Islip Youth Club
   (d) NEC Birmingham

4. State two examples of leisure facilities that Local Authorities might provide.

5. Why might a rugby club and a football club share facilities?

6. State one difference between a health club and a leisure centre.

7. What age groups do community centres cater for?

Exam practice

The Wirral parks and countryside areas

The Wirral, in North West England, has three country parks, four local nature reserves and nine other local parks and countryside areas. It also has a number of beaches, four municipal golf courses (open to the general public) and ten private golf courses.

Arrowe Country Park

Arrowe Country Park is the largest park on the Wirral. Two thirds of it is open parkland and woodland containing trees such as oak, ash, beech, Scots pine, cedar and Indian Bean. The woodland birds include rooks, magpies, jays, nuthatches, tree creepers and greater and lesser-spotted woodpeckers. The park also has a toddlers' play area, a children's adventure playground, an 18-hole golf course, facilities for pitch and putt, tennis, bowls, football, angling and orienteering, and a horse track. It also provides some catering facilities for golfers.

1. Into which two components in the leisure industry might the facilities described above fall? *(2 marks)*
2. What does the map show about Birkenhead Park? *(3 marks)*
3. Using Arrowe Park as an example, explain what is meant by a Country Park. *(4 marks)*
4. Are the Wirral's parks and countryside areas local or national facilities? Give reasons for your answer. *(7 marks)*

Birkenhead Park

Birkenhead Park, Wirral, was designed by Sir Joseph Paxton. It was opened in 1847 and was the world's first ever public park.

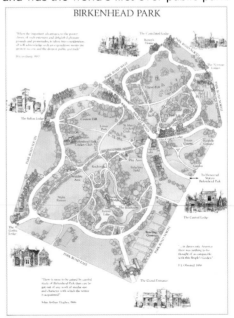

BIRKENHEAD PARK

4 Local leisure facilities 2

Getting started...

People who live in rural locations, such as villages and farms, are likely to enjoy different leisure activities to those living in towns and cities. For example, they may spend a lot of their time using countryside recreational facilities. Many local facilities are only available in towns and cities so if rural residents want to enjoy them, they have to travel. Look at the leisure facilities below.

Blockbuster

Blockbuster rents and sells in-home movies and games entertainment. It has over 700 stores in the UK and its aim is to keep reinventing the 'great night in'. Blockbuster also has a web site where videos, DVDs and games can be bought online. Blockbuster stores are found in most towns and cities.

easyCinema

The first easyCinema opened in Milton Keynes in 2002. It is a 'no-frills' way to watch a film. Seats for advance, online and off-peak bookings can cost as little as 20p. The multiplex has 10 screens but no box office. It does not sell refreshments so you have to take your own.

Point Cinema, Milton Keynes

Which of these local facilities are unlikely to be available outside towns and cities? Explain why not.

The Greyhound

The Greyhound pub is located next to the church in Saxton, North Yorkshire. It is an attractive 13th century, Grade II listed building. It has a cosy bar with a flagged floor and serves Samuel Smith's Old Best Bitter. A colourful plate collection decorates the pub walls and, during the summer, locals enjoy drinks outside surrounded by climbing roses and plants.

The Greyhound, Saxton, North Yorkshire

Frankie & Benny's

Frankie & Benny's is a restaurant chain owned by City Centre Restaurants plc. The restaurant theme is described as a New York  Italian restaurant and bar. There are over 80 of these restaurants in the UK. In 2003, the business had revenue of £64.6 million.

16

Libraries

Reading can be enjoyed by all age groups and most communities have a library. Rural areas are often served by a mobile library. Libraries today provide a lot more than books and their services are provided free by local councils. However, you have to become a member before taking books out.

Croydon, in Greater London, has 13 libraries. One of these is the Central Library located in the town centre. It is a state-of-the-art public facility and offers books, CDs, DVDs, videos, newspapers and magazines. It also provides enquiry services, community information, a children's library, a local studies library and archives service, free access to PCs (including the Internet) and study areas.

Museums

All cities and many towns have local museums. They usually have collections and exhibitions of historic events and past life in the local area. Derby has three museums, one of which is described below.

Derby Industrial Museum

Derby Industrial Museum is on the site of the world's oldest factory - the Silk Mills built by George Sorocold in 1702 and 1717. The foundations

Rolls Royce jet engine

and parts of the tower from the 1717 mill can still be seen. The displays tell the story of the industrial heritage and achievements of Derby and its people. A special feature is about the development of Rolls Royce aero-engines. Other displays show local industries such as the railways, mining, pottery and foundry work.

Galleries

Local galleries, like local museums, are found in towns and cities. The exhibitions vary across the country and often display work by local artists. One typical example is the Glynn Vivian Art Gallery in Swansea.

Glynn Vivian Art Gallery

Swansea's Glynn Vivian Art Gallery contains traditional art, modern art and sculpture, as well as an international collection of porcelain and Swansea china. Painting and sculpture by Hepworth, Nicholson and Nash are displayed alongside local Welsh artists.

The Glynn Vivian Art Gallery

Theatres

Local theatres are used to provide live entertainment to local communities. Some theatres are used by local amateur groups to put on plays, musicals and dramas. They are also used as venues for touring productions. The adverts below are for some attractions at Southport Theatre.

Cinemas

Cinema-going is currently very popular and attendance figures have risen steadily in the last 20 years. In 2003, there were 167 million visits. Some of the top box office attractions were *The Matrix Reloaded*, *Lord of the Rings* and *Calendar Girls*. Modern cinema complexes, with 20 or more screens, can show a range of films all at the same time. This helps to cater for all age groups and tastes.

UCI multiplex cinema, Preston

Video rental shops

Many people enjoy watching DVD and video films at home. The growth in video rental shops allows people to rent a wide range of films. Global Video plc is the second largest video rental company in the UK. It has 250 shops and claims to stock more copies of new releases than any of its competitors. Many video rental shops are located close to take-away restaurants and off-licenses. This makes it easy for people who want to enjoy a film, a take-away meal and a drink at home. Figure 1 shows the VHS and DVD video rental shares by genre in 2002.

Figure 1 *VHS and DVD video rental in 2002*

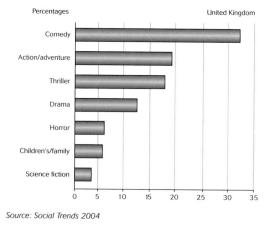

Source: *Social Trends 2004*

Restaurants

Eating out has become a very popular leisure activity. The restaurant industry offers a huge range of choices. A few examples are summarised below including restaurants that also offer a take-away service.

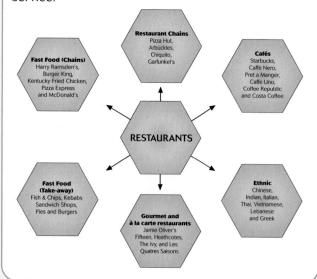

Public houses

Traditionally, pubs sold beer, wines and spirits and the main customers were men. Today, Britain's 65,000 pubs aim a variety of services at everyone, including families. They also offer a much wider range of drinks and most serve food. Many of today's pubs and bars, belong to chains such as Wetherspoon's, Pubmaster, Yates', Rat and Parrot, and Slug and Lettuce.

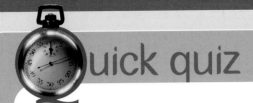

uick quiz

(1) **True or false?**

✪ Most villages have a cinema and a museum.

✪ Comedy was the most popular category of DVD and video rental in 2002.

✪ Harry Ramsden's is an example of an ethnic restaurant.

✪ Library services are free.

(2) State two examples of restaurant chains.

(3) State two types of entertainment showing at Southport Theatre in May/June 2004.

(4) Which of the following is **not** a local leisure facility?
(a) Pizza Express **(b)** Wollaton Library **(c)** Camelot **(d)** The Kings Head, Tackley

Exam practice

Coffee Bars

In recent years, coffee bars have increased in popularity. There has also been a growth in the number of coffee bars provided by chains such as Starbucks, Coffee Republic, Costa Coffee and Caffè Nero. The bar chart in Figure 2 shows approximately how many stores each chain had in 2003.

Costa Coffee was set up by the Italian brothers, Sergio and Bruno Costa in 1971. They started by selling roasted coffee to caterers and Italian coffee shops. The first Costa Coffee bar opened in London in 1978. The business grew and it now has around 300 bars. It has also opened bars in some selected retail outlets, including Waterstone's bookstores, W H Smith, Homebase, Marriott Hotels and Middlesex Hospital. Recently, Costa has also opened coffee bars inside some branches of the Abbey National Bank bringing customers the first ever coffee bar in a bank.

Figure 2 *Number of outlets (approx) for four leading coffee bars 2003*

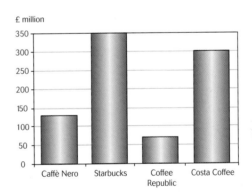

1. Which coffee bar has the most outlets? *(1 mark)*
2. What sort of refreshments do coffee bars such as Costa Coffee offer? *(3 marks)*
3. (i) Explain why coffee bars are local leisure facilities. *(3 marks)*
   (ii) State two reasons why people might use a coffee bar such as Costa Coffee. *(2 marks)*
4. Costa Coffee has set up shops in retail outlets. Discuss whether setting up in (i) libraries and (ii) cinemas, would be an advantage. *(7 marks)*

5 National leisure facilities – recreation centres

Getting started...

National leisure facilities aim to attract visitors from all over the country. Many also appeal to overseas visitors. Britain has an impressive mixture of historic sites and buildings, national museums and galleries, world-class sports facilities, theme parks and other modern attractions. Look at the national facilities below.

Calendar events

The UK has an impressive record for hosting many of the world's most renowned calendar events. Examples include the:

- All England Tennis Championship at Wimbledon.
- London Marathon
- FA Cup Final
- World Snooker Championship at the Crucible Theatre, Sheffield
- British Open Golf Championship at Royal Birkdale Golf Club, Southport
- British Formula 1 Grand Prix at the Silverstone Circuit, Northamptonshire.

These events can be staged because the UK has high quality national facilities.

Royal Birkdale Golf Club

Madame Tussauds

Madam Tussaud's Waxworks is located in London. It is an exhibition of wax models of famous people such as film stars, sports people, politicians and pop stars. Visitors can mingle with the models and pose for photographs alongside them. The visit is enhanced by visual images which are projected around the auditorium. In 2000, 2,388,000 people visited Madame Tussauds.

A waxwork of Beyoncé

Windsor Castle

Windsor Castle, the largest and oldest occupied castle in the world, is one of the Queen's official residences. The castle is 900 years old and covers an area of 13 acres. It contains a royal palace, a chapel and the homes and workplaces of castle workers. Some of the finest works of art from the Royal Collection can be seen including paintings by Rembrandt, Rubens and Gainsborough.

Windsor Castle

(a) Explain why these facilities are national leisure facilities.
(b) Which of the facilities are likely to attract:
  (i) a family with three young children
  (ii) a group of students studying sports science
  (iii) a young couple with an interest in fine art and history?

Recreation centres

Britain has a number of recreation centres. These are sports training grounds or centres of excellence. They are used by the nation's leading sports people and are homes to many national sports bodies. But groups wishing to use them can also book their facilities. The map below shows their locations.

National Sports Centres

Key

1. Lilleshall National Sports Centre, Shropshire
2. Holme Pierrepont National Water Sports Centre, Nottingham
3. Bisham Abbey National Sports Centre, Buckinghamshire
4. Crystal Palace National Sports Centre, London
5. Glenmore Lodge, Aviemore
6. Plas y Brenin National Mountain Centre, Snowdonia

Bisham Abbey - Buckinghamshire

Bisham Abbey is 800 years old and was mentioned in the Doomsday Book. Henry VIII and the exiled Elizabeth I stayed there. These days, it is the training centre for England's football and hockey teams and home to the Lawn Tennis Association, British Amateur Weight Lifting Association, British Judo Association and the English Hockey Association. In 2004, Her Royal Highness, the Princess Royal, opened a £10 million redevelopment at the Abbey.

England players training at Bisham Abbey

Bisham Abbey – Facilities

Seven outdoor floodlit tennis courts

Four indoor tennis courts

Nine-hole par 3 golf course

Three clay tennis courts

Group training studio

One grass tennis court

Harper's Fitness Club

Floodlit artificial turf pitch

Two football pitches

Sailing school

One rugby pitch

Weightlifting competition hall

Two squash courts

Bar, catering and function facilities

Seven conference & banqueting rooms

44 Bedrooms (94 beds)

Crystal Palace - London

The 100 metres at Crystal Palace

Crystal Palace National Sports Centre is one of the largest centres in the country. It is situated in 200 acres of parkland in South East London, just 10 miles from the city. A world famous venue for athletics, Crystal Palace is also home to the Amateur Swimming Association, Amateur Boxing Association, London Towers Basketball Team and British Weightlifting Association.

Crystal Palace – Facilities

Athletics stadium - floodlit 400m eight lane track with warm up areas and central grass area for football, rugby and American football plus seating for 16,500
2 dedicated weight training rooms
2 synthetic artificial turf pitches
Covered practice area
Grass Pitch
4 tennis courts (also used for netball)
4 swimming pools
Indoor track - with jump and pole vaulting areas

Multi-purpose indoor arena with seating for 2,100
4 badminton Courts
5 squash courts
2 training halls
Boxing hall
Group training studio
Harper's fitness club
Climbing wall
3 conference/meeting rooms
86 bedrooms
Bar, catering and function rooms

Glenmore Lodge – Aviemore

Glenmore Lodge is situated in Glenmore Forest, Aviemore, Scotland. Opened in 1995, it has built up a reputation as one of the premier mountain training centres in the world. It provides high quality training courses for instructors in outdoor activities such as mountaineering, climbing, skiing and canoeing. The main attractions at the Lodge are the magnificent mountains, rivers, forests and lochs of the Scottish Highlands. It also has:

- an artificial ski slope
- fitness room
- swimming pool
- climbing wall
- accommodation
- licensed bar.

Scottish Highlands

Holme Pierrepont – Nottingham

The National Water Sports Centre at Holme Pierrepont is located in 270 acres of country parkland, 3 miles from Nottingham on the River Trent. Its main feature is the Regatta Lake with adjustable start positions, timing and commentary boxes, starter's tower, judging and course control tower, electronic scoreboard, photo-finish and electronic timing equipment. The Amateur Rowing Association, British Canoe Union, British Water Ski Association and the English Table Tennis Association, all have a base at the Centre.

Holme Pierrepont

Holme Pierrepont – Facilities

Regatta lake	Multi -purpose sports hall	35 Bedrooms (78 beds)
Canoe slalom course	Fitness training centre	Bar, catering and function facilities
Water ski lagoon - includes cable tow	Six conference & banqueting rooms	

Lilleshall – near Telford

Lilleshall National Sports Centre can cater for nearly all types of sports, from recreational to international and Olympic standard. The Centre's facilities are used by major national sporting associations such as British Gymnastics, the Football Association and the England & Wales Cricket Board. They are also available to the local community.

Premier League players at Lilleshall

Lilleshall – Facilities

4 winter pitches with floodlights	5 squash courts
4 summer pitches	Weight training room
1 floodlit match pitch	Bowls lawn
1 full size water based artificial pitch with floodlights	Studio hall
	Cricket/archery facilities
2 indoor five-a-side areas	8 badminton courts
4 outdoor tennis courts	Chapters restaurant
3 grass tennis courts	15 conference and
Gymnastics training hall	banqueting rooms
2 multi-purpose sports halls	Bar, catering and
Specialist gymnasium	function rooms
2 basketball/netball courts	80 bedrooms

Quick quiz

1. Which of the following National Sports Centres is used mainly for water sports?
   (a) Lilleshall **(b)** Glenmore Lodge **(c)** Holme Pierrepont **(d)** Crystal Palace

2. Which of the following National Sports Centres is famous for athletics?
   (a) Bisham Abbey **(b)** Glenmore Lodge **(c)** Holme Pierrepont **(d)** Crystal Palace

3. Which of the following National Sports Centres is located in Scotland?
   (a) Bisham Abbey **(b)** Glenmore Lodge **(c)** Crystal Palace

4. State three indoor sports that could be played at Lilleshall.

5. State three water sports that can be enjoyed at Holme Pierrepont.

6. State three outdoor activities that could be enjoyed at Glenmore Lodge.

7. State three outdoor sports that could be played at Bisham Abbey.

Exam practice

Plas y Brenin

Plas y Brenin, the National Mountain Centre, is in Snowdonia, Wales. It is an area of high mountains and rivers. Activities enjoyed here include summer and winter hill walking, rock climbing, mountaineering, skiing, abseiling, orienteering, raft building, kayaking and canoeing. The Centre offers a wide range of residential and day instruction courses in all of these activities. Facilities at the centre include:

Plas y Brenin Mountain Centre

- **Equipment Hire** Equipment such as boots, ice axes, crampons and rucksacks can be hired.
- **Canoe Pool** This warm indoor pool is designed to teach canoeing skills such as rolling.
- **Climbing Wall** A state of the art indoor climbing gym with an 11 metre high climbing tower offering lead and top rope climbing.
- **Training Wall** This is smaller than the main climbing wall and is designed for introducing novices to climbing, teaching about climbing and rope work.
- **Ski Slope** This has a variety of slope angles and features, button lift, full mist system for faster, smoother skiing and floodlighting.
- **The Snowdon Bar** A good drinking and eating room with a view of the Snowdon Horseshoe.

Canoeing at Plas y Brenin

- **Self-catering accommodation** Two cottages with up to 16 beds in each.

1. Where in Wales is Plas y Brenin? *(1 mark)*
2. State three outdoor activities that can be enjoyed at the centre. *(3 marks)*
3. What is the difference between the climbing wall and the training wall at Plas y Brenin? *(4 marks)*
4. Using Plas y Brenin and other examples from this unit, explain the purpose of national recreation centres. *(7 marks)*

National leisure facilities – sports venues

Getting started...

In the UK, there is a lot of interest in sport. England won the Football World Cup in 1966 and the Rugby World Cup in 2003. In 2004, the England and Wales cricket team retained the Wisden Trophy, beating the West Indies 3-0. This was the first time that the team had won in the West Indies since 1968. Around the UK there is a variety of world-class sporting stadiums and venues. Look at the venues below.

Villa Park

Villa Park is home to the Premier League football club Aston Villa. It is located in Aston, Birmingham about three miles from the M6 motorway. The stadium has a capacity of 43,000 and, in most years, it is used to host the FA Cup semi-final. In 2002, Villa Park staged an international match between England and Portugal.

Villa Park stadium

Murrayfield

Murrayfield stadium, Edinburgh, is home to the Scottish Rugby Union and the Scottish Claymores American football team. The stadium was first opened in 1925 and now has a capacity of 67,500. Other events staged at Murrayfield include pop concerts, Highland Games, lacrosse and hockey matches.

Murrayfield stadium

The Crucible Theatre

The Crucible Theatre is part of Sheffield Theatres, the largest theatre complex outside London. It is famous for staging the Embassy World Snooker Champion- ship which was first held there in 1977.

World Snooker Final at The Crucible Theatre

It is now snooker's premier venue. The Crucible holds less than 1,000 spectators and has a unique atmosphere because the audience is seated close to the snooker tables.

Which sports are played at each of the venues above and what is the capacity of each venue?

Wimbledon

Wimbledon Tennis Championships

The most famous tennis event in the world is held every year at Wimbledon, which can hold 35,000 spectators. The Lawn Tennis Championships have developed from the garden party atmosphere of the first meeting in 1877, which was only watched by a few hundred spectators, to a highly professional tournament now attracting over 500,000 people.

International sports venues in the UK

The map below shows the main international venues for a range of sports in the UK.

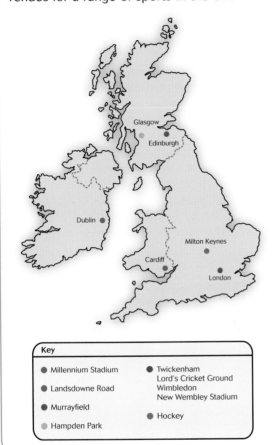

Key

- Millennium Stadium
- Landsdowne Road
- Murrayfield
- Hampden Park

- Twickenham
  Lord's Cricket Ground
  Wimbledon
  New Wembley Stadium
- Hockey

National soccer stadiums

The UK has some of the best soccer stadiums in the world.

Hampden Park

Hampden Park, Glasgow, is home to Queens Park FC and the Scottish National football team. It has a capacity of 52,000 and is classed as a 5 Star stadium by UEFA, football's European governing body. It also houses the world's first national football museum.

Windsor Park

Located in Belfast, Windsor Park is owned by Linfield FC. It has a capacity of 20,332. The Northern Ireland national side use it for their international home matches. There are plans to expand and redevelop the stadium but negotiations between the football, rugby, and athletics bodies about its future use, are causing delays.

The 'New' Wembley

England's international stadium was the world famous Wembley. This was where England won the World Cup in 1966. The old stadium was demolished in 2003 and a new one is now being built. It is expected to cost at least £750 million and will have a capacity of 90,000. Construction work is on schedule and it is expected to open in 2006.

Recent soccer stadium developments

After a number of tragic incidents, such as the Hillsborough disaster in 1989 when 96 Liverpool fans were killed, it was recommended by the Taylor Report that football stadiums should be all-seater. As a result, many top division stadiums were redeveloped and several new stadiums were also built. These include The Stadium of Light in Sunderland, St Mary's Stadium, Southampton and The Reebok Stadium, Bolton. Most top division stadiums now offer modern facilities such as restaurants, bars, souvenir shops, hospitality suites, ISDN links and conference rooms. They also welcome visitors and many organise stadium tours.

Construction of the new Wembley Stadium

Principal Premiership Stadiums

Club	Ground	Capacity	Location
Arsenal	Highbury	38,900	London
Aston Villa	Villa Park	43,000	Birmingham
Chelsea	Stamford Bridge	42,500	London
Liverpool	Anfield	45,362	Liverpool
Manchester Utd	Old Trafford	67,700	Manchester
Newcastle Utd	St James Park	52,000	Newcastle

National rugby stadiums

Every year, England, Scotland, Ireland and Wales compete in the Six Nations Rugby Championships. Each country has its own national rugby stadium.

Landsdowne Road

Landsdowne Road in Dublin is Ireland's national stadium. It is an old stadium and has a capacity of 48,000. It hosts both rugby and football internationals and various other events. For example, Robbie Williams and U2 have both held concerts there in recent years.

Millennium Stadium

Since opening in 1999, the £130 million stadium has received a lot of favourable publicity. It has special features - a fully retractable roof and two huge suspended screens, one at each end. The stadium has a capacity of 72,000 and is located on the banks of the River Taff, right in the centre of Cardiff. The Welsh Rugby Union and Football teams play their home fixtures here. The stadium also hosts the Rugby League Challenge Cup Final and is currently staging the English Domestic cup finals until the new Wembley Stadium is opened.

Cricket match at the Millennium Stadium

Twickenham

Twickenham is the home of England rugby union and is located about 12 miles south west of central London. The stadium currently holds 75,000 but a new South Stand is planned which will increase the capacity to 82,000. The new development also includes a 200 bed hotel, a health and leisure club, a restaurant, a shop, residential flats, and a conference and exhibition centre with basement parking for 200 vehicles.

Cricket grounds

England plays a number of international cricket matches every summer. For example, in 2004 New Zealand played three test matches and the West Indies four. The fixtures were played at a number of grounds around the country.

Lord's

Lord's, the 'home of cricket', is located in St John's Wood, London and has a capacity of 28,000. It is also the home of Middlesex County Cricket Club. Lord's is owned by the Marylebone Cricket Club (MCC) which is the guardian of The Laws of Cricket – the rules which govern the game. In addition to catering facilities, Lord's provides settings for the MCC Indoor School, the MCC Library, and the world-famous MCC Museum.

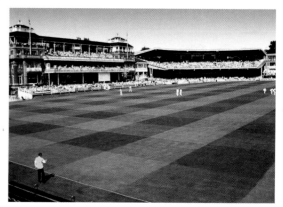

Lord's cricket ground

Other Test Match venues

Ground	Capacity	Location
Edgbaston	17,500	Birmingham
Headingley	14,000	Leeds
Old Trafford	19,000	Manchester
The Oval	18,500	London
Trent Bridge	15,350	Nottingham

Hockey

The National Hockey Stadium, opened in 1996, is based at Milton Keynes. It has a capacity of 10,000 and currently provides a temporary home to Wimbledon Football Club. The Stadium prides itself on being one of the UK's best conference and banqueting centres.

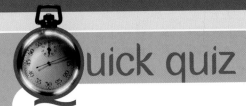

Quick quiz

1 **True or false?**

- ✪ Wimbledon is the home of the National Hockey Stadium.
- ✪ Old Trafford, home of Manchester United, has the largest Premier League stadium.
- ✪ Murrayfield is the home of Scottish football.

2 Match the venues with the sports in the box.

- ✪ Twickenham
- ✪ Lord's
- ✪ Hampden Park

Football	Snooker
Tennis	Cricket
Rugby Union	Golf

3 Apart from Lord's, state three other grounds where England plays test cricket.

Exam practice

The Manchester Commonwealth Games 2002

In 2002, Manchester hosted the Commonwealth Games. The Games were enormously successful and helped to promote and improve Manchester's image.

The Games:

- ✪ had a global TV audience of over 1 billion
- ✪ sold over 90% of the tickets for events (almost 750,000 tickets in the UK alone)
- ✪ was the largest Commonwealth Games ever held with 17 sports, 5,900 athletes and officials
- ✪ met its revenue targets.

By hosting the games, Manchester enjoyed a number of benefits.

- ✪ Over £600m of investment was attracted into the area, particularly East Manchester.
- ✪ Thousands of jobs were created.
- ✪ £800m was spent on transport in the area.
- ✪ New sports venues such as the Manchester Aquatics Centre, the Bolton Arena, the Heaton Park Bowls Centre and The National Squash Centre, were built.
- ✪ The City of Manchester Stadium was built. This was the main centre for the games. It is now home to Manchester City FC and its capacity has been increased from 38,000 to 48,500.

Final medals table (top 10)

	Gold	Silver	Bronze
Australia	82	62	62
England	54	51	60
India	32	21	19
Canada	31	41	42
New Zealand	11	13	21
South Africa	9	20	17
Cameroon	9	1	2
Malaysia	7	9	18
Scotland	6	8	16
Nigeria	5	4	11

City of Manchester Stadium during the English Commonwealth Games trials, 2002

1. How many people watched the Games on TV? *(1 mark)*
2. How did England perform in the Games? *(2 marks)*
3. Suggest four types of jobs that were created by the Games. *(4 marks)*
4. What were the benefits of the Games to (i) sport and (ii) the city of Manchester? *(8 marks)*

National leisure facilities – museums and galleries

Getting started...

The UK has some of the most impressive museums and galleries in the world. These celebrate our historical and cultural heritage. National museums and galleries attract visitors from all over the country. Many overseas tourists also enjoy the exhibitions and collections. Look at the museums below.

Natural History Museum

The Natural History Museum, Cromwell Rd, London, is the UK's national museum of nature.

It aims to promote discovery, understanding, responsible use and enjoyment of the natural world. Its main exhibitions include the Earth Galleries, Life Galleries, a wildlife garden and the new Darwin Centre. This provides world-class storage facilities for precious collections, new laboratories, and access behind the scenes for visitors. The Museum also has special exhibitions for which a small entrance charge is sometimes made.

Skeleton of a diplodocus dinosaur in the entrance to the Life Galleries

National Museum of Photography, Film & Television

The National Museum of Photography, Film & Television is the most visited national museum outside London. Located in Bradford, it attracts around 750,000 visitors each year. It has a collection of over three million items of historical, social and cultural value. This includes the world's first photographic negative and the earliest television footage. Visitors can also obtain a hands-on experience of the media.

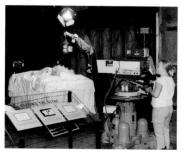

Using a TV camera

Ironbridge Gorge

Ironbridge

The Ironbridge Gorge in the Severn Valley is known as the birthplace of the industrial revolution. The iron bridge, built in 1779, is the centrepiece of a six square mile area that has been designated a World Heritage site. The attractive, steep-sided valley has 10 museums containing nationally important collections of machines, fine china, tiles and ironwork that were among the first ever modern mass-produced articles.

(a) *Why might people throughout the country be attracted to these museums?*

(b) *Describe each museum's collection briefly.*

Beamish

The Beamish pit mining museum stands in over 300 acres of beautiful countryside nine miles from Newcastle upon Tyne. It recreates life in the North of England in the 1800s and early 1900s.

Beamish pit mining museum

British Museum

The British Museum in Great Russell Street, London was founded in 1753. It holds in trust, for the nation and the world, a collection of art and antiquities from ancient and living cultures. Housed in one of Britain's architectural landmarks, the collection is one of the best in the world. It spans two million years of human history.

The British Museum

The Royal Armouries

The Royal Armouries is housed in the Tower of London, one of the most famous buildings in the world. It is responsible for all the displays in the White Tower, the central keep of the castle. The displays contain armours of Henry VIII, Charles I, Charles II and James II. The Royal Armouries has also reconstructed many of the historical displays of arms and armour for which the Tower is famous, including the Grand Storehouse which was destroyed by fire in 1841.

Henry VIII's horse armour at the Royal Armouries

Science Museum

The Science Museum, founded in 1857, is located in South Kensington, London. It contains around 20 collections of scientific interest.

The Gemini submarine car at The Science Museum

Science Museum – subject collections

Air transport	Agricultural engineering
Pictorial	Environmental science
Road transport	& technology
Materials science	Chemistry
Bioscience	Mechanical engineering
Civil engineering	Astronomy & mathematics
Classical physics	Space technology
Clinical medicine	Water transport
Computers and IT	Public health

The National Gallery

The National Gallery houses one of the finest collections in the world of paintings, sculptures and graphic arts from the Middle Ages to the present time. The Gallery's aim is to encourage the public throughout the UK, and beyond, to value and enjoy its pictures.

The Gallery has a Collection Features section which presents different ways of looking at the paintings in the collection. There might be surprising details or unusual facts to discover in familiar pictures. The features are:

The National Gallery

- ✪ Painting of the Month
- ✪ Cupid's Box of Delights
- ✪ Puzzling Pictures
- ✪ The Art of Science.

The National Gallery is located in Trafalgar Square, London

The Tate Galleries

The Tate Galleries is a family of galleries operating on four sites. They house the national collection of British art from the sixteenth century to the present day, including the Turner Bequest, and the national collection of international modern art.

Tate Britain Located in Millbank, London, The Britain has five key displays:

- ✪ British Art 1500-1900
- ✪ British Art 1900-2004
- ✪ Duveen Galleries
- ✪ Gallery Extras
- ✪ Turner Collection.

Tate Modern Located in Bankside, London. Its display themes include:

- ✪ Concourse
- ✪ History/Memory/Society
- ✪ Landscape/Matter/Environment
- ✪ Nude/Action/Body
- ✪ Still Life/Object/Real Life.

Tate Liverpool This gallery is located in the Albert Dock, Liverpool. Its current displays include:

- ✪ International Modern Art, June 2004-2005
- ✪ The Shape of Ideas, December 2003-May 2004.

Tate St Ives Located in the Cornish town of St Ives. This small gallery houses temporary collections of modern contemporary art.

Facilities at galleries and museums

As well as collections and exhibitions, museums and galleries offer a wide range of other facilities. These include:

- ✪ catering facilities such as restaurants, cafés and kiosks
- ✪ souvenir shops
- ✪ detailed information about the collections and exhibitions
- ✪ guided tours
- ✪ digital audio guides
- ✪ printed programmes of collections
- ✪ sign language communicators for the deaf
- ✪ special activities, talks, discussions, and other events
- ✪ research facilities
- ✪ reading rooms.

Quick quiz

1. **True or false?**
   - ✪ All of the national museums and galleries are located in London.
   - ✪ The Royal Armouries is based in Buckingham Palace.
   - ✪ Beamish is an open-air museum.

2. Match the collections in the box with the correct museums or galleries.
   - ✪ Tate Britain
   - ✪ The Science Museum
   - ✪ The Natural History Museum

Agricultural engineering	*Turner Collection*
Life Galleries	*Modern Art*

3. State briefly what can be found in the British Museum.

Exam practice

National Railway Museum

The National Railway Museum (NRM) in York is the largest of its kind in the world. Its huge collection consists of:
- ✪ locomotives and powered units
- ✪ rolling stock e.g. carriages and wagons
- ✪ railway road vehicles
- ✪ railway tools and equipment
- ✪ signaling and telecommunications
- ✪ miniature locomotives
- ✪ railway shipping artifacts
- ✪ railway time pieces
- ✪ railway models
- ✪ tickets, documents, records and pictures.

Figure 1 *Reasons for not visiting museums and galleries*

Percentages

- Nothing I particularly wanted to see
- Museums are boring places
- I find it difficult to get out / health reasons
- Admission charges too high
- Poor local transport / too far to travel
- Not open when I have time to visit
- My children wouldn't be interested
- No time / too busy

0 5 10 15 20 25 30 35 40 45

Source: Mori survey 2001

The Interactive Learning Centre

The Interactive Learning Centre at York contains two full-size locomotive driving cabs. One is a training cab for a steam locomotive from the 1950s. A sound guide explains the controls in the cab and tells the listener how to drive a steam locomotive. The other is an InterCity 125 diesel-electric power car from the 1970s. Although only 20 years apart, the two cabs are entirely different in layout and environment.

1. What is the main reason for not visiting museums and galleries? *(1 mark)*
2. State three other facilities that the NRM might have. (3 marks)
3. Describe the general purpose of museums using the NRM as an example. *(4 marks)*
4. A friend has written to you asking where you could go for a day out together. Write a letter back suggesting reasons why a visit to the NRM might be interesting. *(7 marks)*

Locomotives at the National Railway Museum

National leisure facilities – major visitor attractions

Getting started...

The UK has some very big attractions such as zoos, safari parks and seaside resorts. They attract millions of visitors every year. The attractions offer a variety of activities, amusements and facilities for all different age groups and tastes. Look at the two attractions below.

Blackpool Tower and Pleasure Beach

Blackpool is the UK's top tourist attraction. In 2003, 5,737,000 people visited the resort. However, this was 10% down on 2002. Some of its attractions include:

- ✪ The 158 metres tall Blackpool Tower.
- ✪ Various indoor attractions such as a playground, aquarium and zoo.
- ✪ A listed ballroom with a Wurlitzer organ.
- ✪ The Pleasure Beach with five roller coasters including a twin track racer.
- ✪ Plus many other attractions including travelling to the Times of the Dinosaurs, Alice in Wonderland, the Greatest Show on Earth, the Big One and the Log Flume.
- ✪ Three piers and sandy beaches.

- ✪ The famous Blackpool Illuminations (from September to early November).

There are also plans to build a casino and new hotels in Blackpool to provide Las Vegas style facilities.

The Big One at Blackpool Pleasure Beach

Jorvik Viking Centre

Jorvik was the name given to York by Vikings who conquered and settled in the Anglo-Saxon kingdom of Northumbria. Between 1976 and 1981, archeologists discovered remains of the Viking world. These included wooden houses, fence lines, alleyways, backyards and thousands of objects from the Viking Age, many of them in excellent condition. The Jorvik Viking Centre opened in 1984 and has had over 13 million visitors to see its collections. Visitors can get face-to-face with staff dressed as Vikings and discover what life was like in York over 1000 years ago.

Jorvik Viking Centre

A Viking woman feeding geese

(a) State two reasons why Blackpool gets more visitors than the Jorvik Viking Centre.
(b) State one possible reason why visitors to Blackpool fell by 10% in 2002.

Major visitor attractions

Key
- Blackpool Tower and Pleasure Beach
- Bristol Zoo
- Chester Zoo
- Jorvik Viking Centre, York
- London Zoo
- Longleat Safari Park
- Madam Tussaud's
- NEC Birmingham
- Palace Pier Brighton
- The London Eye
- Woburn Safari Park

Number of visitors to attractions in 2003

Attraction	Visitors	Change from 2002
Blackpool Pleasure Beach	5,737,000	-10%
British Museum	4,584,000	-0.5%
Tate Modern	3,895,746	-16%
Natural History Museum	2,976,783	-3%
Science Museum	2,886,859	6%
Victoria & Albert Museum	2,257,325	2%
Tower of London	1,972,263	-3.6%
Eden Project	1,404,737	-19%
Legoland Windsor	1,321,128	-4%
National Maritime Museum	1,305,150	8%
Edinburgh Castle	1,172,534	1%
Tate Britain	1,106,911	-4.5%
Kew Gardens	1,079,424	9%
Chester Zoo	1,076,000	2.5%
Canterbury Cathedral	1,060,166	-4.5%
Westminster Abbey	1,002,718	-5%
Roman Baths	983,392	-1%
London Zoo	839,865	-8%
Stonehenge	776,279	-1%
St Paul's Cathedral	710,975	-9%

Source: Manchester online.co.uk

Brighton Pier

The Palace Pier, Brighton is over 100 years old and a mile long. It is located on the East Sussex coast and during the summer the pier is open until 2.00 am. Its attractions include the following.

- Traditional funfair with a new Ghost Train in 2004.
- 250-seater fish and chip restaurant.
- Three bars with free entertainment.
- A variety of take-away outlets.
- Side stalls such as Tin Can Alley.
- Arcades with games such as Star Wars, Ocean Hunter, Time Crisis II.
- Free children's entertainment on a purpose-built stage with costume characters, music and dancing.
- Fortune tellers, bingo hall and a night club.

The Palace Pier

Zoos

Zoos continue to attract people in large numbers. In 2003, London Zoo and Chester Zoo were both in the top 20 attractions.

London Zoo

London Zoo was the world's first scientific zoo. It opened in 1828 and housed exotic animals that were studied by scientists. In 1847, the Zoo opened to the public and became the most famous zoo in the world. It houses a huge range of reptiles, fish, invertebrates, birds and mammals. Of the more than 650 species at London Zoo, 112 are listed as threatened. The Zoo also participates in breeding programmes for 130 species.

Chester Zoo

In 2003, Chester Zoo won the Zoo of the Year Award and enjoyed more visitors than London Zoo. It was founded in the 1930s by George Mottershead. He wanted to create a zoo without any bars or cages. It is now known for its innovative enclosure designs and breeding successes. Chester Zoo also plays an important conservation role. It works to protect threatened plants and animals in the wild. For example, it supports the conservation of wildlife in the Forest Reserves of China.

Bristol Zoo

Bristol Zoo Gardens won the Zoo of the Year Award in 2004. It is described as a 'must see' destination with lots to see and do at excellent value. There are over 300 species and the Zoo is committed to conservation. For example, it supports the Cameroon Wildlife Aid Fund.

A baby orangutang and his mother at Chester Zoo

Zoo admission prices – 2004

	London	Chester	Bristol
Adult	£13.00	£12.00	£9.50
Child 3-15	£9.75	£9.50	£6.00
Family	£41.00	£39.50	£28.00
Senior Citizens	N/A	£9.50	£4.25
Under three	Free	Free	Free

Safari parks

Safari parks offer similar attractions to zoos but tend to have more wide open space. One of the main differences is that you can get close to the animals by driving through the park where they are free to roam.

Longleat Safari Park – Wiltshire

Longleat is both a stately home and a safari park. Longleat House, home to the 7th Marquess of Bath, is one of the best examples of Elizabethan architecture in Britain. Other attractions include grounds and gardens, an adventure castle, mazes, Longleat Railway, Motion Simulator, Pets' Corner, Old Joe's Mine, Postman Pat Village and safari boats.

Woburn Safari Park – Bedfordshire

The attractions at Woburn include animal reserves, Woburn Abbey (home of the Earls and Dukes of Bedford for over 375 years), Deer Park, Woburn Golf and Country Club and Woburn village. Once inside the park, visitors can drive through the animal reserves as often as they like. The animals in the reserves include rhinos, elands, antelopes, giraffes, ankoles, zebra, elephants, camels, bison, ostriches, lions, tigers, wolves, black bears, grass and Colobus monkeys, Barbary apes and hippos.

Longleat Safari Park

Quick quiz

1 Where is the Jorvik Viking Centre located?
(a) Wiltshire **(b)** Birmingham **(c)** Bristol **(d)** York

2 How much would entrance into London Zoo cost a 14 year old?
(a) £10 **(b)** £9.75 **(c)** £9.50 **(d)** £6.00

3 Which is the oldest zoo in the world?
(a) Dudley Zoo **(b)** Chester Zoo **(c)** Bristol Zoo **(d)** London Zoo

4 **True or false?**

○ Brighton Pier is in Surrey.

○ Five of the top 10 attractions in 2003 were museums.

○ There is a nightclub on Brighton Pier.

5 What is the difference between a safari park and a zoo?

Exam practice

NEC Birmingham

The National Exhibition Centre (NEC) is the busiest exhibition centre in Europe. It stages more than 180 annual exhibitions including the Crufts Dog Show, the Motor Show and numerous international trade fairs. Up to four million people visit the NEC each year. It has its own main line railway station, is just a few miles from Birmingham International Airport and is close to the M6, M45 and M42 motorways, in the centre of England. The complex has several venues.

British International Motor Show, NEC

The NEC
The exhibition centre has 20 flat-floored, interconnected halls and can cater for all types of exhibitions and events.

The NEC Arena
The 12,300 seated NEC Arena is used for shows and concerts. Pop stars such as Sir Cliff Richard, Status Quo, Tina Turner, Diana Ross, Elton John and David Bowie have all appeared on stage here. It is also home to the Horse of the Year show.

The National Indoor Arena
The National Indoor Arena is one of the busiest indoor sporting and entertainment venues in Europe. Since 1991, over 4 million visitors have enjoyed over 30 different sports and a huge variety of entertainment.

Best in Show winner at Crufts in the NEC

The Symphony Hall
The Symphony Hall is said to be the UK's finest concert hall and one of the best in the world. The auditorium has superb acoustics and in 2001, a 6,000-pipe symphony organ was installed.

1. Which of the above venues is likely to stage (i) an opera (ii) a trade fair? *(2 marks)*
2. State four reasons why people visit the NEC. *(4 marks)*.
3. What evidence is there to suggest that the NEC is a major visitor attraction? (4 marks)
4. Discuss the quality of the NEC's transport links. *(6 marks)*

Getting started...

The first theme park was built in America by Walt Disney in 1955. Today there are plenty to choose from in the UK. Most theme parks attract visitors with thrilling 'white knuckle rides'. They are called theme parks because they are usually divided into zones or areas, each of which has a different theme. For example, all the amusements and exhibitions in one area might show life in a particular country, such as Mexico. Because theme parks are so big, they can offer attractions for all age groups and tastes. The most popular theme park in the UK is Alton Towers.

Alton Towers

Alton Towers is located in Staffordshire, a short drive from the M6 motorway. It lies in 200 acres of attractive gardens and features a Chinese Pagoda Fountain and the towers themselves, as well as amusements, rides, restaurants and shops. It is one of the top five attractions in the UK and has about 2.7 million visitors each year. It is divided into ten areas which include Forbidden Valley, X-Sector, The Towers/Gardens, Ugland, Kantanga Canyon, Gloomy Wood, Merry England, Cred Street, Old MacDonald's Farmyard and Adventure Land. These areas cater for different age groups and tastes.

Riding upside down on the 'air' rollercoaster at Alton Towers

The swing carousel at Alton Towers

New for 2004
Spinball Whizzer

'This ride is themed like a giant pinball machine. Riders rattle like a ball as they are catapulted down the 450m track at speeds of up to 60km per hour. Over the 1 minute 30 second duration of the ride, each car can spin up to 90 times!'

Top Rides

Alton Towers has 15 of the country's most thrilling rides. Examples include:

✪ Nemesis ✪ Blackhole ✪ Blade ✪ Ripsaw
✪ Enterprise ✪ Submission ✪ Oblivion ✪ Air

(a) Where is Alton Towers?
(b) Why is Alton Towers suitable for a family day out?

Camelot

Camelot was voted the Lancashire Family Attraction of the Year in 2002. It is located in Charnock Richard, Chorley and enjoys over one million visitors a year. The park is divided into five lands each with its own attractions.

King's Realm Go-Karts, Pendragon's Plunge, Log Flume and Cats of the Round Table.

Knight's Valley Jousting arena, Kingdom in the Clouds, The Galleon, Merlin's School of Wizardry and the Dragon Flyer.

Merlin's Playground Suitable for young children with a Junior Galleon, Carousel, Sky Divers, Junior Dragon Coaster, Kiddies' Indoor Playground and Cup 'n' Sorcerer.

Land of the Brave Gauntlet, The Rack, The Quintain, Whirlwind and Dungeon of Doom.

Squire Bumpkin's Farm Horse grooming, sheep shearing and bottle-feeding lambs.

The park has numerous restaurants including a food court offering four different styles of meals.

A sword fight in the jousting arena at Camelot

Entrance fees

Adults and Children	£15
Family (4 guests)	£50
Senior citizens and disabled guests	£11
Children under 1m	Free

Chessington World of Adventures

Chessington is the South's main theme park. It is located in Chessington, Surrey. Its themed areas include Animal Land, Beanoland, Forbidden Kingdom, Land of Dragons, Market Square, Mexicana, Mystic East, Pirates' Cove, Toytown and Transylvania.

Like all theme parks, Chessington has a huge choice of places to eat and drink. Caffè Nero, Cadbury Castle, Fizz and Burp Café, Casbah Café, Decadent Donuts, KFC, Pizza Hut, Greedy Goblin BBQ, Greedy Goblin Family Inn, Mexican Diner, Orient Express, Golden Donuts, Coca Cola Pagoda, Chips Ahoy and Alpine Café are some examples.

Rameses Revenge ride at Chessington

Night time Special Events

Chessington provides facilities for night-time parties and other functions. In addition to food and drink they may provide:

- ✪ Discos
- ✪ Magicians
- ✪ Comedians
- ✪ Casino tables
- ✪ Guest speakers
- ✪ Extreme artists
- ✪ Bands
- ✪ Giant games.

Drayton Manor

Drayton Manor Family Theme Park is one of the oldest parks in the country. When it first opened in 1949, it was described as an 'Inland Pleasure Resort'. The park is still 'Family Run for Family Fun'. It has five 'thrill' rides called Apocalypse, Cyclone, Shockwave, Stormforce 10 and Maelstrom. The park also has a zoo with over 100 species from all over the world. These include big cats, reptiles, bats, monkeys, owls, eagles, parrots – plus an exotic creature reserve. Drayton Manor is located in Tamworth, Staffordshire.

*Girl band B*Witched launching the Apocalypse ride at Drayton manor*

Apocalypse

Apocalypse was the world's first stand-up tower. It takes riders to a height of 54 metres and tilts them forward at an agonising 20 degree angle as they are hoisted skyward on a half-ton launch shuttle. Then they drop at the mercy of gravity at over 4Gs. With no footrest at all, 'thrill-seekers' hang from 54 metres with nothing to hold them but their shoulder restraints!

Thorpe Park

Thorpe Park is located in Chertsey, Surrey, just 20 miles from London. It is one of Europe's leading leisure parks and is enjoying rising visitor numbers. In the last decade, Thorpe Park has changed from an exhibition style park to a leisure attraction particularly popular amongst families. A summary of the changes in the Park is given below.

1994 Ranger Country opened with two new rides.

1995 Two more rides opened in Ranger Country. Project X construction began.

1996 No Way Out opened. It was one of the biggest investments ever for the park.

1997 Voted the most parent-friendly leisure park in the UK.

1998 The Dino Bumper Boat Ride and Wet! Wet! Wet! opened.

1999 Tussaud's Group bought the park. Pirates 4D cinema opened starring Leslie Neilson.

2000 Tidal Wave opened. Fantasy Reef was re-named and re-themed.

2001 Three new thrill rides opened – Zodiac, Vortex and the 100 ft high drop tower, Detonator.

2002 Colossus opened, the world's first ten looping coaster, and Ribena Rumba Rapids.

2003 Continuing the trend of large coasters, Nemesis Inferno was introduced.

2004 The Samurai from Chessington replaced Calgary Stampede.

100 students breaking the world record for riding naked on a rollercoaster at Thorpe Park

Extract from 2003 survey carried out by Thorpe Park

What was your favourite thrill ride at Thorpe?

Colossus	33%
Detonator	16%
Nemesis	48%
Quantum	1%
Tidal Wave	1%
Vortex	9%
No Way Out	2%
Zodiac	0%

Quick quiz

1. Where is Drayton Manor located?
   (a) London **(b)** Tamworth **(c)** Surrey **(d)** Chorley

2. How much would an individual pay to get into Camelot?
   (a) £15 **(b)** £50 **(c)** £11 **(d)** £20

3. Which theme park has the Apocalypse as an attraction?
   (a) Alton Towers **(b)** Camelot **(c)** Thorpe Park **(d)** Drayton Manor

4. Which was the most popular ride at Thorpe Park in 2003?

5. What happened in 1999 at Thorpe Park?

6. What are the five lands at Camelot?

7. Where will you find the Greedy Goblin Family Inn?

Exam practice

Legoland

Legoland is located in Windsor and has over 50 rides and attractions suitable for the 2-12 age groups. Older children are likely to enjoy the coasters, each with its own LEGO theme. They can also build, program and test their own robots. Younger children can enjoy the Kid Power Towers, pedal a monorail car around an elevated track or earn their very first licence at the popular Driving School. Toddlers are provided with their own Playtown, with a model village jam-packed with rides and activities. The major attraction is Miniland, a detailed and animated depiction of life in various European cities. The park has spectacular models made entirely from LEGO bricks and has eight shops for souvenirs, sweets and LEGO.

Legoland showing Big Ben and Nelson's Column

Additional facilities

There are wheelchairs, pushchair hire, cash dispensers, kennels, 'Lost Parents' meeting points and a First Aid Centre staffed by qualified nurses. The well-equipped Baby Care Centre provides a peaceful haven for nursing and nappy changing.

Age and height restrictions

Children under the age of 12 must be accompanied by an adult. Some rides and attractions have height restrictions. Height restrictions are shown at the entrance to each ride.

1. State two additional facilities that Legoland provides. *(2 marks)*
2. What evidence is there to suggest that Legoland caters for very young children? *(3 marks)*
3. Like all theme parks, Legoland has age and height restrictions. Explain the purpose of these. *(4 marks)*
4. Describe the activities that the following age groups might enjoy at Legoland. (i) 2-5 (ii) 5-8 (iii) 9-12. *(6 marks)*

Getting started...

The UK has many historic attractions. Dinosaur remains have been found as well as evidence of life in the Stone Age and the Bronze Age. Both the Romans and the Vikings settled in parts of the UK and consequently, there are a variety of historic sites that attract visitors from all over the country. Look at the attractions below.

Hadrian's Wall

Hadrian's Wall near Housteads, Northumberland

In 122 AD, the Roman Emperor Hadrian, built a 73 mile-long fortified wall to mark the northernmost boundary of Roman Britain. It stretched from Wallsend, near Newcastle in the east to Bowness-on-Solway in the west. Warring tribes were contained behind it for over 350 years.

Parts of Hadrian's Wall can still be seen today and visitors to the site can explore a range of interesting forts and museums. The Wall is also the centre of Hadrian's Wall Country, a rich and varied corridor of land which contains some of Britain's most beautiful scenery.

Stonehenge

Stonehenge is an ancient monument of huge stones standing on the Salisbury Plain in Wiltshire, England. A lot of mystery surrounds the monument. For example, who built it? Some think it might have been the Druids, or the Greeks, or the Phoenicians, or the Atlanteans. Why was it built? There are a variety of possible answers ranging from human sacrifice to astronomy. Investigations over the last 100 years show that Stonehenge was built in several stages from 2800-1800 BC. It seems to have been built to observe astronomical events such as summer and winter solstices and eclipses.

Stonehenge

(a) *Where are Hadrian's Wall and Stonehenge?*
(b) *Do you think these attractions would be suitable for toddlers? Explain your answer.*
(c) *What are the attractions of these two historic sites?*

Beaulieu

Beaulieu is situated in the heart of the New Forest and has three main attractions.

Palace House

This was the 14th century Great Gatehouse of Beaulieu Abbey. It overlooks the Beaulieu River and has been owned by Lord Montagu's family since 1538. It has a mixture of Victorian Gothic, medieval Gothic and 18th century fortification styles.

Beaulieu Abbey

Beaulieu Abbey

Beaulieu Abbey was founded in 1204 by Cistercian monks on land given to them by King John. Visitors can see modern, embroidered wall hangings showing scenes from medieval monastic life and the history of the Abbey since 1204. The Abbey Cloister is a place of tranquillity, planted with fragrant herbs.

The National Motor Museum

National Motor Museum

Managed by the National Motor Museum Trust, the museum has a collection of 250 vehicles. They range from some of the earliest examples of motoring to more recent World Record Breakers such as Bluebird and Golden Arrow. Visitors can also see the James Bond Experience where various vehicles and props used in the Bond films are displayed, including the Jaguar XKR Roadster from the film *Die Another Day*. Beaulieu is also the home of the world famous Beaulieu International Autojumble and Automart.

Buckingham Palace

Buckingham Palace, London, is the Queen's official residence. It is also the administrative centre for the monarchy. The Palace is a venue for great royal ceremonies, state visits and investitures. Although the Palace is furnished and decorated with priceless works of art, it is not an art gallery and nor is it a museum. However, parts of the Palace are open to the public. Many people come to see the changing of the guards which takes place in the forecourt of Buckingham Palace at 11.30am every day in the summer. Since 1660, Household Troops have guarded the Sovereign and the Royal Palaces. The Queen's Guard is made up of Foot Guards in full-dress uniform of red tunics and bearskins.

Household troops

Chatsworth

Chatsworth Estate in the Peak District National Park covers 35,000 acres spreading over more than 20 miles of Derbyshire and Staffordshire. It is one of the treasure houses of England and the home of the Dukes of Devonshire. A 1,000 acre park surrounds Chatsworth and is open all year round. People are welcome to walk, play and picnic in the park. The house, which is open to the public, has 175 rooms, 3,426 feet of passages, 17 staircases and 359 doors, all lit by 2,084 light bulbs. Throughout the house, there are displays of paintings, including work by Rembrandt and Gainsborough, furniture, silver, tapestries and porcelain and a gallery of neo-classical sculptures.

Chatsworth – the house and park

Hampton Court Palace

Hampton Court Palace on the banks of the River Thames in Surrey, is famously linked to Henry VIII even though he only spent 811 days here during his 38 year reign. With over 500 years of royal history, costumed guides and audio tours bring the palace to life and people can see what the state apartments and Tudor kitchens would have been like in the time of Henry VIII. The Palace contains an important part of the largest private collection of art in the world – the Royal Collection. This covers 500 years and contains material from the 16th, 17th and early 18th centuries. There is also a famous maze which was planted as part of the gardens laid out for William of Orange between 1689 and 1695.

Hampton Court maze

Quick quiz

1. How long is Hadrian's Wall?
   (a) 37 miles **(b)** 173 miles **(c)** 137 miles **(d)** 73 miles

2. Where is Beaulieu situated?
   (a) New Forest **(b)** Sherwood Forest **(c)** Black Forest **(d)** Forest of Bowland

3. In which National Park is Chatsworth situated?
   (a) Lake District **(b)** Peak District **(c)** Exmoor **(d)** Dartmoor.

4. **True or false?**
   - Buckingham Palace is **not** open to the public.
   - Henry VIII lived at Hampton Court Palace during his reign of England.
   - Buckingham Palace is home to David and Victoria Beckham.

5. State the three main visitor attractions at Beaulieu.

Exam practice

Tower of London

Founded by William the Conqueror in 1066-67, the Tower of London has been used in a number of ways. It has been an armoury, a royal palace and fortress, a prison and place of execution, a mint, a menagerie (housing lions, bears, and, to this day, flightless ravens) and a jewel house. It is now a famous tourist attraction and, like many of the UK's historic sites, a World Heritage Site.

The Jewel House

This is where the Crown Jewels are kept. They are said to be priceless. The crowns are made of real gold and have many diamonds, rubies and pearls that sparkle and shine.

Beefeaters

Beefeaters is the name for the Yeoman Warders who look after the Tower and the Crown Jewels. They usually wear blue coats with red trim, or on special occasions, bright red coats with gold trim. They are helpful and will answer visitors' questions.

The Ceremony of the Keys

Every night at 21.30, the Yeoman Warders and military guard lock the outer gates of the Tower of London and deliver the keys to the Resident Governor of the Tower.

1. Who founded the Tower of London? *(1 mark)*
2. State three uses the Tower has been put to in its history. *(3 marks)*
3. Using the Tower of London as an example, explain what is meant by an historic site. *(4 marks)*
4. Explain why a family from Leeds, with two teenage children, might visit the Tower of London. *(7 marks)*

Beefeaters at The Tower of London

11 Products and services in the leisure industry

Getting started...

People use leisure facilities, such as sports centres, parks and the natural environment, to enjoy their leisure time. But to make the most of the facilities, they often need certain products and services. For example, for a camping expedition in the Lake District, you would need a tent, a rucksack, waterproof clothing, hiking boots, a map and other essential equipment. A huge range of products and services is provided by the leisure industry. Look at the examples below.

Fishing

Lakshmipathy Singh and Anil Pactor, both aged 15, enjoy fishing. They live in Newark and fish in the River Trent. They also visit nearby lakes and ponds when they can get a lift from their parents. A lot of the money they earn from their paper rounds is spent in the local fishing tackle shop.

Canoeing

Kelly Palmer is 16 and mad about canoeing. She lives in Ross-on-Wye and spends many hours practising on the River Wye. She is a member of a local canoeing club which allows her to hire its equipment for a small charge. One day, she would like to be able to buy her own canoe and wetsuit.

Swimming

Billy Jennings and Gillian Dodds are both 5 years old. They are learning to swim at the Crowtree Leisure Pool, Sunderland. The lessons cost £30 for a 15 week course. Each lesson lasts for 30 minutes. They enjoy the lessons because the swimming coach is really friendly.

Swimming coach

What products or services are being used by the children in the above leisure activities and where do they get them from?

Catering facilities

Most leisure facilities and visitor attractions sell refreshments. This provides extra revenue for the business and adds to the customer's enjoyment. Cinemas and theatres, for example, often sell confectionery and have a bar. Leisure centres, parks and fitness clubs might have a café or a bar where drinks and meals are served. Vending machines with drinks, confectionery and snacks are also common. Major visitor attractions and sports venues often provide a wide range of restaurants, cafés, bars, kiosks, food and drink vendors and fast food outlets.

Conferencing, banqueting and functions

Many leisure centres, sports clubs and visitor attractions can cater for large group functions. Businesses, groups and families can book function rooms for conferences, business presentations, weddings, children's parties and other special occasions. Details of the facilities provided are usually available on their web sites. In addition to a range of dining services, they might also offer audio visual and multi-media facilities for conferences and presentations, and entertainment such as live music or a comedian for parties. Some centres, such as outdoor activity centres, provide accommodation for people attending residential courses.

Equipment hire

Leisure centres, outdoor activity centres and sports clubs usually hire out equipment to customers or members. Squash rackets, golf clubs and trolleys, lockers, canoes, camping equipment, wet suits, ice-skates and snorkelling gear are just a few examples of the wide range available. Hiring equipment is helpful to people who just want to try out a new activity or who can't afford to buy expensive items. It also helps to increase revenue for the centres.

Special rates and discounts

Charges at clubs and centres vary. For example, discounts are often available for:

- 'off-peak' times e.g. during the day
- children, students, senior citizens and the disabled
- group bookings e.g. a 14 year old pays £27 for a day at Alton Towers but as part of a large group, the entrance fee falls to £20.

Many clubs, centres and attractions offer membership schemes. By paying an annual fee, the facilities can be used all year round, any number of times. For example, the entrance charge to London Zoo is £9 for a 15 year old whereas annual membership only costs £35 and allows unlimited visits. Members often get other benefits such as cheap rates for hiring equipment.

Lessons and classes

People can go to centres and clubs to learn different sports and pursue a variety of leisure activities. For example, many leisure centres provide lessons and classes in such things as squash, badminton, aerobics, yoga, keep-fit, swimming and circuit training. They are often offered at different levels – beginners, intermediate and advanced – so that people can choose the one that best suits them.

Many lessons and instruction will also focus on health and safety issues. For example, the importance of doing warm-up exercises to avoid injury before playing sport.

Sports and specialist shops

Sports shops such as JJB Sports, sell a wide range of equipment and sportswear for popular sports such as football, cricket and rugby. But some activities require specialist equipment. For example:

- ✪ fishing
- ✪ skiing
- ✪ golf
- ✪ camping
- ✪ surfing
- ✪ craft and model making
- ✪ water sports such as canoeing
- ✪ caving and potholing
- ✪ boxing
- ✪ hiking, climbing and mountaineering.

Outdoors – a specialist shop for camping, hiking and climbing

Products and services for home-based leisure activities

Businesses provide many products and services so that people can enjoy home-based leisure activities. Generally, products and services can be bought from shops, by telephone, by mail order or online. Some common examples are shown below.

Video rental shops
Videos and DVDs can be rented or bought from local shops or big chains such as Blockbuster. Supermarkets also sell them and they can be borrowed from libraries.

Bookshops and libraries
People who enjoy reading can borrow books from libraries. Magazines and newspapers can be bought from shops. There are also bookshops such as Waterstone's and Borders.

Computer games
Computers and computer games can be bought from supermarkets and specialists like HMV, Game and PC World. Some games can be downloaded from the Internet.

Take-away food
There is a huge range of ethnic restaurants such as Chinese, Thai, Indian and Italian many of which offer a take-away service. Supermarkets also sell take-away meals.

HOME-BASED LEISURE ACTIVITIES

Gardening products
Local garden centres, DIY stores and supermarkets sell plants, seeds, shrubs, tools, equipment, garden furniture and other accessories, for gardening enthusiasts.

Entertaining friends
Food and drink for dinner parties, birthday parties, BBQs and other social gatherings, can be bought from a range of outlets. Supermarkets and off-licenses for example.

Games and crafts
Games such as chess, Scrabble, Monopoly and cards can be bought from shops, as can materials for crafts and model making. Equipment for home sports such as table tennis and snooker, can be bought from sports shops.

DIY products
Tools, materials and other DIY items can be bought from big stores such as B & Q, Homebase and Wickes. Heavier tools and machinery can be hired from specialist shops.

Quick quiz

1 **True or false?**

- ✿ A council-run swimming pool is likely to offer ethnic take-away foods.

- ✿ A specialist shop might sell equipment for water skiing.

- ✿ Building a fish pond in the garden might be a home-based leisure activity.

2 Who of the following is **not** likely to be entitled to a discount at a visitor attraction?
(a) 29 year old **(b)** Full-time student **(c)** Toddler **(d)** 67 year old

3 Which of the following is a service in the leisure industry?
(a) Computer game **(b)** Squash lesson **(c)** Charcoal for a BBQ **(d)** A magazine

4 State three products that might be bought for a home-based leisure activity.

5 State two advantages of being a member of a leisure centre or sports club.

Exam practice

Westbridge Leisure Centre

Westbridge Leisure Centre is owned by the local council. It wants the centre to make more money and has carried out a customer survey. Five hundred customers completed the questionnaire. Some of the main findings are shown below.

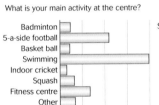

What is your main activity at the centre?

Which classes or lessons do you attend?

How satisfied are you with the leisure centre?

Which if the facilities do you use regularly on your visits?

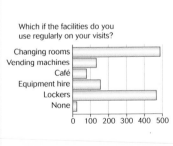

Playing squash

A selection of customer comments

- ✿ 'The lessons are too expensive.'
- ✿ 'Drinks in the vending machines are warm.'
- ✿ 'The food in the café is awful.'
- ✿ 'The café is too dear and untidy.'
- ✿ 'Staff are very friendly and helpful.'
- ✿ 'I'm going to join a private club next month.'

1. Which is the most popular activity at the leisure centre? *(1 mark)*

2. (i) Which facilities are used most at the centre? *(2 marks)*
   (ii) State one reason why these facilities are used the most. *(1 mark)*

3. Do you think people are satisfied with the leisure centre? Explain your answer. *(4 marks)*

4. How do you think the centre could be improved and make more money? *(7 marks)*

Getting started...

People spend their leisure time in different ways. This may be because they belong to different groups and have different circumstances. For example, a family with three young children might enjoy going to Legoland but this is unlikely to appeal to a 23 year old single man who enjoys sport. Look at the leisure activities below.

Children's activities

Leroy and James are both 8 years old. When they get home from school, they like to play in Leroy's back garden where there is a tree house. On Wednesday nights, they go to Cub Scouts. At Cub Scouts they do various activities such as swimming, music, exploring and computing. They also go on trips to places like the zoo or a farm and sometimes they go camping with the rest of their Pack.

Cub scouts

Surfing

Jake and Kim are both single, 25 years old and live in St Ives, Cornwall. They spend most of their leisure time surfing on the local beaches. They are very good surfers and both have won competitions. They love the outdoor life and often go to new beaches at the weekend where they camp overnight.

Disabled archery

Robin McSheffrey is a member of the Bullingdon Archery Club. He is the best archer at the club and practices nearly every day. He hopes to qualify for the Disabled Olympics. He likes the Bullingdon Club because it caters for his needs. There is wheelchair access to all parts of the club, special toilet facilities and archery equipment that has been adapted to cope with his disability.

Wheelchair archery contest

What factors have influenced the choice of leisure activity in each of the cases above?

How do people choose their leisure activities?

Age group

Some leisure activities may appeal to different age groups. Toddlers will enjoy children's activities such as playgrounds. Young teenagers might enjoy computer games, football or the pop music scene. 20 and 30 year-olds might enjoy wine bars and nightclubs. As people get older, their interests and leisure activities tend to change. There are some activities that appeal to nearly all age groups, such as watching television, but the programmes they watch may be quite different. For example, the table in Table 1 shows that more of the over 65s enjoy watching news programmes than the other two age groups. It is also possible for someone to enjoy an activity that is not normally associated with their age group. For example, in 2004, 93 year-old Fauja Singh ran the London Marathon in 6 hours and 7 minutes.

Table 1 *Interest in TV programmes by age*

	16-24	25-64	65 and over
News	83	94	97
Factual	69	87	84
Drama	75	80	87
Entertainment	89	76	70
Regional	50	72	85
Current affairs	57	68	79
Educational	45	61	52
Sports	51	54	53
Arts	30	33	43
Children's	41	33	17
Religious	11	19	51

Source: Social Trends 2004

Culture

People belong to different cultures. This means they have different backgrounds, traditions, beliefs, values, religions and lifestyles. As a result, they may enjoy different leisure activities. For example, Asians are likely to be interested in Indian 'Bollywood' films. Muslim women are unlikely go to a public swimming pool because their religion requires personal modesty. Orthodox Jews would only eat at a kosher restaurant where the food has been prepared in accordance with Jewish dietary laws.

Special needs

Some groups of people have special needs. Unless their needs are met, they may be prevented from enjoying certain activities.

The disabled may require specially adapted equipment. For example, visually impaired people play cricket with an oversized ball which has a bell inside. Some disabled groups need ramps, lifts, widened doors and corridors to gain access to facilities.

Ethnic minorities may be not be able to enjoy a tennis coaching session because of language difficulties.

The unemployed may not be able to enjoy the facilities in a leisure centre unless charges are reduced.

Men's 400 metres, Paralympic Games

Single parents might need crèche facilities before they can enjoy many leisure activities.

Type of household

The type of household that people live in can affect their choice of leisure activities. Some examples include the following.

Families might enjoy going to visitor attractions where there is entertainment and other facilities for young children.

A couple might enjoy leisure activities that they can do together – sailing, going to restaurants, the theatre or bowling, for example.

Single people may choose leisure activities where they are likely to make new friends. They may join a sports or fitness club, for example. Single people probably have the greatest choice of all when choosing leisure activities. This may be because they do not have any family or personal household ties.

Other types of household Students often live in shared accommodation. An adult may live with, and care for, a parent. Some elderly people live in nursing homes. Some households are made up of extended families. These living arrangements might affect the choice of leisure activities.

Gender

Many years ago, men and women were more likely to enjoy different leisure activities. For example, only men drank in pubs and played sports whereas women's activities tended to be centred on the home – shopping, cooking and such like. Today, due to Equal Opportunities legislation, changes in attitudes and culture, there are no leisure activities that cannot be enjoyed by both genders. However, men and women do not compete against each other in some sports activities such as rugby and boxing.

British Universities Rugby Union Championship Women's Final

Socio-economic groups

People can be categorised according to their marital status, education, jobs and income. It is common for people with similar jobs and income to enjoy the same leisure activities. Table 2 shows how people are grouped according to socio-economic status by the Institute of Practitioners in Advertising.

Table 2 *Social status and leisure activities*

Group	Social status	Occupation	Possible leisure activities
A	Upper middle class	Solicitors, directors	Golf, opera, gourmet food
B	Middle class	Teachers, managers	Theatre, galleries, squash
C1	Lower middle class	Supervisors, clerical	Major visitor attractions
C2	Skilled working class	Train drivers, chefs	Football, theme parks
D	Working class	Waiters, fitters	Fast food, videos
E	The poorest in society	Unskilled, pensioners	Home-based activities

It is important to remember that all leisure activities can be enjoyed by anyone. Although there are factors that affect the choice of leisure activity, there will always be people who enjoy activities that do not necessarily fit into their age group, social group or type of household. For example, a middle-aged solicitor who takes part in freestyle Motocross every weekend.

Quick quiz

1 **True or false?**

❂ Families with young children are not likely to join a golf club.

❂ Women do not enjoy playing football.

❂ Single people probably have a wider choice of leisure activities.

2 Match the most likely leisure activity with the age group.

❂ Under 5s

❂ 14-16s

❂ Over 65s

Playing squash   Listening to pop music
Playing bowls   Attending a playgroup

3 State two leisure activities that could be enjoyed by all the age groups in number 2 above.

Exam practice

Windermere Lake Cruises Ltd

Lake Windermere is the largest lake in England. It is 10.5 miles long and 200 feet deep. It attracts a large number of visitors. Windermere Lake Cruises Ltd provides trips on the lake throughout the year. Details of fares and a map of the lake are shown below.

1. What are the fares for (i) an adult going from Bowness to Ambleside (single) (ii) a family going from Bowness to Lakeside (return)? *(2 marks)*

2. Give details of any special discounts offered by Windermere Lake Cruises Ltd. *(4 marks)*

3. To what extent does Windermere Lake Cruises Ltd cater for people with special needs? *(4 marks)*

4. Do you think there are any groups of people that might not enjoy this type of leisure activity? Give reasons for your answer. *(7 marks)*

2005 TIMETABLE

WINDERMERE LAKE CRUISES

Fares €

Red Cruise
(Red dotted line on map)
BOWNESS TO AMBLESIDE OR VICE VERSA

	Adult	Child (5-15yrs)	Family*
Single	£4.70	£2.80	
Return	£6.95	£3.60	£19.00

Yellow Cruise
(Yellow dotted line on map)
BOWNESS TO LAKESIDE OR VICE VERSA

	Adult	Child (5-15yrs)	Family*
Single	£4.80	£2.90	
Return	£7.20	£3.70	£19.50

Freedom of the Lake
ROUND THE LAKE FROM ANY PIER
INCLUDES ALL ROUTES SHOWN AS DOTTED LINES ON MAP

Our best value cruise ticket is valid on all scheduled sailings for a period of 24 hours from the time of purchase including Islands Cruises from Bowness and cruises to Brockhole, boat passengers enjoy free entry.

Adult £12.50 Child(5-15yrs) **£6.25 Family* £32.00**

Children under 5 free. Well behaved dogs travel free. Bicycles £1 between any two piers. Season Tickets available.

* Family ticket 2 Adults and up to 3 children. Tickets strictly not transferable. Break of journey is permitted on all scheduled sailings, check return times.

We sail 364 days a Year! - ask for our Winter Brochure or see our website - www.windermere-lakecruises.co.uk

♿ FACILITIES FOR WHEELCHAIR USERS
Our steamers are suitable for wheelchair users but on board toilet facilities can only be reached by means of stairs. However there are adapted toilets at Lakeside, Bowness and Ambleside, and 'Radar' facilities close to Ambleside and Bowness piers. The main saloons are wheelchair accessible on Teal and Swan but not on Tern (although there is ample covered accommodation).

13 Factors affecting choice of leisure activity 2

Getting started...

Unit 12 showed how different groups of people might enjoy different leisure activities. There are a number of other factors that can affect how people spend their leisure time. For example, people are interested in different activities. Someone who is not interested in sport is unlikely to enjoy going to Lord's to see a Test Match. The availability of local facilities and the amount of money that people have to spend are also important factors. Think about the factors that are important below.

Rally driving

Tyrone Young is aged 32 and enjoys rally driving. He owns a Ford Cosworth that has been specially adapted for the sport. In the last three years, he has spent £27,500 on maintaining and improving the car. Tyrone says, 'All my spare cash goes on the car. I know it's a lot but it's worth every penny. Last year, I came second in a national rally. It was brilliant.'

Bell ringing

Claire O'Donnell enjoys bell ringing at her local church in Mallow, near Cork. She says, 'All my friends are bell ringers. I started when I was 14 when my best friend, Shelly, persuaded me to go. Two of my other friends from school are also bell ringers. We have a great laugh together.'

Bell ringers

Ice hockey

Sam Hussein is aged 16 and plays ice hockey for a team in Newcastle. Sam first got interested when he went ice-skating at the age of 10. He was quite good at it and after watching ice hockey on TV, he persuaded his parents to let him try it. He joined a local club and got hooked. Now, he is ice hockey mad. He plays three times a week, watches it on TV, goes to see Newcastle Vipers play in the Findus British League and he also buys all the ice hockey magazines. Sam has no other interests and his dream is to play for the Vipers.

An ice hockey game

What factors may have influenced each of the above people in their choice of leisure activity?

Availability of local facilities

People are influenced by the availability of leisure facilities in their local area. If someone lives 85 miles from the coast, they are unlikely to be interested in sea fishing. Remote rural places do not have a local leisure centre or a lot of restaurants, pubs and nightclubs to choose from. People tend to pick leisure interests that match the available facilities. Town and city dwellers will enjoy different leisure activities to those who live in the countryside.

Times Square, New York

Walking the dog in the countryside

Availability of transport

People are more likely to use leisure facilities if there are good transport systems to get them there. The increase in car ownership and improvements in transport have made people much more mobile. However, some forms of transport may be expensive, time-consuming, unreliable and infrequent. This may restrict the choice of leisure activities. For example, it may be possible to get a bus to a local cinema, but there may not be a late bus to get back home. People in rural areas tend to be particularly disadvantaged in this way.

Personal interests

One of the most important factors affecting choice of leisure activity is personal interest. People will only choose leisure activities that give them pleasure. Different people have different interests. Some have varied interests and may enjoy a number of different activities whereas others may just have one that they are really passionate about. Just like Sam Hussein, the ice hockey player in the case study above, they may find many ways of enjoying the same activity.

A rock climber

Fashion

Different leisure activities rise and fall in popularity. A lot of people enjoy leisure activities that are fashionable or trendy at the time. TV programmes often help to popularise certain leisure activities. In 2004, some of the fashionable leisure activities included extreme sports such as bungee jumping and parachuting, snowboarding, membership at health or fitness clubs, interior and garden design, gourmet cooking, yoga and shopping. England's triumph at the 2003 Rugby Union World Cup created a lot of interest and made the game more fashionable.

The Trafford Centre, Manchester – a shopper's dream

The influence of family and friends

Young children will usually take part in family activities. If families go camping and enjoy the outdoor life, children may continue to enjoy these activities as they get older. Parents who play tennis regularly may encourage their children to do the same. Children often support the same sports team as their parents. But as children get older, they may reject their parents' leisure activities in favour of the things that their friends are interested in. It is quite common for children to 'go along with the crowd'.

Money

Some leisure activities are expensive and many people cannot afford them. For example, to go skiing you need to travel to a country where there is snow and you also have to buy or hire special equipment and buy a ski pass. This can cost hundreds of pounds. Other expensive leisure activities include horse riding, paragliding, rally driving, power boating, sailing, mountaineering and scuba diving.

Some groups of people such as pensioners, the unemployed, single parent families and students cannot afford leisure activities that others often take for granted. Activities like going to visitor attractions, eating out at restaurants and going to football matches may cost too much. However, there are some activities that nearly everyone can afford such as walking, reading, watching TV, playing board games, jogging, playing football, train spotting and swimming.

Expensive leisure activity

Scuba diving

Inexpensive leisure activity

Playing football in the park

Quick quiz

1 **True or false?**

✪ As children get older they are more likely to choose the same leisure activities as their friends.

✪ People living in towns and cities are more likely to visit the theatre.

✪ Better transport facilities mean that more leisure activities are available.

2 Which is the most expensive leisure activity?
(a) Listening to the radio **(b)** Reading **(c)** Playing golf **(d)** Yoga

3 Which of these leisure activities have gone out of fashion?
(a) Playing football **(b)** Skateboarding **(c)** Fitness training **(d)** Listening to Punk Rock

4 If you lived in a city centre, for which of these facilities would you need transport?
(a) Country Park **(b)** Cinema **(c)** Theatre **(d)** Restaurant

5 State three leisure activities that would be difficult to enjoy if you lived in the countryside.

Exam practice

Ann Sweeney

As a youngster, Ann Sweeney enjoyed reading and family outings to the countryside. They would go for walks together and have a picnic. Ann also enjoyed playing in the woods with her brother. At 18 she left home and got a job in London as trainee journalist. She lived in a flat and had very little money for leisure. Trips to the country were too expensive. So were many of the London attractions such as theatres, restaurants and nightclubs. However, she did go to a few free visitor attractions in the city. When Ann was 20, she met Danny at work who was a member of a North London Amateur Dramatic Society. He dragged Ann along and to her surprise, she enjoyed it. And it was only £4 a week. Later, she got a part in a play. Ann was good at acting and got a mention in a local newspaper. She now lives in Suffolk and is the editor of the *Ipswich Herald*. She belongs to another drama group and often plays the leading role. She can now afford to go to the theatre every week and see some of her favourite plays.

1. State two free visitor attractions that Ann might have gone to in London. *(2 marks)*

2. Would a lack of transport have stopped Ann from enjoying any leisure activities in London? Explain your answer. *(3 marks)*

3. Do you think it is expensive to become a member of drama group? Explain your answer. *(4 marks)*

4. Explain two factors that have affected Ann's choice of leisure activities. *(6 marks)*

A performance of Dick Turpin by an amateur dramatic society

Getting started...

Over two million people are employed in the leisure industry. Many of them are part-time workers which means that they work say, between 10 to 16 hours a week. The industry also employs seasonal workers. For example, a student that works at a theme park for two months during the summer vacation. The range of jobs in the leisure industry is huge. Think about the jobs at a council-run swimming pool below.

Angela Walton

Angela is a lifeguard at the swimming pool. She is a single parent and works 14 hours a week. It is a very responsible job. Last month, she had to rescue a boy from the deep end who could not swim. She spends a lot of time making sure teenagers do not break the pool rules such as 'No Running and No Diving'. Angela has life-saving and first-aid qualifications.

Amanda Mutambara

Amanda is in charge of the café at the pool. She works long hours, sometimes 50 hours a week. She has a number of duties which include supervising other staff, preparing food and drinks, ordering foodstuff, handling cash and dealing with customers.

Lucy Burgess

Lucy is a student at a sixth form college. She works at weekends in the reception area. She has to take money from customers, answer the telephone, deal with customer enquiries and do the cashing up at the end of the day. She sometimes helps with cleaning the pool. During the busy summer holidays, Lucy works full time at the pool.

(a) In what ways do the pool workers have important responsibilities?
(b) State which of the pool workers are (i) part-time (ii) full-time (iii) seasonal.

What jobs are there in the leisure industry?

Leisure assistants

Leisure assistants work in leisure centres. Their work will vary depending on what facilities the centre provides. In most cases, leisure assistants will be required to carry out a wide range of tasks. Examples might include setting up equipment such as badminton nets, working on reception, dealing with bookings, helping with the supervision of groups and special sessions, handling cash, equipment maintenance and cleaning the pool. Most of the work is unskilled and needs few, if any, qualifications. Training will be given 'on-the-job'. Pay rates will also be fairly low.

2.0m

Fitness instructors

Fitness instructors might work for a leisure centre or a private health club. They are trained to teach certain activities and supervise group sessions. These might be aerobics, keep fit, weight training or circuit training. Instructors need to be fit and well qualified with good people skills and the ability to motivate.

Some instructors work for themselves as private fitness instructors. They might go to a client's home or have a one-to-one session in a private health club. They are often called personal trainers and their services may include:

✪ fitness and health assessment

✪ designing a training programme

✪ suggesting a new diet

✪ ensuring that clients exercise safely

✪ providing motivation for individuals

✪ measuring fitness progress.

Lifeguards

By law, wherever the general public are allowed to swim, there must be a lifeguard in attendance. The main duty of a lifeguard is to ensure the safety of swimmers.

A lifeguard must have a proper qualification such as the National Pool Lifeguard Award and will also need training in first aid.

A lifeguard has to:

✪ oversee the safety of bathers

✪ enforce safety rules

✪ rescue people if necessary

✪ clean the pool

✪ check safety equipment

✪ attend training sessions

✪ supervise swimming groups

✪ record accidents

✪ report maintenance requirements

✪ attend management meetings.

Ground staff

Ground staff are employed at sports grounds. Football, rugby, hockey, tennis, bowling, cricket and golf clubs all need people to look after the grass surfaces on which the games are played. Football pitches, tennis courts and golf courses for example, need constant attention and proper preparation for important matches. At a professional level, the job of ground staff is particularly important and sometimes quite specialised. For example, the maintenance of greens on golf courses needs years of experience and knowledge of up-to-date treatments and techniques – it's not just about cutting the grass! Ground staff are also employed in parks, gardens and other open spaces to maintain flowerbeds and lawns, for example.

A green-keeper working on a golf course

Restaurant manager

In 2002, 545,400 people were employed in restaurants and cafés in the UK. Some of these jobs will have been restaurant managers. The job requires long hours, experience in the restaurant industry, catering training, perhaps some formal qualifications like NVQs and good people skills. Also, different types of restaurants may require different

The manager of the Bangla Fusion Restaurant, Much Hoole, near Preston

skills. For example, running a fast-food restaurant is not the same as running a restaurant in a five-star hotel. Management tasks in a restaurant might include:

- recruiting, training and supervising staff such as waiters, chefs, cleaners and dishwashers
- planning menus with the head chef
- dealing with customers
- buying food, wine and other provisions
- handling complaints
- administration
- handling and accounting for cash.

Park rangers

Park rangers work in countryside recreation areas. Their job is to look after countryside resources such as forests, lakes, ponds, walks and coastal walkways. They work to protect the natural environment from damage by people or the elements. Their duties might include:

- fire protection
- maintaining property such as gates and huts
- forestry work
- conservation work
- protecting endangered species
- gathering natural, historical, or scientific information
- enforcing local guidelines and regulations
- maintaining and operating camp sites
- dealing with the public.

Park rangers do not require formal qualifications but they must enjoy working outdoors.

Quick quiz

1. Which of these jobs requires a formal qualification?
   (a) Leisure assistant **(b)** Park ranger **(c)** Lifeguard **(d)** Ground staff

2. Which of these jobs is **not** likely to require people skills?
   (a) Ground staff **(b)** Restaurant manager **(c)** Fitness instructor **(d)** Leisure assistant

3. Which of these tasks is **not** likely to be done by ground staff?
   (a) Mowing grass **(b)** Repairing football nets **(c)** Handling complaints
   (d) Marking pitches

4. What is the most important job of a lifeguard?

5. State three tasks that a park ranger might be involved with.

6. Why might a second language be useful for a restaurant manager working in London?

7. Suggest four services a personal trainer might provide.

Exam practice

The Boulevard

The Boulevard is a popular restaurant in Bristol. It serves a range of Mediterranean style food and employs 18 staff, 12 of whom are part time. In the last two years, the restaurant has become very busy. In 2003, for the first time, it was recommended in a national restaurant guide. This meant that the manageress needed an assistant to cope with the extra workload. She had been working up to 70 hours a week and was beginning to tire. The advert shown here was placed in a local newspaper.

The Boulevard
12 Bath St, Bristol

Assistant Manager Required

Due to the popularity of the restaurant, an assistant manager is now required. You will work alongside the current manager and be expected to run this busy restaurant at least two days a week. You must be hard-working, able to perform well under pressure and work as part of a team. Experience in restaurant management would be preferable. However, applicants with other catering experience will be considered because full training is given.

- Permanent position.
- 5 weeks paid holiday.
- References required.
- Salary negotiable.
- Apply in writing.

1. Why has The Boulevard become more popular? *(2 marks)*
2. Apart from the restaurant manager, state three other jobs in the restaurant. *(3 marks)*
3. What does the term 'salary negotiable' mean? *(3 marks)*
4. Explain the skills and personal qualities that might be needed to do the job of the assistant manager. *(7 marks)*

Getting started...

A big part of the leisure industry is travel and tourism. Travel is about the movement of people from one place to another using various types of transport. For example, how a family gets from Glasgow to London for a weekend break. Tourism is to do with being away from home for a short time. For example, overnight on a business trip or for a two-week holiday. The people in the cases below are all leaving home for a while.

John and Kevin

John and Kevin are both in their 30s. On July 31st, they plan to travel from Southport to Birmingham by train and then stay overnight in a hotel. The next day, they will take a short taxi journey to Edgbaston to see a cricket match between England and Pakistan.

Edgbaston, Birmingham

The Campbell family

Mr and Mrs Campbell and their three teenage daughters are going to France for a two-week holiday. On the first day, they plan to drive from their home in Swindon to Paris. They will stay in a hotel and then the next day, drive down to Montpellier where they have rented a cottage.

Angela Tiler

Angela lives in Coventry. She is a university lecturer in physics. She has to give a lecture at the University of London. She plans to travel down by train the night before and stay with a friend who lives in Balham.

Angela quite often stays overnight when travelling on business because she feels fresher when she starts work the next morning.

Nazmul Huda

Nazmul Huda owns a cash and carry business in Leamington Spa. He has a lot of relatives who live in Bangladesh. He plans to take his family for a three-week holiday to visit

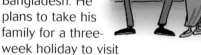

them in Chittagong. They will fly to Dhaka from Birmingham Airport and then get a bus from Dhaka to Chittagong. The flight will take about ten hours and the bus journey eight.

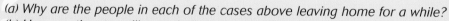

(a) Why are the people in each of the cases above leaving home for a while?
(b) How are they travelling to their destinations?

Why do people spend time away from home?

A holiday

People that work are entitled to paid holidays of at least four weeks a year. They may take an annual holiday. There is a wide range of holidays to choose from. Examples include:

- a seaside resort in the UK, such as Newquay
- salmon fishing in Scotland
- camping in the New Forest
- cruising around the Mediterranean
- a beach holiday on a Greek Island
- a fly-drive to Florida.

Holiday-makers on a cruise ship

Most people take their main annual holiday in the summer. But increasingly, people are taking other holidays during the year because costs are lower outside the main holiday season. Perhaps a weekend break to a European City such as Prague or into the countryside to stay at a quiet hotel. Winter holidays in the sun and winter skiing holidays are also popular.

Sightseeing

People might go sightseeing when they are on holiday. It means that they travel around their holiday area and visit places of interest. For example, a family on holiday in the Spanish resort of Lloret de Mar might go sightseeing in nearby Barcelona. They could see Las Ramblas, an area full of street performers and vendors, and the Barri Gotic which is famous for its gothic architecture.

Barcelona Cathedral

People can do these kinds of activities on their own or take a guided tour.

At home, it is common to go sightseeing for the day or for the weekend. Going to London or the Lake District, for example. There are plenty of interesting things to see in the UK.

Visiting an attraction

Visitor attractions include theme parks, zoos, historic sites, art galleries, National Parks, museums and the countryside. A family may spend the whole day at an attraction such as Alton Towers, or a young couple may just spend an hour or two looking at a new exhibition in the Tate Modern Art Gallery. Many people enjoy travelling to a big shopping complex such as the Trafford Centre. This £900 million shopping and leisure destination has restaurants, bars, pubs, cinemas, hotels, 10-pin bowling, turbo dodgems, gaming machines and a laser tag game in addition to the hundreds of shops and stores.

The Trafford Centre, Manchester

Visiting friends and relatives

In the UK in recent years, the number of nights, and the amount of money spent visiting friends, has increased. This is shown in Figures 1 and 2.

Figure 1 *Visiting friends and relatives in the UK – number of nights in millions*

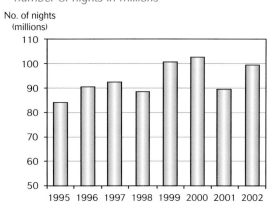

No. of nights (millions)

Figure 2 *Visiting friends and relatives in the UK– spending in £ millions*

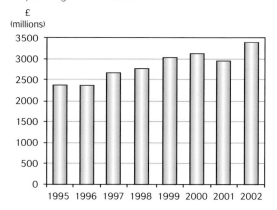

£ (millions)

Source: UK Tourist Survey

When people visit friends and relatives it is usually like a holiday. Although they may not stay in holiday accommodation, they often spend extra money going out to pubs, restaurants and other attractions.

Going to a sports event

People who enjoy watching sport usually have to travel, especially to away matches and international fixtures. Increasingly, spectators travel to watch sport and stay overnight. For example, thousands of Irish rugby supporters stay in London when Ireland play England in the Six Nations championship at Twickenham. A number of holiday companies specialise in the sale of packages that include travel, match tickets and accommodation for sports fixtures.

English rugby supporters at Twickenham watching England v France

Some people travel and stay away from home to take part in sporting events. For example, an amateur football club might go on a short tour playing matches in the Isle of Man.

Business

Business people at a meeting

Some people have to travel and stay away from home because of their jobs. Executives and managers may attend meetings and conferences. Sales people may have to visit customers, and other employees may have to attend training courses. They often stay overnight because their destinations are a long way from home or because the meetings and conferences last for more than one day. During the week, hotels in London are packed with business people. At weekends, they are less busy and attract different kinds of visitors, such as people taking a weekend break to see the sights.

Quick quiz

1 **True or false?**

- ✪ When people visit their friends or relatives for a few days, they normally stay in a hotel.
- ✪ Spending three weeks walking and camping in the Atlas Mountains, Morocco is an example of a holiday.
- ✪ Visitors to the Trafford Centre might go to the cinema and stay overnight.

2 How many nights were spent visiting friends and relatives in 2000? (see Figure 1)

3 State two reasons why Sunderland FC supporters travelling to Exeter for an FA Cup fixture, might stay overnight.

4 State two possible reasons why people spend more money than usual when visiting friends and relatives.

5 Suggest three sights that you might see in London.

Exam practice

Liz Berry and Chantelle Nixon

Liz Berry and Chantelle Nixon work for a large telecommunications company. They live and work in Burnley, Lancashire. They were sent on a training course to Birmingham to learn about a new IT system that they would have to use at work. They travelled from Burnley to Birmingham by train. The course was for three days and they stayed in a hotel for two nights. They were both given a £50 per day allowance to pay for an evening meal and other expenses. On the first night, they spent most of their money in a bistro and various wine bars on Broad Street, Birmingham's popular night scene. On the second night, they went to see a film and then had a Balti (Pakistani curry dish) in a restaurant on Ladypool Road.

1. (i) How many trips were made for business purposes in 2001? *(1 mark)*

   (ii) How much money was spent on business trips in 2000? *(1 mark)*

2. (i) Explain why Liz and Chantelle's business trip is classified as tourism. *(3 marks)*

   (ii) State two other purposes of tourism. *(2 marks)*

3. Explain how the travel and tourism industry might benefit from Liz and Chantelle's business trip to Birmingham. *(9 marks)*

Figure 3 *Business and work tourism in the UK – number of trips in millions*

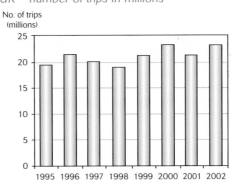

Figure 4 *Business and work tourism in the UK – spending in £ millions*

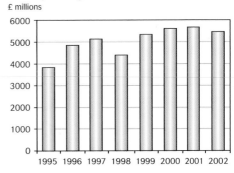

Source: UK Tourist Survey

Getting started...

> The travel and tourism industry is made up of many different organisations. Most of them are businesses. They provide services to people who want to travel and spend time away from home. They give information and advice, help people with choices, arrange holidays and trips, transport people, cater for people's accommodation needs and provide entertainment. Look at the services provided by the businesses below.

easyJet

Callum McIvor runs a software design company in Edinburgh. He has a business appointment in London on May 24th. He plans to fly with easyJet and stay overnight. He booked a return flight to London Gatwick on the Internet. His outward flight leaves Edinburgh at 08.25 and arrives at Gatwick at 10.00 and cost £96.49. His return flight leaves London the next day at 14.55 and arrives in Edinburgh at 16.25. This cost £56.99.

The Airds Hotel – Port Appin

Carl has planned a special 40th birthday surprise for his wife Melanie. He has booked a night at the Airds Hotel, Port Appin, on the west coast of Scotland. It is a luxurious hotel set in stunning scenery and offers the very best in service, décor and dining. Carl has booked a superior double room for £280. This includes dinner and a full Scottish breakfast. He thinks it will be worth the money because the food is said to be outstanding.

The restaurant at The Airds Hotel

Going Places

Dilshan, Manik, Jo and Sarah are all 17. They have booked their first holiday abroad. The travel agents, Going Places, sold them a two-week package holiday to Ibiza costing £399 each. The package includes a return flight from Luton Airport, transfers between Ibiza Airport and the resort and 14 nights accommodation in a two-star hotel. They spent 2½ hours at Going Places while they made up their minds where to go. They listened to suggestions from the sales assistant and looked at endless brochures.

(a) What services are being provided by the businesses in each of the above cases?

(a) How much have the services cost?

What are the key components in the travel and tourism industry?

The diagram in Figure 1 shows that there are seven key components of the travel and tourism industry. There is a relationship between the components. For example, tour operators buy transport and accommodation and put them together as a package holiday which travel agents then sell to customers. This unit looks at travel agents, tour operators, tourist information and guiding services.

Figure 1 *A summary of the travel and tourism industry*

Transportation
e.g. flights, trains and coaches.

Travel agents
e.g. Thomas Cook, Lunn Poly and Going Places.

Attractions
e.g. excursions to places of interest such as historic sites and theme parks.

Tour operators
e.g. Thomson Holidays, First Choice and JMC.

Key components of travel and tourism

Accommodation and catering
e.g. hotels, apartments, caravans, motels, guest-houses and restaurants.

Tourist information and guiding sevices
e.g. regional and local tourist boards.

Online travel services
e.g. websites on the Internet.

Travel agents

Travel agents make money by selling services, such as holidays and travel insurance, that others provide. For example, they might charge a 10% commission on a holiday they sell for a tour operator. Travel agents usually have shops in towns and cities. They:

- sell package holidays for tour operators

- sell and issue tickets for flights, coach tours, trains and ferry crossings

- sell holiday insurance for insurance companies

- sell foreign currency to travelers

- plan travel itineraries

- give advice and information about visas, destinations and travel options

- book accommodation.

Most travel agents are owned by chains such as Going Places, Travelcare and Lunn Poly but there are also many small, local agents that operate independently. One thing they all have in common is that they do not charge the customer for providing their services. They are paid commission by the companies whose products and services they sell.

Part of a national chain of travel agents

An independent travel agent

Tour operators

A tour operator's job is to put together all the components of a holiday and sell it as a single product. This is done for the customer's convenience and is called a package holiday. The different components may include:

- ☺ travel to the holiday destination – by plane, train, ferry or coach, for example

- ☺ transfers from the airport to the accommodation – coach, minibus or taxi, for example

- ☺ accommodation – hotel, villa, guesthouse or apartment complex, for example

- ☺ excursions – optional day trips to attractions and places of interest.

Tour operators pay other businesses such as airlines, hotels and coach companies for their services. They are able to negotiate cheap rates for making huge block bookings. They advertise their holidays in brochures and sometimes on TV. They then rely on travel agents to sell them. But increasingly, customers can book holidays direct themselves. Some tour operators such as First Choice, are travel agents as well.

Holiday brochures

Types of tour operators

Inbound tour operators provide services for visitors to the UK.
Outbound tour operators provide services for UK residents who plan to travel overseas.
Domestic tour operators provide services for UK residents visiting other parts of the UK.

Tourist information

In addition to travel agents, there are other places that provide information. There are around 560 Tourist Information Centres (TICs) located around the UK and each one provides information about the local area. TICs give out brochures, leaflets, maps, timetables and other information to tourists. They may also offer booking services for local hotels and other accommodation. TICs are also responsible for promoting and monitoring tourism in their local areas.

Tourist Information Centre, Salisbury

Guiding services

Some people like to use guiding services when they are visiting places of interest. Guided tours are often available at such places as museums, galleries, stately homes and castles. Tour guides may be volunteers with a special interest in a local attraction, or people who are trained and paid to accompany groups of tourists. They point out interesting details and answer questions. Guided tours are also common in open-top buses and coaches where a running commentary is given as the vehicle travels along.

Quick quiz

1. Which of these is **not** a component of the travel and tourism industry?
   (a) Tourist information **(b)** Tour operators **(c)** Travel agents **(d)** Video rental shops

2. Which of these is **not** a service provided by a travel agent?
   (a) Selling foreign currency **(b)** Booking a flight **(c)** Running a hotel
   (d) Booking accommodation

3. Which of the following is a tour operator?
   (a) Thomson Holidays **(b)** easyJet **(c)** British Airways
   (d) The Tourist Information Centre

4. Which of these is **not usually** a component of a package holiday?
   (a) Transfer **(b)** Hotel accommodation **(c)** Flight **(d)** Meals in local restaurants

5. Why do people buy holiday insurance?

6. Why do people need foreign currency?

7. State the difference between inbound, outbound and domestic tour operators.

Exam practice

Halesowen Travel Ltd

Halesowen Travel Ltd is an independent travel agent. It employs seven staff and provides a range of travel and tourist services to local people. John Wozniac and his wife Theresa, have booked a holiday to Sri Lanka. They fly from Birmingham Airport leaving at 10.00 and arrive at Bandaranaike Airport, Colombo at 09.30. On arrival, they will be transferred by taxi to The Galle Face Hotel. The holiday is being provided by Golden Sun Tours at a cost of £680 each. During their stay, John and Theresa hope to see:

A beach in Sri Lanka

- ✪ The Dambulla Caves
- ✪ The Pinnewala Elephant Sanctuary
- ✪ a tea plantation
- ✪ Adam's Peak
- ✪ surfers at Hikkaduwa.

The sales assistant at the travel agent also advised them to ask their doctor what injections they would need before going to Sri Lanka to protect themselves from diseases such as malaria and tetanus. She also recommended that they take American dollars with them to change into the local currency on arrival.

1. How much commission will Halesowen Travel Ltd receive from Golden Sun Tours if they charge 10%? *(2 marks)*

2. John and Theresa hope to go on some excursions in Sri Lanka. Using examples from the case, explain what this means. *(3 marks)*

3. Explain what is meant by an independent travel agent. *(4 marks)*

4. Using examples from the case, explain the difference between a travel agent and a tour operator. *(7 marks)*

Getting started...

When people travel away from home they usually spend more money than they would normally. The travel and tourism industry benefits from this spending. Businesses that provide transport, accommodation, catering and tourist attractions probably gain the most. Think about the spending in the cases below.

Ellen Buschbacher

Ellen Buschbacher is going to spend Christmas with her daughter's family in Dunedin, New Zealand. She has not seen them for six years. She has saved up for ages to pay for the 26 hour flight. The return fare from London Heathrow to Christchurch, New Zealand is £1,360. She is flying with Quantas, the Australian airline.

A Quantas Airways Boeing 747

The Thomas family

The Thomas family are going to Euro Disney, Paris for a holiday. They are going to drive from their home in Newport and stay in budget self-catering accommodation. They have bought four 3-day Disney Park Hopper tickets for £74 each. Their three children, all in their early teens, have saved up £100 each which they plan to spend in Euro Disney's shops.

Main Street, Euro Disney

Chris Chambers and June Simmonds

Chris and June have booked a weekend trip to Milan. They are both very keen on Italian food and the main purpose of their break is to eat in some of Milan's finest restaurants and experience some authentic Italian food. They expect to spend around £500 on eating out during their trip.

An Italian restaurant

(a) *What are the main items of spending described in each of the above cases?*
(b) *Into which of the key components of the travel and tourism industry does the spending fall?*

The key components in the travel and tourism industry

Figure 1 is a copy of Figure 1 in Unit 16. In this unit, transportation, accommodation and catering, attractions and online travel services will be discussed.

Figure 1 *A summary of the travel and tourism industry*

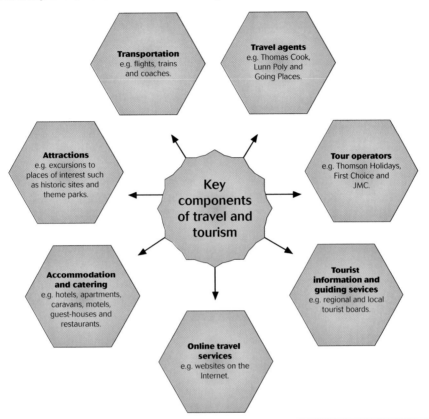

Transportation

When people travel, they have a number of transport methods to chose from.

Many people prefer cars. Car ownership has increased significantly in recent years and people use their cars for leisure purposes. Examples include driving to leisure centres, visiting friends and relatives, picking up videos and take-aways and driving to visitor attractions.

Some people take their cars overseas using ferry services or on the train through the Channel Tunnel. Car hire is popular with people who fly to overseas destinations. Two very different methods of transport used in

The old and the new – a traditional rickshaw and a modern coach in Thailand

the travel and tourism industry are shown in the photograph. In some Asian countries, the rickshaw – a small, two or three-wheeled passenger vehicle drawn by one or two men – is a popular method of transport.

Accommodation

When people stay away from home, they may stay with friends or relatives. But if not, there is a wide range of accommodation to choose from.

Hotels The size and standard of hotels varies considerably. Some are very large with up to 600 rooms but others are small with say, only 6 rooms. Some are luxurious whilst others are basic. The facilities hotels offer also vary. Large ones have restaurants, cafés, swimming pools, fitness centres, spas and shops. Others have none of these.

Guest-houses are usually family run and they are often smaller and cheaper than hotels. The rooms may be situated in the owner's home and provide a 'homely' atmosphere. Many bed-and-breakfast operations are run from guest-houses. Some are farmhouses or inns.

Holiday homes might include apartments, villas, cottages and chalets. Many are self-catering with kitchen facilities included. There are a number of holiday villages, such as Pontin's and Center Parcs, in the UK. They offer a variety of holiday homes all in one location. They often have shops, restaurants, recreational and other facilities.

Motels provide fairly basic accommodation. They are located on the roadside and are geared up to serve motorists who just want to stay overnight. Motels are more popular in the US and Australia where motorists travel much greater distances than in the UK.

Caravans and tents Caravan and camping sites allow people to bring their own caravan or tent. Some are quite large with good washing facilities, a shop, a restaurant and recreational facilities. Others have fixed tents and caravans and offer facilities like holiday villages.

Youth hostels These provide beds in different sized rooms, sometimes in dormitories. There are also cooking facilities and a social area. Youth hostels are specifically aimed at young people but they are actually used by all age groups.

Catering

Whilst a lot of accommodation provides meals or facilities to prepare meals, some people prefer to eat out or buy a take-away meal. The choice of restaurants, pubs, bistros and fast-food outlets is huge. Eating out is often a very important part of a holiday or a trip away from home. When people are away from home, they often treat themselves by eating out more often than they would normally.

Attractions

The range of attractions that people like to visit is enormous. Some of them have been described in previous units. For example, in the UK, people travel to historical sites, museums, galleries, countryside locations, parks, theme parks and seaside resorts. They also travel to see major sporting events such as the Open Golf Championship, the FA Cup Final and Test Matches. When people go on holiday, they sometimes like to go on excursions that are organised by tour operators. Other people prefer to hire a car and make their own way to attractions.

Online services

There is an enormous amount of information about travel, holiday destinations and attractions on the Internet. It is also possible to book flights, holidays, train and coach journeys, accommodation, tickets for major visitor attractions, sports fixtures and the theatre. It is often cheaper to book on the Internet. For example, when booking a flight with easyJet on the Internet, it is £5 cheaper per person. Credit cards are used to pay for Internet purchases and an email is sent to confirm the booking – the tickets are then sent by post. Sometimes, tickets can be printed off immediately using a computer.

Quick quiz

1 State three services in the travel and tourism industry that can be booked on the Internet.

2 State two types of holiday accommodation that might be suitable for people on a very low budget.

3 State three major sporting events that people might travel to.

4 Match the most likely transport method with the journey described.

- ✿ A two-mile trip to a video rental shop
- ✿ A business trip from Leeds to London
- ✿ A holiday journey from England to Barbados

Ferry	Train	Car
Coach	Tram	Plane

5 What type of accommodation would you choose for one night if you were driving through California in the USA?

Exam practice

A trip to Birmingham

Ken and Joyce Brennan want to stay in Birmingham overnight. They are visiting their daughter at university and also want to see Birmingham Cathedral, the botanical gardens and the Birmingham Museum and Art Gallery. They would like some reasonably priced accommodation, preferably in a small hotel. They plan to drive down from their home in Bradford.

On the same day, Jacques Bredoteau and his business partner Frank Pearson, are attending a conference at the NEC. They are travelling from Exeter and would like to stay in the city centre, within walking distance from the city's amenities. Their hotel expenses will be met by the business. They plan to book their travel and hotel on the Internet.

Hotel	Star Rating	Room per night	Distance to city centre	Size (Rooms)	Brief description
Copthorne	4 Star	£102	0.2 miles	212	Modern accommodation
Burlington	4 Star	£135	0.5 miles	112	Luxurious, Victorian style
Quality Hotel	3 Star	£60	1.2 miles	213	Practical accommodation
Hagley Court	N/A	£66	1.3 miles	24	Family atmosphere
Plough and Harrow	3 Star	£128	1.5 miles	44	Fine old Victorian building

1. State two ways in which Jacques Bredoteau and Frank Pearson may have travelled from Exeter to Birmingham. *(2 marks)*

2. What attractions might Ken and Joyce Brennan enjoy visiting in Birmingham? *(3 marks)*

3. Explain two advantages of using the Internet to book travel and tourism services. *(4 marks)*

4. Which hotels do you think would be most suitable for the two sets of travellers? Explain your answers. *(7 marks)*

The Copthorne Hotel, Birmingham

Getting started...

People look forward to their annual holiday. Part of the fun is choosing where to go and making all the plans and preparations. There is a huge variety of holidays to choose from which cater for different tastes, age groups and interests. Think about the holidays below.

Backpacking

Paul Crowley and Helen Cotterill have just finished their university courses. Before getting a job, they are going to spend a year backpacking. They have booked flights which allow them to stop off at Hong Kong, Beijing, Bangkok, Sydney and Wellington. These long haul flights have cost £1,050 each. They have packed all their luggage into two large backpacks. They will find accommodation as they travel around.

All-inclusive

Greg and Laura Tomlinson are going on their honeymoon to the Maldives for two weeks. They are staying on a small island and have paid £2,250 each for an all-inclusive holiday. This means that all their travel, 5-star accommodation, food, drinks, water sports, excursions and insurance are included in the price.

Weekend away

Jacek Novak and his family are going to The Lake District for a long weekend. They will stay in a guest house in Ambleside for three nights. They plan to walk in the hills, take a boat out on Lake Windermere, visit some old country pubs and eat in some interesting restaurants. They have booked bed-and-breakfast accommodation and plan to drive from their home in Warwick on Friday afternoon.

(a) Describe briefly the type of holiday in each case.
(b) Which of these holidays might be unsuitable for an elderly, retired couple?

Types of holiday

Package holiday

Package holidays are put together by tour operators such as Thomas Cook. Basic packages include flights, transfers and accommodation but there are other packages available that might also include the following:

- ✿ Holiday insurance
- ✿ Excursions
- ✿ Car hire
- ✿ Free travel for children
- ✿ All food and drinks
- ✿ All entertainment and water sports.

When people choose a destination, they also have to decide what type of accommodation they want. They may be offered self-catering, bed-and-breakfast, half board (includes lunch or evening meal) or full board (includes all meals). Package holidays are popular because they are convenient and cheap. They are cheap because tour operators block-book flights and accommodation and can negotiate low prices.

Independent travel

Instead of buying a package holiday, some people prefer to make all their own holiday arrangements and travel independently. They book their own travel, accommodation and other requirements. This type of holiday is often popular with single people and couples without children. They often take guidebooks with them to help in finding suitable accommodation, restaurants and other places of interest. One advantage of this type of holiday is that it is flexible. People can go wherever they like and decide what they want to do as they go along. However, it might be more expensive and there is a chance that hotels might be fully booked when they arrive at a destination.

Guide books

Domestic holidays

Although there has been a huge growth in the number of people taking holidays abroad, many people still like to take a holiday in the UK. This may be because it is cheaper, there is less travelling, no language difficulties, no money to exchange and more predictable. But in the UK, the weather can be unreliable, new cultures cannot be experienced and there is often congestion on roads and at resorts.

Inbound and outbound holidays

Inbound tourists are those coming into the UK from other countries. Figure 1 shows that most visitors to the UK are from the EU. In 2003, 14,800,000 EU residents visited the UK. Outbound tourists include people from the UK who travel overseas.

Figure 1 *Inbound tourists 2003*

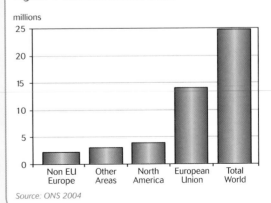

Source: ONS 2004

Short haul and long haul holidays

Holidays are sometimes categorised according to the distance traveled. Short haul flights go to holiday areas that are less than five hours flying time from the UK so mainly, they are to European destinations. Long haul flights take longer than five hours and go to such places as India, the USA and Australia. For example, a flight to Australia can take up to 24 hours and is likely to involve a stop in Singapore or Hong Kong for the plane to refuel.

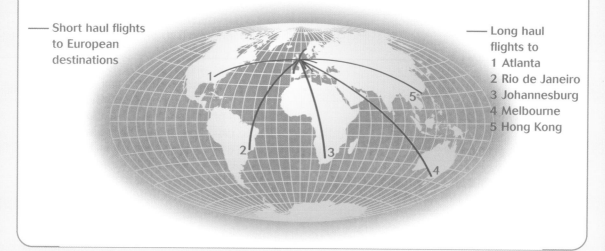

—— Short haul flights to European destinations

—— Long haul flights to
1 Atlanta
2 Rio de Janeiro
3 Johannesburg
4 Melbourne
5 Hong Kong

Special interest holidays

Some people like to combine a hobby or interest with their holiday. Others might decide to try a completely new activity that requires tuition and equipment. Specialist tour operators often provide this type of holiday. For example:

✪ Red Spokes Adventure Tours offers cycling holidays in places like Peru, Tibet, Nepal, Pakistan and Thailand.

✪ Will 4 Adventure provides outdoor trips and adventures around the world, e.g. white water rafting on the Nile.

✪ Italian Cookery Weeks Ltd provides people with accommodation and Italian cookery lessons in Venice.

✪ Ebookers provides specialist tours for cricket, football and rugby supporters following the England team abroad.

A wide range of interests can be enjoyed on specialist holidays such as skiing, sailing, mountaineering, painting, yoga, scuba-diving, golfing, bird-watching and fishing.

Short break holidays

Many people take short breaks as well as an annual holiday. Due to cheaper air and ferry travel and the Channel Tunnel, short breaks to places such as European cities, have become very popular.

BARCELONA 2nts
3★ HOTEL ABVILADOMAT
Deps 10 May - 27 June 04
£^fr 175

PRAGUE 2nts
3★ TYL HOTEL
Deps 02 - 30 July 04
£^fr 189

ROME 2nts
3★ WINDROSE HOTEL
Deps 11 July - 30 August 04
£^fr 199

DUBLIN 2nts
4★ CLARION HOTEL DUBLIN
Deps up to 30 December 04
£^fr 199

Short breaks to UK destinations are also common. These include breaks at countryside hotels, health farms, country clubs, UK cities, seaside resorts and sporting venues. Some people are prepared to travel as far away as places like New York, Boston, Dubai and North Africa for short breaks. Christmas shopping in New York is very popular.

Quick quiz

1 **True or false?**

⚙ An American visiting the UK to see some of the historic sites is an example of outbound tourism.

⚙ Most inbound tourists to the UK in 2003 were from the European Union.

⚙ Going on a package holiday to the resort of Torremolinos in Spain is a special interest holiday.

2 Which of these is a long haul destination?

(a) Melbourne **(b)** Paris **(c)** Madrid **(d)** Prague

3 Which of these is a disadvantage of domestic holidays?

(a) Cheaper **(b)** Less travelling time **(c)** No currency to exchange **(d)** Unpredictable weather

4 Which of these is **not** normally included in a package holiday?

(a) Accommodation **(b)** Meals in restaurants **(c)** Flights **(d)** Transfers

5 State one advantage and one disadvantage of independent travel.

Exam practice

Cyprus and Glasgow

CYPRUS

Mayfair Hotel and Apartments

- KIDS go FREE
- **Self catering, Bed and breakfast, Half or Full board sleeps up to 3, 4 & 6.**

A modern, popular complex, the Mayfair offers good value accommodation with good standards of service. Situated only 700 metres from the Kato Paphos resort centre and approximately 15 minutes stroll away from the Lighthouse beach.

Fast Facts
Facilities: 2 outdoor swimming pools • Sun terrace • Restaurant • 2 bars (24 hours) • Poolside bar • Lounge bar • Reception.
Children's facilities: Paddling pool • Activities programme • Animation programme • Highchairs.
Entertainment: Daytime activities programme • Evening entertainment programme • TV room.
Sports: Bowling green • Mini-golf • Table tennis • Volleyball.
Health & Fitness: Gym • Fitness centre • Massage • Sauna • Whirlpool.
Nearest beach: 1.5 kilometres.
Transfer time by coach (approx): 40-50 minutes.

Glasgow and Edinburgh Christmas Shopping

Glasgow boasts the United Kingdom's second biggest shopping district and retail centre. The huge Buchanan Galleries, Princes Square and the Italian Centre combine all the famous high street names with Italian designer excellence where you will also find many stylish cafés and restaurants.

3 Day Itinerary

Friday: Travel directly to Glasgow with the afternoon free for shopping and sightseeing. The evening is free to either dine in the Campanile or to visit one of Glasgow's many fine restaurants.
Saturday: After breakfast, depart for Edinburgh with the day free to do as you please before returning to Glasgow.
Sunday: Returning from Glasgow, a stop will be made at Gretna Outlet Village. Here it is possible to buy well-known branded goods and clothing at discounted prices. Arrival home will be late afternoon.

3 Day Coach Tour - No 45 Glasgow
Price per person includes 2 nights bed & continental breakfast
November 12: £89   December 3:   £89
November 19: £89   December 10: £89
November 26: £89
Supplements per person: single room £35

1.   What types of holiday are described above? *(2 marks)*

2.   Explain the difference between self-catering, half-board and full-board accommodation. *(3 marks)*

3.   Explain why the holiday to Cyprus is suitable for children. *(4 marks)*

4.   Explain why an independent traveller may not be interested in either of these holidays. *(7 marks)*

Getting started...

Although methods of travel have not changed very much in recent years, the amount of travelling has increased and people's transport preferences have changed. Look at the methods of travel chosen in the cases below.

Jack McIlvanney

Jack is a pensioner and lives on his own in Toxteth, Liverpool. He is going to visit his sister who lives in Birmingham. He always travels by coach because it is cheap. The fare from Liverpool to Birmingham is £11.25. To go by train would cost twice as much. He booked his ticket with National Express two weeks before the journey.

National Express coach

Sikha Ray

Sikha Ray lives in Cardiff and is a sales rep for a large electronics manufacturer. She drives around 50,000 miles a year on business. She has a hectic schedule and usually visits about five or six customers a day. She uses a car because it is flexible and quick. She would not be able to visit as many customers in a day if she used public transport.

The Hackett family

The Hackett family are having a camping holiday in France. They are going to drive from their home in Guildford to Dover, and then take the ferry across the Channel to France.

   The children, who are aged seven, ten and twelve, enjoy the trip. They like to explore the ferry and sit on the top deck watching other boats and ships. The ferry costs £448 for their return trip and leaves on August 1st. They could have gone by Euro Tunnel which is quicker but much more expensive at £745.

P & O ferry

(a) What methods of transport are being used in the above cases?
(b) Give reasons why these methods have been chosen.

How can people travel to their destinations?

Air travel

The popularity of air travel is shown by the graph in Figure 1. The number of passengers flying between the UK and the rest of the world has increased from 82,949,900 in 1992 to 143,569,600 in 2002. Most people travelling overseas prefer to fly. It is safe, fast, becoming less expensive and there is a large choice of airports in the UK. The main airports are shown in Figure 2. One disadvantage of air travel is that flights may be delayed due to strikes, bad weather or airport congestion. Air travel is provided mainly by scheduled or charter flights.

Scheduled flights run to a regular timetable throughout the year. Flights go ahead even if the plane only has a handful of passengers. This makes them more expensive to operate than charter flights.

Charter flights are usually booked by tour operators for their package holidays but some tickets are also sold to independent travellers.

Flights are sometimes consolidated. This happens when all the seats on a plane have not been sold and passengers from various departure airports are combined to fill one plane. This saves the airline or tour operator money but it can be very inconvenient for the passengers.

Air taxi services transport a small number of passengers. Their service is tailored specifically to the passenger's requirements. For example, a business executive might use an air taxi if they cannot find a convenient scheduled flight.

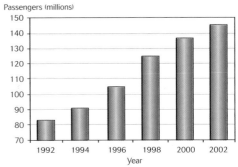

Figure 1 *Air traffic between the UK and the rest of the world 1992 - 2002*

Source: Annual Abstract of Statistics 2004

Figure 2 *Main UK airports*

Rail travel

Despite the problems of delays, rail crashes, rising fares, and a poor image, rail travel has increased in recent years. Figure 3 shows that the number of journeys made on the national rail network has increased from 770 million in 1992 to 976 million in 2002. Inter-city travel is particularly popular. The main advantages of rail travel over the car include:

- ✪ less tiring – it is possible to sleep on the train
- ✪ tickets can be booked on the day or in advance
- ✪ refreshments are provided on most journeys
- ✪ work can be done on a train, e.g. using a laptop
- ✪ quicker on some long distance journeys
- ✪ more environmentally friendly.

The disadvantages include:
- ✪ lacks flexibility due to fixed rail routes
- ✪ restricted timetable, e.g. few late-night journeys
- ✪ some journeys are very expensive
- ✪ some trains are busy with standing room only
- ✪ trains may be delayed or cancelled.

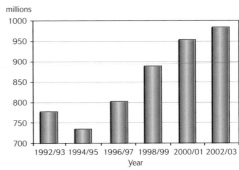

Figure 3 *Rail passenger journeys 1992-2002*

Source: Annual Abstract of Statistics 2004

Sea travel

Some people use the ferry to get to overseas destinations such as France, Belgium, Spain, Ireland and Scandinavia. Although the ferry is slower than flying, it is still quite popular. The ferry allows people to drive their own car to overseas destinations and saves them from having to hire a car when they get there. There are some parts of the UK where the ferry link is the main means of transport. For example, the Isle of Man, the Isle of Wight, the Hebrides and the Shetlands. Some ferries provide short cuts to destinations – the Corran Ferry in Scotland takes passengers and vehicles on the short crossing between Corran and Ardgour on Loch Linnhe thus avoiding a 36 mile road trip. It was thought that when the Channel Tunnel opened, ferry services would find it difficult to compete. But they have survived and the extra competition has reduced the price of crossing the Channel. The major ferry ports are shown in Figure 4.

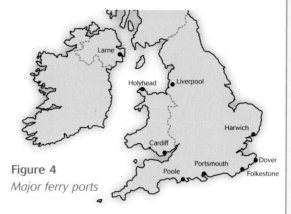

Figure 4
Major ferry ports

Road travel

Car Road travel by car is extremely popular and continues to grow as shown in Figure 5. Between 1992 and 2002, new car registrations rose from 1,528,000 to 2,528,800. The UK has a very good road and motorway network and most places can be reached easily in one day. Figure 6 shows the main motorways.

Advantages	Disadvantages
Cheap per mile	Tiring on long journeys
Highly flexible	Congestion can cause delays
Carry lots of luggage	Cannot work while travelling
Cars can be hired	Parking may be difficult
	High initial cost of buying a car

Coaches When travelling on public transport, some people might choose a coach rather than a train because it is cheaper. But coaches are slower than trains and a journey must be pre-booked to guarantee a seat. Like cars, coaches may also get delayed by traffic. Modern coaches have a toilet, telephones, videos and serve light refreshments.

Taxis may be used by people when they reach their destination. They are quick, convenient and particularly useful in unfamiliar locations, such as a foreign city.

Figure 5 *New car registrations*

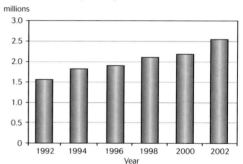

millions

Source: Annual Abstract of Statistics 2004

Figure 6 *UK motorway network*

Quick quiz

1 **True or false?**
- Coach travel is more expensive than rail travel.
- The M4 links London and Cardiff.
- The nearest ferry port to Bristol is Dover.

2 Which of these motorways links Birmingham and Carlisle?
(a) M25 **(b)** M6 **(c)** M25 **(d)** MI

3 Which is the nearest airport to Edinburgh?
(a) Liverpool **(b)** Newcastle **(c)** Glasgow **(d)** East Midlands

4 Which two ferry ports could you use to travel to Ireland?
(a) Portsmouth **(b)** Harwich **(c)** Holyhead **(d)** Liverpool

5 What is the difference between scheduled and charter flights?

Exam practice

Travel from Preston to London

Mark and Janice Belushi want to travel from Preston to London for a weekend break. They plan to leave on Friday morning at about 9.00 am and return on Sunday at about 11.00 am. They own a car but they don't want to drive the 500 miles round trip because they think they will get caught in traffic. They would prefer a more relaxed journey. The departure and arrival times, the duration of each journey, and the prices are shown in the table below.

	Preston Depart	London Arrive	Duration hrs/mins	London Depart	Preston Arrive	Duration hrs/mins	Price
Train	9.20	12.21	3.01	11.30	16.18	4.48	£113.60
Coach	9.15	15.05	5.50	11.00	16.35	5.35	£100.00

Virgin train

National Express coach

1. Which motorways would the coach use travelling from Preston to London? *(2 marks)*

2. (i) The Belushi's car does 40 miles to the gallon. Calculate the cost of the 500 miles round trip if petrol costs £3.90 per gallon. *(3 marks)*

   (ii) Which is the cheapest travel option of the three? *(1 mark)*

3. State three disadvantages of using the car for the journey. *(3 marks)*

4. Compare the train and the coach as a means of getting from Preston to London and suggest which one they should use. *(9 marks)*

Getting started...

People from the UK and tourists from abroad can enjoy a wide variety of tourist destinations in the UK. There are seaside resorts, attractive coastlines, National Parks, Areas of Outstanding Natural Beauty, tourist towns and cities. There are also the attractions that have been discussed in previous units such as theme parks, museums, galleries, historic sites and sporting venues. Think about the destinations below.

Llandudno

Llandudno in North Wales is a fine example of a traditional Victorian seaside resort. It has a long crescent promenade, wide shopping streets, sweeping sands and a variety of attractions for all the family including:

- Alice in Wonderland centre
- Victorian shopping centre
- Award-winning tearoom
- Oriel Mostyn Gallery
- Bodafon Farm Park
- Great Orme Tramway (Britain's only cable-hauled public road tramway)
- Llandudno Superbowl
- Haulfre Gardens
- Miniature golf course
- Llandudno cable car.

Llandudno

Bath

Bath is said to be one of England's tourist gems. It is 2000 years old and is a World Heritage Site. Visitors can see fine examples of Georgian architecture, the famous Roman Baths and the ancient thermal springs, which is now one of the UK's top five tourist attractions. There are also many museums, restaurants and pubs.

The Roman Baths at Bath

Cornwall

Most people visit Cornwall to enjoy its attractive beaches and beautiful coastal scenery. The north coast attracts surfers. Lands End is the most westerly point in mainland Britain with rugged, wave-lashed cliffs, stunning views, the Longships Lighthouse and the Wolf Rock Lighthouse. In Cornwall, there are castles, fishing villages, moors, old tin mines, gardens, golf courses, the Eden Project and much more.

A beach in Cornwall

(a) For each of the above destinations, state two specific attractions.
(b) Which of the destinations might an American tourist, with an interest in historic Britain, be most likely to visit?

Seaside towns in the UK

Blackpool attracts more visitors than any other seaside resort. It is famous for its tower, illuminations, pier, sandy beaches, shops, bars and pleasure beach. It is a popular venue for stag and hen-nights and attracts holiday-makers, day-trippers and people taking a short break. Unit 8 has more information about Blackpool.

Bournemouth has seven miles of golden beaches, attractive parks and gardens, a pier, an Oceanarium, a museum and a number of facilities for businesses.

Brighton is a lively seaside resort and is popular with all types of people from young clubbers to families. It has a famous pier, lots of restaurants and night clubs and a pebble beach. Unit 8 has more information about Brighton.

Portrush is Northern Ireland's most popular seaside resort. Its attractions include sandy beaches, Royal Portrush Golf Course, Barry's Amusement Park, Dunluce Castle, Waterworld and Portrush Countryside Centre. The surrounding area has some attractive countryside and the Old Bushmills Distillery is nearby.

Scarborough has been a seaside resort for almost 400 years. It has two large bays separated by the castle headland and an elegant Victorian Esplanade. Its attractions include the Atlantis Waterpark, Eden Camp (a museum located in a former prisoner of war camp where visitors can experience life in wartime Britain), Kinderland amusement centre, the Alexandra Indoor Bowls Centre and the Stephen Joseph Theatre.

Tenby is in Pembrokeshire, South Wales. One of the main attractions is the Pembrokeshire Coast Path National Trail which has 186 miles of spectacular coastal scenery. There are also many other things to see and do including Folly Farm, Dinosaur Park, Oakwood Leisure Park, Tenby Museum, Silent World Aquarium, Tenby Lifeboat Station and the Heatherton Country Sports Park.

Torquay seafront is lined by palm trees and has Italian style white villas perched on the surrounding hillside. Yachts are moored in a modern marina which helps to create a continental atmosphere. Torquay has attracted the rich and the famous for over a hundred years and offers a wealth of tourist facilities.

Bournemouth beach

Figure 1 *Seaside resorts*

Torquay – the town and harbour

National Parks in England and Wales

A National Park is a large area of beautiful and relatively wild countryside. The aim of these parks is to preserve and enhance their natural beauty for the benefit of the whole nation. Free access is provided to all members of the public. All wildlife, buildings and places of historic interest are also protected. There are 12 National Parks in England and Wales and they provide a wide variety of countryside scenery such as mountains, lakes, moors, forests and rugged coastline. National Parks provide services such as:

- ✪ car parks, picnic sites and toilets

- ✪ information centres providing leaflets maps, books and other information

- ✪ park rangers and wardens who are responsible for the upkeep and maintenance of the parks

- ✪ assistance to conservation and voluntary groups

- ✪ improved access through footpaths, stiles, signposts and nature walks.

Areas of Outstanding Natural Beauty (AONB)
These are similar to National Parks but they do not get the same level of protection from development. For example, a wind farm might be built in an AONB but probably not in a National Park. These areas are run by The Countryside Agency. There are over forty AONBs including Cannock Chase, the Cotswolds, Cornwall, Forest of Bowland and the Isle of Wight. Like National Parks, the main aim of AONBs is to conserve and enhance their natural beauty.

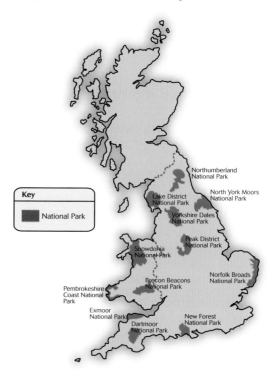

Figure 2 *National Parks in England and Wales*

Key

▮ National Park

Northumberland National Park
North York Moors National Park
Lake District National Park
Yorkshire Dales National Park
Peak District National Park
Snowdonia National Park
Norfolk Broads National Park
Brecon Beacons National Park
Pembrokeshire Coast National Park
Exmoor National Park
New Forest National Park
Dartmoor National Park

Heritage Coasts are also managed by The Countryside Agency. There are 43 coastal areas that are protected from development because of their scenic and environmental value. Some examples include Exmoor, North Devon, The Lizard and West Dorset. Some of the Heritage Coasts are inside National Parks.

Other countryside areas that are protected from development include:

- ✪ Forest Parks
- ✪ Nature Reserves
- ✪ Sites of Special Scientific Interest
- ✪ Marine Nature reserves.

Table 1 *National Park statistics*

	Brecon Beacons	Dartmoor	Exmoor	Lake District	Norfolk Broads	Northumberland
Area (hectares)	135,144	95,570	69,280	229,198	30,292	104,947
Population	32,000	29,100	10,645	42,239	5,500	2,200
Visitors per year	7 million	4 million	1.4 million	22 million	5.4 million	1.5 million

	North York Moors	Peak District	Pembrokeshire Coast	Snowdonia	Yorkshire Dales
Area (hectares)	143,603	143,833	62,000	214,129	176,869
Population	25,500	38,100	22,842	26,251	17,980
Visitors per year	8 million	19 million	4.7 million	10.5 million	9 million

Note: New Forest became a National Park in 2005, after these statistics were compiled.

Source: The Countryside Commission 1998

Quick quiz

(1) **True or false?**

- ✪ Scarborough is further north than Blackpool.
- ✪ The nearest seaside resort to London is Torquay.
- ✪ National Parks get more protection from development than Areas of Outstanding Natural Beauty.

(2) Which of these is **not** a National Park?
(a) Cannock Chase **(b)** Peak District **(c)** Snowdonia **(d)** Dartmoor

(3) Which of these is **not** a seaside resort?
(a) Blackpool **(b)** Tenby **(c)** Liverpool **(d)** Portrush

(4) Which National Park had the most visitors in 1998?
(a) Exmoor **(b)** Peak District **(c)** Lake District **(d)** Snowdonia

(5) Which is the largest National Park?

Exam practice

Brecon Beacons

The Brecon Beacons National Park has some of the most spectacular scenery in Britain. Situated amongst hills and mountains, the Park covers an area of 520 sq miles. Stretching from Hay-on-Wye in the east to Llandeilo in the west, it contains the Black Mountains, the Central Beacons and Forest Fawr as well as moorland, forests, valleys, waterfalls, lakes, caves and gorges. The National Park Authority looks after the Park, helps the public to enjoy it and works with local communities towards a sustainable future.

Visitors can enjoy a range of outdoor activities such as walking, cycling, horse riding, climbing, gliding, sailing, windsurfing, canoeing and fishing. There are also castles, show caves, museums, ancient hill-forts, burial sites, Roman roads, heritage centres and the Brecon Mountain Railway.

The Countryside Code

- ✪ Enjoy the countryside and respect its life and work.
- ✪ Guard against all risk of fire.
- ✪ Fasten all gates.
- ✪ Keep your dogs under close control.
- ✪ Keep to public paths across farmland.
- ✪ Use gates and stiles to cross fences, hedges and walls.
- ✪ Leave livestock, crops & machinery alone.
- ✪ Take your litter home.
- ✪ Help keep all water clean.
- ✪ Protect wildlife, plants and trees.
- ✪ Take special care on country roads.
- ✪ Make no unnecessary noise.

Brecon Beacons

1. Does the Brecon Beacons have a coastline? *(1 mark)*
2. Using the Brecon Beacons as an example, explain the aims of a National Park. *(3 marks)*
3. State three activities that outdoor enthusiasts might enjoy in the Brecon Beacons. *(3 marks)*
4. Using examples, explain the purpose of the countryside code. *(4 marks)*
5. What are the advantages in having protected areas such as National Parks and Areas of Outstanding Natural Beauty? *(7 marks)*

Getting started...

The previous unit looked mainly at seaside towns and countryside destinations but the UK also has a number of towns and cities which attract tourists. This unit looks at the reasons why tourists visit them. Think about the attractions of the cities below.

Cambridge

Cambridge is situated in the heart of the fens (flat marshland) and was occupied by both the Romans and the Normans. It is modern but picturesque and historic. It is famous for its university colleges, some of which were founded in the fourteenth century. Cambridge is at the cutting-edge of science and technology but it also has a bustling nightlife with many pubs, bars, restaurants, clubs, theatres, cinemas and sporting facilities.

Durham

Durham is another historic city. Its main attractions are Durham Castle, dating from 1072, and the Norman Cathedral, founded in 1093. The castle now houses University College, the foundation college of Durham University. Other attractions include the Durham University Museum of Archaeology, the medieval Crook Hall, river cruises, the botanical gardens and other museums.

Durham Cathedral

York

York Minster is the city's most famous attraction. It is the largest gothic cathedral north of the Alps. The Minster was built on what was originally the headquarters of a Roman fortress. Other attractions in this historic city include the Bar Walls (the medieval walls that surround the city), York Dungeon, the National Railway Museum, the Shambles (one of the world's best preserved medieval streets), the 13th century Clifford's Tower, many other historic buildings and churches, museums and galleries and the Jorvik Viking Centre.

York Minster

(a) What is a major attraction in each of these cities?
(b) What do all these cities have in common?

Chester

Chester, the gateway to the coast and castles of North Wales, is the most complete walled city in Britain. It is 2,000 years old and has some unique attractions. It is home to the largest stone-built amphitheatre in Britain, a 900 year old cathedral and the Victorian Eastgate Clock (the most photographed timepiece after Big Ben). It has a compact shopping centre and the Three Old Arches in Bridge Street is the oldest shop front in England. The city has a town crier and a racecourse which dates back to Tudor times.

Chester Cathedral

Figure 1 Tourist destinations

Edinburgh

Edinburgh is dominated by Castle Rock, a volcanic crag with three vertical sides. It was probably this natural defensive position that first attracted settlers in 850 BC. Edinburgh first began to grow in the 11th century when markets developed at the foot of the fortress. Today, Edinburgh's attractions include:

- ✪ Calton Hill
- ✪ Edinburgh Castle
- ✪ Grassmarket
- ✪ Greyfriars Kirk
- ✪ Holyrood Park
- ✪ Museum of Childhood
- ✪ Royal Museum of Scotland
- ✪ Royal Observatory
- ✪ St Giles' Cathedral
- ✪ University of Edinburgh.

Edinburgh Castle

Edinburgh is also famous for its festivals. Edinburgh International Festival, in August, is one of the world's largest and most important arts festivals. The Fringe Festival runs at the same time and has become the largest such event in the world. Over 500 amateur and professional groups present every possible kind of avant-garde entertainment in venues all around the city. There is also the Edinburgh Military Tattoo, which takes place on the Esplanade of Edinburgh Castle. This is an extravaganza of daredevil displays, regimental marching and swirling bagpipes and ends with a single piper playing a lament.

London

London is a popular tourist destination for both domestic and overseas tourists. In 2002, there were 11,600,000 visits to London by overseas tourists. London is the capital of England, one of the biggest cities in the world and has a huge range of attractions. Some of London's historic attractions include the Houses of Parliament, the Tower of London, the Monument, Nelson's Column, Trafalgar Square, St Paul's Cathedral, Buckingham Palace and Westminster Abbey. Other attractions include The Southbank, Shakespeare's Globe Theatre, Neasden Temple, The Thames' Barrier, London Eye, Madame Tussauds, London Zoo, Covent Garden, Greenwich, Abbey Road Studios and dozens of museums and galleries. London also has a lively night-life with hundreds of theatres, cinemas, restaurants, bars, pubs and nightclubs. There is plenty for the whole family and all different age groups.

The Houses of Parliament

Stratford-upon-Avon

Stratford-upon-Avon is on the banks of the River Avon in Warwickshire. Most visitors come to see the historic houses maintained by the Shakespeare Birthplace Trust. These are Shakespeare's Birthplace, Nash's House and Hall Croft.

Out of town is Ann Hathaway's Cottage at Shottery and Mary Arden's House in Wilmcote. There is also the Shakespeare Countryside Museum and three theatres owned by the world famous Royal Shakespeare Company. Visitors can also see

William Shakespeare

Shakespeare's final resting place at the Holy Trinity Church. Stratford is within easy reach of Oxford, Warwick Castle, Henley-in-Arden, the Cotswolds, the Malverns and Blenheim Palace in Woodstock.

Other towns and cities

In addition to the historic towns and cities already mentioned, there are numerous others that people choose to visit. For example, Manchester, Birmingham, Liverpool, Leeds, Newcastle, Glasgow, Cardiff, Nottingham, Sheffield, Dublin and Belfast all attract visitors. Each one has its own collection of attractions.

Other tourist destinations

Sporting venues People from home and abroad visit various sporting venues in the UK to watch important fixtures. For example, in June, thousands of people come to Wimbledon to watch the world's most famous tennis tournament. Unit 6 has more information on sporting venues.

Theme parks Theme parks such as Alton Towers and Camelot and other major visitor attractions such as Madame Tussauds attract millions of visitors each year. Units 8 and 9 have more information on these attractions.

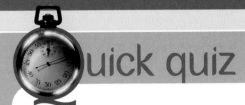

Quick quiz

1 **True or false?**
- The first settlers in Edinburgh arrived in the 11th Century.
- The Victorian Eastgate Clock is in Cambridge.
- Stratford-upon-Avon lies on the banks of the River Cherwell.

2 Which of these is **not** an attraction in York?
(a) Hadrian's Wall **(b)** York Minster **(c)** The Shambles **(d)** National Railway Museum

3 Which of these castles is within easy reach of Stratford-upon-Avon?
(a) Corfe Castle **(b)** Warwick Castle **(c)** Durham Castle **(d)** Edinburgh Castle

4 Which of these is **not** a London attraction?
(a) Ann Hathaway's Cottage **(b)** Greenwich **(c)** Thames' Barrier
(d) Westminster Abbey

5 State three festivals that take place in Edinburgh.

Exam practice

Oxford

The historic city of Oxford lies about 45 miles north-west of London. It is rich in ancient architecture and is surrounded by beautiful countryside. It is sometimes known as the City of Dreaming Spires. It is world famous for its university colleges and its unique place in history. For 800 years it has been home to royalty and scholars. It is very popular with overseas visitors and its attractions include:

- Numerous university colleges
- Christchurch Cathedral (built in 1280)
- Carfax Tower (with its 'quarter boys' clock)
- Ashmolean Museum
- Museum of the History of Science
- Oxford University Museum of Natural History
- Pitt Rivers Museum (world famous anthropology collection)
- Museum of Modern Art
- The Bate Collection of Musical Instruments
- Botanical Gardens
- Punting on the River Isis.

Figure 2 *Overseas visitors to historic towns and cities 2002*

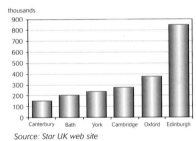

Source: Star UK web site

Woodstock

People visit Woodstock to see Blenheim Palace and Sir Winston Churchill's grave in nearby Bladon. Before the Norman Conquest, English kings had lodges in Woodstock - 'a clearing in the woods' and possibly where the name of the town came from. King Alfred is said to have stayed at Woodstock in 890. Ethelred the Unready held a council in the town which suggests that it had grown big enough to accommodate a king.

There are also many attractive and historic towns and villages in Oxfordshire such as Witney, Henley, Banbury, Burford, Chipping Norton and Woodstock.

1. What evidence is there to suggest that Oxford is popular with overseas tourists? *(1 mark)*
2. Name three Oxford museums that could be visited. *(3 marks)*
3. Explain why someone might want to visit Woodstock. *(4 marks)*
4. Discuss whether a weekend in Oxford would suit a family with an 11 year old daughter. *(7 marks)*

22 The impact of tourism and sustainable development

Getting started...

Tourism is the fastest growing industry in the world. It provides products, services and opportunities for people to enjoy their leisure time. Tourism also creates jobs for people and helps to generate income for communities. But unfortunately, tourism can also have a negative impact. It might attract unwanted development, intrude on attractive landscapes and damage the environment. Think about the effects of tourism in the cases below.

Greenhouse gas emissions

Greenhouse gases are found naturally in the air. Some of them are natural gases such as carbon dioxide and methane, whereas others are man-made – for example, the gases that come from burning coal and oil for electricity. They trap heat in the atmosphere and this causes the earth's temperature to rise. This warming effect is called the 'greenhouse effect' and scientists believe that it has contributed to an increase in global temperatures and sea levels. In the last 200 years, greenhouse gases have increased due to human activities. Around 3.5 per cent of greenhouse gas emissions come from air travel which has risen sharply in the last ten years, as shown in Figure 1. Greenhouse gas emissions are expected to rise much faster in the future as air travel increases.

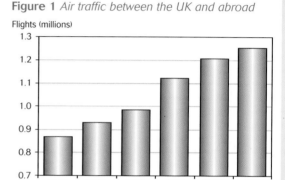

Figure 1 *Air traffic between the UK and abroad*

Flights (millions)

Source: Annual Abstract of Statistics 2004

Bluestone Holiday Village

In 2004, outline planning permission was granted for Bluestone Holiday Village. If the development goes ahead, it will have 340 log cabins, 60 holiday flats, a 'Snowdome', a 'Waterworld' and a sports centre. The Holiday Village will be located in the Pembrokeshire Coast National Park. With up to 2,000 residents and 5,000 day visitors, campaigners are worried about the impact of the development on the area. It will be the third largest settlement in the National Park with all the infrastructure, traffic and waste equivalent to that of a small town. It is anticipated that over 1,000 full-time jobs would be created in the area which suffers from high unemployment.

Holidaybreak plc

Holidaybreak plc is a leading provider of specialist holidays. It has three divisions – Eurocamp, Hotel Breaks and Adventure Holidays. In 2003, it increased its staff from 1,702 to 1,958. Most of the people employed are couriers. The amount of money paid to shareholders (the owners of the company) went up from 20p per share to 22p.

Eurocamp courier greeting new holiday-makers

Describe briefly the impact that tourism may have in each of the above cases.

Impacts of tourism

Social impacts

Some of the impacts of tourism are social. This means that society, or the way of life, can be affected. For example, if a derelict building in London is converted into a stylish restaurant for tourists, this might improve the urban landscape and benefit local residents. This is a positive social impact. But if the increased demand from tourists increases prices in nearby shops, this would be a negative social impact for local people. More examples of the positive and negative social impacts of tourism are given below.

Positive social impacts

- Investment in facilities for tourists is likely to improve the infrastructure for local residents as well. For example, better transport links and safer road crossings.
- Tourism might help to preserve cultural activities such as dance, crafts, art, cuisine, dress, events and festivals. Tourists often visit destinations to experience new cultures.
- Cultural exchange can be two-way. Tourists might bring with them their own customs which locals can enjoy. For example, Bangladeshi people enjoyed singing with the 'Barmy Army' when they toured with the England cricket team in 2003.

Negative social impacts

- Tourism in some areas has led to more crime. This happens when tourists are seen as soft targets for theft.
- Some tourist destinations provide opportunities for the suppliers of illegal gambling, drugs and prostitution. In some tourist areas, the sex industry is huge.
- In some cases, tourism takes over completely and leads to overcrowding, a loss of identity, a loss of language and the isolation of local people.

Economic impacts

The economic impacts of tourism are those that affect the financial well-being of people and communities.

Positive economic impacts

- Tourist destinations, regions and whole countries can benefit from the extra income that comes from spending by tourists.
- Tourism creates jobs which improve living standards and provide security for locals.
- People who take up jobs in the tourist industry may receive training. This gives them skills which they might be able to use in future jobs.
- The government benefits from tourists because they pay taxes such as VAT.

Travel agents at a convention

Negative economic impacts

- Some of the jobs created by tourism are seasonal. This means that people get laid off when the tourist season ends. This creates insecurity and uncertainty.
- If tourist destinations get too busy, prices may rise. This might raise the cost of living for locals.
- Many jobs in the tourist industry are low paid.
- Some places might become too dependent on tourism so, if there is a downturn in the number of visitors, the area may suffer.

Tourist workers in the winter

- A lot of the money 'leaks' from local destinations. It goes to large holiday companies, for example.

Environmental impacts

The environmental impact of tourism is concerned with the effect of tourism on the natural environment. For example, the coral on the Great Barrier Reef in Australia has been badly damaged in certain parts by tourist activity.

Positive environmental impacts
- ✪ Money is raised to help protect the environment.
- ✪ Conservation areas are created which stop development and provide protection.
- ✪ Tourists may be given guidance about how to care for the environment.
- ✪ Resources which might otherwise decay and spoil the environment, are reused. For example, derelict buildings are renovated.

Always observe the
Country Code
Take your litter home.
Always close the gate

Negative environmental impacts
- ✪ Tourists create more traffic, road congestion and air pollution.
- ✪ Crowded resorts may suffer from more noise, litter, sea pollution and unruly behaviour.
- ✪ Natural attractions might suffer from soil erosion caused by walkers and cyclists, the loss of wildlife habitats, wildlife disturbance and other detrimental effects on the landscape.

Sustainable tourism

Sustainable tourism attempts to address the effects of tourism by maximising the positive impacts and minimising the negative ones. It aims to meet the needs of tourists whilst, at the same time, protecting local communities. This means that the development of tourism must be planned and controlled. How might this be done?
- ✪ Restrict the number of hotels, restaurants and other tourist facilities that are built. This will prevent resorts from becoming too big and swamping the local residents.
- ✪ Control the design of tourist infrastructures by, for example, restricting the height of buildings so that the environment is not spoilt.
- ✪ To reduce congestion, provide clearly marked tourist routes around destinations and encourage more people to use public transport.
- ✪ In countryside areas, provide footpaths and encourage people to use them.
- ✪ Provide cycle-ways for cyclists so that walkers can use paths and tracks safely.
- ✪ Control the flow of tourists by siting car parks in places where visitors cannot cause damage.
- ✪ Employ local people and use local resources such as locally grown food. This will help to reduce the 'leakage' of money from the local economy.
- ✪ Pay local workers fair wages and provide them with proper training.
- ✪ Try to restrict the numbers of people going to certain destinations.

Quick quiz

1 **True or false?**

- If tourist destinations get too busy, prices might rise.
- Many jobs in the tourist industry are highly paid.
- One of the aims of sustainable tourism is to soften the impact on local residents.

2 Match these impacts with the correct description in the box.

- Tourists create more traffic, road congestion and air pollution.
- Tourism creates jobs which improve living standards and provide security for locals.
- Tourism in some areas has led to more crime. This happens when tourists are seen as soft targets for theft.

> *Negative economic impact*
> *Negative social impact*
> *Positive economic impact*
> *Negative environmental impact*

3 State three ways in which sustainable tourism might be achieved.

Exam practice

The Blackpool Resort Masterplan

There are far-reaching plans to develop Blackpool, the UK's most famous seaside resort. The Blackpool Masterplan aims to create 'a year-round entertainment destination with world-class facilities'.

The Conference and Casino Quarter
This brand-new development will include a luxury casino, top quality hotels, facilities for conferences and exhibitions, along with fashionable bars and restaurants. It aims to attract visitors throughout the year rather than the traditional summer season.

Artist's impression of The Conference and Casino Quarter

Developing existing facilities The Masterplan aims to develop the town centre with tree-lined streets, town squares and bigger and better shopping facilities. The famous Blackpool Illuminations will be developed and extended throughout the town. The seafront promenades will be redesigned and reconstructed. And the transport network will be developed – for example, the existing tram network will be extended.

The results The Masterplan anticipates that these developments will double the number of visitors to Blackpool, create 20,000 new jobs, reduce the present high level of unemployment in the off-season winter months and revitalise the entire resort.

1. How might The Masterplan attract new types of visitors in addition to the traditional holiday-makers? *(3 marks)*

2. Explain one possible negative social impact of the development. *(3 marks)*

3. Identify two positive economic impacts that the development could have. *(4 marks)*

4. What do you think could be done to make this development sustainable? Give reasons for your answer. *(8 marks)*

Getting started...

There is a wide range of jobs for people to choose from in the travel and tourism industry. Many jobs are seasonal such as in hotels, airports, pubs, restaurants and theme parks. Jobs in travel and tourism often involve close contact with customers. Think about the jobs in the cases below.

Paul Brayshaw

Paul Brayshaw is a student at Manchester University. He has a summer job working at Manchester Airport as a baggage handler. He has to load cases and other baggage on to the aircraft. He has to work very hard. Loading baggage quickly is important because the aircraft must take off on time. Part of his training involved being shown how to lift heavy baggage without damaging his back.

Rhona Bradley

Rhona works full-time for a large tour operator. Her job is to meet groups of holidaymakers at Palma Airport on the island of Majorca. She escorts them to their hotel in Cala D'or and tells them about the island during the coach journey. The next day, she holds a welcome meeting to give out important information and answer any questions. Rhona has to make sure that people enjoy their holiday and deal with any problems. She works with hoteliers, coach companies, airport staff and local tour operators.

Tariq Venkat

Tariq runs a taxi business which specialises in taking people to and from Gatwick Airport. He is based in Aldershot and most of his customers are from that area. He charges £20 per person for a return journey. He works long hours and sometimes has to get up in the middle of the night to drop off, or pick up, customers from the airport.

(a) Which of the jobs in the above cases involves direct contact with tourists?
(b) Which of the people in the above cases is likely to receive the most training?

Jobs in travel and tourism

Travel consultants

Travel consultants are usually employed by travel agents or tour operators. They normally deal with customers before they go on a trip but sometimes they also have to deal with customers when they return – for example, if they have a complaint about their holiday. Travel consultants may arrange people's travel and accommodation and give information about destinations and visas, for example. They sell package holidays, flights, coach tours, train tickets, ferry crossings, holiday insurance and, in many cases, foreign currency. Some travel consultants might be paid commission when they sell a package holiday or flight. Travel consultants need:

Travel consultant

- ✪ effective communications skills
- ✪ a good telephone manner
- ✪ competent IT skills
- ✪ a smart appearance
- ✪ to be able to work on Saturdays
- ✪ to enjoy working with the public.

Conference organiser

A conference is a meeting where people come together to discuss ideas and information or to attend lectures or presentations given by guest speakers. Conferences are attended by groups of people with something in common. They might belong to the same organisation or work in the same field of business. Some conferences are very big, with hundreds of delegates attending – a political party conference, for example. Organising a conference might involve:

- ✪ booking a venue and accommodation for delegates
- ✪ booking caterers to provide meals and refreshments
- ✪ making sure that speakers have the equipment they need such as overhead projectors
- ✪ arranging security, if necessary
- ✪ sending out information such as programmes and itineraries
- ✪ greeting guests and delegates at reception.

This sort of job may be done by someone with experience in tourism, hospitality or marketing. It is a management position that requires good leadership, communication, organisational and administrative skills. A conference organiser must be able to work under pressure and meet deadlines.

Coach drivers

A coach driver may be employed by a tour operator to take parties on a tour. Coach trips are popular to seaside resorts, National Parks and many European destinations. Drivers are required to transport people safely, stick to timetables and care for their passengers. Most tour operators have driver-couriers who give a commentary, pointing out places of interest, as they drive along. On overseas trips, two coach drivers take it in turns to drive because the law restricts the number of hours that one person can drive. Coach drivers need:

- ✪ a public service vehicle (PSV) licence which proves that they are qualified to drive buses and coaches
- ✪ good people skills to deal with customers
- ✪ a thorough knowledge of routes and places of interest when giving commentaries
- ✪ a foreign language if travelling overseas (preferably).

Air cabin crew

Some people think that working for an airline is glamorous because it often involves flying all over the world and staying in good hotels. In reality, it is hard work and staff may work long hours on back-to-back flights with few breaks. Air cabin crew are responsible for the safety and comfort of passengers on flights. They welcome passengers aboard, direct them to their seats, give out safety information, serve meals and refreshments, answer passengers' questions and deal with any problems. Airlines give their crews a lot of training but applicants must:

✪ be at least 20 years old
✪ have 5 GCSEs
✪ be able to work away from home
✪ have a good sense of humour
✪ be able to swim
✪ be a good team member
✪ speak a foreign language, preferably.

Air cabin crew

Tourist guide

Tourist guides escort groups of people around tourist attractions such as museums and historic buildings or towns and cities. They may also drive coaches as mentioned earlier. Tour guides need:
✪ a sound knowledge of the attraction where they work
✪ a friendly and open personality
✪ good people skills.

Many tourist guides working in London are registered and have been awarded a Blue Badge. This means that they are qualified guides and have met certain standards.

Tourist guide

Resort representatives

Resort representatives usually work for a tour operator. They welcome holiday-makers to their resort and ensure that their stay is comfortable and enjoyable. If people enjoy their holiday, they are more likely to book with the same tour operator again in the future. A resort representative may carry out the following tasks:
✪ meeting holiday-makers at the airport and escorting them to their resort
✪ holding a welcome meeting to provide information about the local area, health and safety issues and excursions
✪ dealing with customer problems and complaints
✪ selling resort excursions, organising car hire and encouraging tourists to spend money at the resort.

Resort representatives must be friendly, confident, flexible, tolerant and enjoy working with people. It is a demanding job and they are often on 24-hour call. They receive a lot of training and may not need any formal qualifications.

Tourist rep

Quick quiz

① **True or false?**

✪ Travel consultants usually work for travel agents or tour operators.

✪ People working in travel and tourism need very good numeracy skills.

✪ Resort representatives are likely to hold a Blue Badge.

② State three qualities that a travel consultant might need.

③ State three tasks that a conference organiser might have to carry out.

④ State three qualities that air cabin crew need.

⑤ Why are two drivers usually needed for overseas coach tours?

Exam practice

MediTours Ltd

MediTours Ltd is a small tour operator specialising in package holidays to destinations in the Mediterranean. The company has recently placed an advert in a regional newspaper inviting applications for jobs as trainee resort representatives. The company will send successful applicants on a four-week training course in Spain. After that, they will get on-the-job training. Two letters of application are shown below.

Dear Sir or Madam,

I would like to apply for the job of trainee resort representative with MediTours. I am 20 years old, hold a current driving licence and have an AS Level in Biology. I am currently working as an assistant in a local market garden. I work in the greenhouses and I am involved in the production of tomatoes. I also deliver goods to customers. I am young, enthusiastic and work well without supervision. I am keen to learn new skills and I am very hard-working. I can attend an interview at any time.

Yours faithfully

Alan Parkinson

Dear Sir or Madam,

I am very interested in the job advertised for a trainee resort representative with MediTours Ltd. I am 20 years old and I have an AVC in Travel and Tourism and an AS level in IT.

I am interested in the travel and tourism industry and have worked for the last two years in a local leisure centre. I have experience in dealing with customers and have recently been supervising children's 5-a-side football games. Now that I am old enough, I would like a more challenging job and to preferably work abroad. I am keen to learn new skills and want to take some responsibility. I would very much welcome an interview.

Yours faithfully

Anna Yousef

Table 1 *Employment in tourism related industries 1992-2002 (thousands)*

	Hotels and other tourist accommodation	Restaurants cafés etc.	Bars, public houses and nightclubs	Travel agents tour operators	Libraries museums and other cultural activities	Sport and other recreation activities	All
1992	311.0	303.0	414.2	69.2	74.8	320.8	1671.0
2002	418.0	545.4	535.9	133.6	81.4	412.9	2127.2

Source: Department for Culture, Media and Sport

1. (i) How many people were employed by travel agents and tour operators in 2002? *(1 mark)*

   (ii) How has the number of people employed by travel agents and tour operators between 1992 and 2002 changed? *(2 marks)*

2. What does the term 'on-the-job training' mean? *(3 marks)*

3. State four tasks that a MediTours resort representative might have to carry out. *(4 marks)*

4. Which one of the two applicants do you think is most likely to be given an interview with MediTours? Give reasons for your answer. *(7 marks)*

Getting started...

So far, the components of the leisure industry and those of the travel and tourism industry have been discussed separately. However, it is important to recognise that there are strong links between the two industries. For example, catering is a component of both the leisure industry and the tourism industry. A London restaurant may serve both local residents a meal and tourists from France who are visiting for the weekend. Think about the links between leisure and tourism in the cases below.

The Penford Golf Society

The Penford Golf Society has 20 members. They all live in Shrewsbury and play golf regularly at different courses in the area. Every year, they go on a five-day golf trip. In 2004, they decided to go to Portugal. Each member paid £460 which included:

✪ return flight to Faro Airport

✪ airport transfers

✪ four nights half-board hotel accommodation

✪ all green fees for golf rounds

✪ insurance.

Palheiro Golf Course, Madeira, Portugal

Jill Stepanek and Sally Groves

Jill and Sally are both in their early 20s. They spend a lot of their leisure time hillwalking and belong to the mountain rescue team in the Lake District. Most of their free weekends are spent camping in the hills and attending training courses. In February, they decided to go walking in Glencoe in the Scottish Highlands. They wanted to experience walking in a winter landscape. They were looking forward to snow-capped peaks, wild deer and golden eagles. They drove up to Glencoe by car and stayed at the Clachaig Hotel for two nights.

Scottish Highlands

For each case, identify two components from the tourism industry and one from the leisure industry.

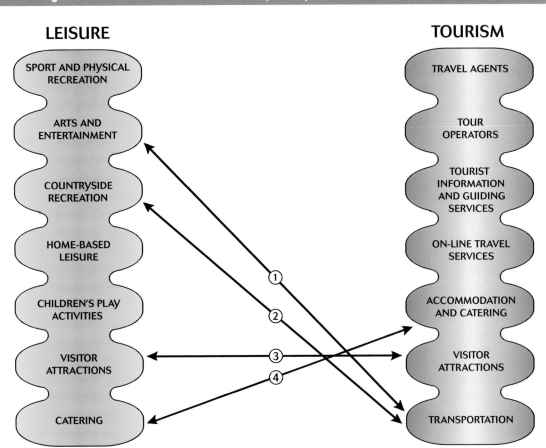

Figure 1 Some links between the key components of leisure and tourism

1 The diagram in Figure 1 shows some of the obvious links between the leisure industry and the tourism industry. Both industries are dependent on each other for customers. The first link shows that people will often need transport to enjoy the arts and entertainment. For example, people living in Norwich may travel by coach to visit the Ashmolean and Pitt Rivers museums in Oxford.

2 The second link also involves transport. It shows that some people will need to use transport to enjoy the countryside. For example, people living in cities will have to travel to rural locations to enjoy activities such as camping, canoeing and mountaineering. Transport is a key link between the two industries.

3 The third link shows that visitor attractions are important components of both industries. People living in Bradford may visit the National Museum of TV and Photography. Tourists from Italy may also visit the same museum.

4 Catering is a very important component of both industries. In 2002, 545,400 people were employed in the catering industry. This is about 25% of all the people employed in the leisure and tourism industries. Eating out at restaurants is a popular leisure activity and many restaurants cater for tourists. This is an important link between the two industries.

Examples of links between the leisure and tourism industries

Test Match at Trent Bridge

England usually plays a Test Match at Trent Bridge, Nottingham every summer. Some supporters travelling by train from Halifax, might stay over night in the Talbot House Hotel, have a few drinks in the Trip to Jerusalem pub and book all their travel and accommodation online. They would be using the following components from the leisure and tourism industries.

Leisure	Tourism
Sport	Accommodation
Catering	Transport
	Online services

A Test Match at Trent Bridge

Coach trip to the Norfolk Broads

Robinson's is a tour operator that organises coach trips to many destinations. One of its holidays is a seven-day trip to the Norfolk Broads. Amongst other things, this includes a visit to the historic village of Walsingham and a cruise on the Norfolk Broads. Holiday-makers will stay in the Hotel Elizabeth in Great Yarmouth. This holiday involves a tour operator, accommodation, catering and transport in the tourism industry. The countryside and visitor attractions are components of the leisure industry.

The Norfolk Broads

Center Parcs

Center Parcs has 19 holiday villages in Europe. People can stay in different types of accommodation and choose from various types of restaurant. They can relax in the forested grounds or enjoy water activities such as rapids, hot whirlpools, a wave pool and the exotic Aqua Mundo. There are sports facilities such as zip wire, abseiling, archery, climbing, skiing, snowboarding, diving, cycling and sailing. Children are well catered for with a children's farm, kids' club, pony riding, special play areas and entertainment. A holiday at Center Parcs booked online would involve:

Center Parcs

- ✪ sport and physical recreation, entertainment, countryside recreation, children's play activities and catering – components from the **leisure industry**.

- ✪ online travel services, accommodation, attractions and transportation – components from the **tourism industry**.

Quick quiz

1 **True or false?**

- Children's play activities are a component of both the leisure and tourism industries.
- Reading a magazine at home does not provide any link between the leisure and tourism industries.
- Tourist Information Centres will only serve tourists.

2 Decide whether there are any links between the leisure and tourism industries in the following events.

- A hen-night in Blackpool enjoyed by a group of women from Doncaster.
- Booking a flight from Birmingham to Dublin online to see the Irish Grand National.
- A family enjoying a BBQ in their garden.
- A two-day business trip to the National Exhibition Centre, Birmingham.

Exam practice

Southport

Southport is on the north-west coast in Merseyside. It provides a wide range of facilities and attractions for both locals and tourists. It is an important conference centre and the best location for a golfing holiday in England. It has a marine lake, an attractive shopping boulevard, Pleasureland with the Traumatizer as its main 'white knuckle ride', beaches, a newly renovated pier, a new seafront development, dozens of restaurants, bars, nightclubs and more.

Southport town centre

1 Scarisbrick Hotel
2 Tourist Information Centre
3 Travelcare
4 Pleasureland
5 Valentino Italian Restaurant
6 Arts Centre

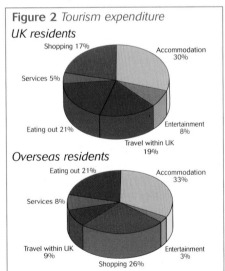

Figure 2 *Tourism expenditure*

UK residents

- Shopping 17%
- Accommodation 30%
- Services 5%
- Entertainment 8%
- Eating out 21%
- Travel within UK 19%

Overseas residents

- Eating out 21%
- Accommodation 33%
- Services 8%
- Travel within UK 9%
- Entertainment 3%
- Shopping 26%

1. State one item of expenditure in the **tourism** industry where foreign residents spend more than UK residents. *(1 mark)*

2. State one item of expenditure in the **leisure** industry where UK residents spend more than foreign residents. *(1 mark)*

3. For each of the facilities in the key, state which component of the leisure **or** tourist industry they fall into. *(6 marks)*

4. Choose two facilities from the key and explain why they fall into both the tourism **and** leisure industries. *(4 marks)*

5. Explain why transport is such an important component for the **leisure** industry. *(4 marks)*

Getting started...

MARKETING is a very important business process. It is concerned with identifying customers' needs and supplying the right products and services in the right place, at the right time, at the right price and using the right promotion. Organisations in the leisure and tourism industries have to market their products and services. Marketing requires businesses to communicate with their customers to find out what they want and also to tell them about the products and services that are available. Look at the two organisations below.

The Caravan Club

The Caravan Club has over 850,000 members and operates 200 Club caravan sites in the UK. The Club carries out an annual survey of its members to find out the needs of different customer groups. In 2003, 70,000 questionnaires were sent out and 30% – 35% of the members completed them. The survey helped The Caravan Club to find out things such as:

✪ who wanted family-friendly sites
✪ who wanted to escape from the kids
✪ who expected to take their dogs with them and who were not keen on dogs.

As a result of the survey, the Club brought out some leaflets giving its members advice on choosing a suitable site. One was aimed at families, one at dog owners and another on rural, peaceful sites.

CT2 Holidays

Based in Manchester, CT2 was founded in 1984 as Club Travel 2000. It is now one of the UK's fastest-growing tour operators. It offers holidays and flights to popular sunshine destinations such as the Canary and Balearic Islands, mainland Spain, the Algarve, Cyprus and Malta. CT2 offers customers a variety of choices from its flight-only and holiday programmes. With a staff of over 100 people, it claims to have the right products at the right prices. CT2 placed this advert in the *Sunday Times* in October 2003.

BOOK BY 31ST OCT
SAVE £200 PER PERSON†

CT2 Holidays

SOUTH AFRICA

Two week holiday from

£599 * *pp*

CAPE TOWN – Fly direct from Manchester.
DURBAN – Fly from Newcastle or direct from Manchester.

Please quote code S81

08451 22 11 26

WWW.CT2-SAFRICA.COM

*Based on 2 weeks Durban, 2 adults sharing. See brochure for details.
†Selected departures to Cape Town only (subject to availability).

ABTA V1854

(a) How are each of the two organisations communicating with customers?
(b) What is the purpose of the communication in each case?

What is marketing?

Marketing is about satisfying customers. It involves:

- finding out what customers want or need
- developing and supplying the products and services that they want
- selling products in the right place at the right price
- making sure people know about the products
- selling products at a profit.

Marketing activities are aimed at customers. It is their needs that drive organisations in the leisure and tourism industries. Tour operators, hotels, theme parks, fitness clubs, restaurants and train operators, for example, will only succeed if they satisfy customers. It they do not, customers will go elsewhere. Marketing is said to be an ongoing process because businesses need to continue their marketing activities all the time. For example, by continually collecting information from customers to make sure that they are satisfying their needs.

The need for marketing

Marketing is very important for a number of reasons.

- **Competition** The leisure and tourism industries are very COMPETITIVE. This means that many organisations, especially businesses, are trying to sell products and services to the same customers. One way of beating competitors is to market products more effectively by charging a lower price or having better promotion, for example.
- **Fashion changes** People's tastes are likely to change in the leisure and tourism industries. Holiday destinations, pubs, restaurants and different leisure activities, for example, fluctuate in popularity. In the early 2000s, garden design, gourmet food and fitness clubs were all very popular. Businesses have to keep collecting information from customers to make sure that their products are still popular and to see whether any changes are needed.
- **Launching new products** Businesses in the leisure and tourism industries often launch new products. Tour operators find new destinations, restaurants change their menus and new computer games are developed, for example. Launching new products is very risky because they are expensive to develop and they might not sell. But if a business has thoroughly researched what customers want, this is likely to be much less risky.

Marketing objectives

Organisations in the leisure and tourism industries are likely to use marketing to achieve certain objectives or goals. Examples might include the following:

○ **To increase or keep their MARKET SHARE** For example, a tour operator might try to increase its share of the market from 10% to 12% with a special promotion.

○ **To help introduce new products** McDonald's used TV advertising in 2004 when introducing a range of 'healthier' fast foods.

○ **To increase sales** In recent years, the Scottish Tourist Board has used a TV advertising campaign aimed at increasing the number of visitors to Scotland.

○ **To target a new group of customers** For example, Pontin's, the holiday camp operator, has traditionally catered for families but it is now trying to attract other groups, such as the over 50s.

Pontin's advert for the over 50s

○ **To encourage early booking** Train operators sometimes offer discounts on tickets if passengers book in advance. Most sports clubs such as football clubs, and some attractions such as zoos, offer discounts to customers who buy season tickets. This helps to improve their cash flow.

○ **To improve customer satisfaction** For example, many tour operators use questionnaires to find out whether customers have enjoyed their holiday. The information they collect may be used to improve the holidays in the future.

○ **To improve the image of a product or business** For example, many professional football clubs now have grounds with all-seater stadiums, shops, museums, guided tours and catering facilities.

Satisfying customers profitably

Although marketing is all about satisfying customers, organisations must do this profitably. The PROFIT is the amount of money left over after all expenses such as wages, rent and raw materials have been paid. If they do not make a profit, they may go out of business. To calculate its profit, a business must subtract its COSTS from its REVENUE. The diagram in Figure 1 shows the revenue, costs and profit for an Indian restaurant, The Aysha. The profit made by the business is £46,000. It is found by:

$$\text{Profit} = \text{revenue} - \text{costs}$$
$$= £206,000 - £160,000$$
$$= £46,000$$

Figure 1 *Revenue, costs and profit for The Aysha*

Revenue £206,000

Profit £46,000

Costs £160,000

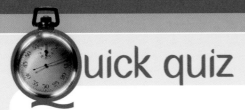

Quick quiz

1 **True or false?**

⚙ Marketing activities are aimed at suppliers.

⚙ Marketing is needed because there is a lot of competition in the leisure and tourism industries.

⚙ Organisations collect information from customers to find out what they want.

2 State four marketing objectives.

3 Why is marketing needed when launching new products?

4 In 2004, the revenue for a video shop was £187,000 and its costs were £142,000. What is the profit?

Portfolio practice

Antequera Villas

Joseph Matthews owns Antequera Villas. Four years ago, he bought six properties in Andalucia, southern Spain, and converted them into luxury villas. He used to rely on an agent to let the villas for him but they were empty for a lot of the time. In 2004, Joseph placed this advert in a Sunday newspaper. He wanted to increase lettings and attract new groups of customers.

To help improve customer satisfaction, Joseph telephones every customer when they return to find out whether they had a good time. He also has a suggestion box in each villa. If people have any complaints or suggestions, they can put a note in the box before they leave.

Antequera Villas

We have six luxury villas set in secluded mountain locations. Each has its own private pool and BBQ area and is furnished to a very high standard. The romantic settings are ideal for couples, honeymooners and special occasions.

1. What new groups of customers is Joseph trying to attract? *(2 marks)*

2. Why is it important for businesses like Antequera Villas to market their services profitably? *(2 marks)*

3. (i) Explain how Joseph gathers information from his customers. *(4 marks)*

   (ii) Why do you think Joseph collects information from his customers? *(4 marks)*

4. Using examples from the case, explain what is meant by marketing objectives. *(6 marks)*

key terms

Competitive – many different businesses trying to sell products and services to the same customers.

Costs – the expenses incurred by businesses such as wages and rent.

Marketing – finding out what customers want and then providing them with it at a profit.

Market share – the proportion of sales that a business has compared with the total sales in the market.

Profit – the amount of money remaining after costs have been met.

Revenue – the amount of money a business receives from selling its products and services.

Getting started...

Organisations in the leisure and tourism industries often target their products and services at particular groups of people. People that belong to these groups will have similar wants and needs. For example, many train operators offer students a special railcard that allows them to travel at a discount. All the people in this group are students – they have limited income and travel fairly regularly. By offering students discounts, the train operators can attract more customers. Without railcards, students might choose other methods of travel such as the coach. Look at the groups being targeted below.

Great Days Out for Schools

NEW FOR 2004

Educational Cruise

We operate a 45 minute Circular Cruise departing from the Lake District Visitor Centre at Brockhole.

ADULT £5.25 CHILD £3.00 (5-15)

Price includes educational worksheets for each child.

Windermere Lake Cruises advert

Holmes of Natland Ltd

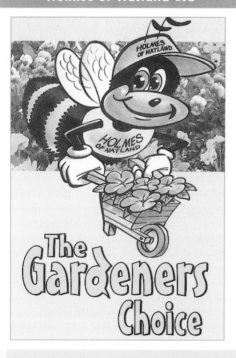

The Gardeners Choice

Fishing

Fishing at Hawkshead in the Lake District.

Beginner or expert we can cater for your needs. Our friendly and knowledgeable staff will offer a warm welcome and ensure your day on Esthwaite Water is enjoyable.

Rod hire and tuition available

Which groups are being targeted in each of the cases above?

Market segments

Tour operators know that families with young children are not likely to want the same type of holiday as retired couples. Families might want a package holiday by the beach with self-catering accommodation. Retired couples might want a special-interest holiday in Egypt where they can learn about ancient Egyptian culture.

Tour operators therefore try to cater for different MARKET SEGMENTS. A market segment is a group of customers who are similar in certain ways and therefore likely to have similar needs and wants. Once a business has segmented its market in this way, it has to decide which segment to aim at. This is called TARGETING and the segment chosen by the business is called its 'target market'. Some businesses aim different products and services at different target markets at the same time. Figure 1 shows some of the ways in which customers might be grouped.

Figure 1 *Market segments*

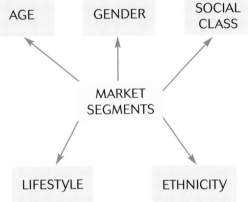

AGE   GENDER   SOCIAL CLASS

MARKET SEGMENTS

LIFESTYLE   ETHNICITY

Grouping by age

Infants, teenagers, 40 year olds and the over 80s all have different needs so it is common for businesses to target people according to their age. For example, Thomas Cook caters for the 18-30 year old age group with its Club 18-30 holidays. The Club is aimed at young people who want a lively resort with beaches, night-life and lots of activities.

Saga Holidays caters for the over 50s. It offers a wide range of holidays such as cruises, resorts, activity and special-interest holidays.

Pontin's caters for children in a variety of ways. For example, by arranging for popular children's TV characters such as Postman Pat, Sooty and Barney to appear at its holiday camps.

Grouping by gender

Males and females often prefer different products and services in the leisure and tourism industries so businesses may decide to target either men or women. For example, leisure centres may offer women-only sessions for yoga, swimming or aerobics. In the media, publishers target magazines such as *Loaded* and *Nuts* at men and *Company*, *Cosmopolitan* and *She* at women.

An advert aimed at women

Grouping by social class

People are often grouped according to education, occupation and income. Such groups are called SOCIAL CLASS or SOCIO-ECONOMIC groups. One system of classifying people in this way is used by the Registrar General for government statistics. It is shown in Table 1. A tour operator selling luxury cruises around the world might target people in Class 1 because they may be the only group that could afford such expensive holidays.

Table 1 *Registrar General's socio-economic groups*

Class 1	**Higher managerial and professional occupations**
	1.1 Employers in large organisations *(company directors or senior civil servants)*
	1.2 Higher professionals *(doctors or lawyers)*
Class 2	**Lower managerial and professional occupations** *(nurses, musicians, actors or prison officers)*
Class 3	**Intermediate occupations** *(clerks or secretaries)*
Class 4	**Small employers and own-account workers** *(publicans, farmers or taxi drivers)*
Class 5	**Lower supervisory, craft and related occupations** *(printers, plumbers, train drivers or bakers)*
Class 6	**Semi-routine occupations** *(shopworkers or cooks)*
Class 7	**Routine occupations** *(waiters or refuse collectors)*
Class 8	**Never worked/long term unemployed**

Grouping by lifestyle

It is possible to categorise people according to the way that they live their lives. It is not easy to measure someone's lifestyle so there are different ways of doing this. For example, people can be segmented according to their interests and hobbies such as sport, DIY, gardening and fashion. One method used is ACORN (A Classification of Residential Neighbourhoods), a computer database which places people into four lifestyle groups.

○ **Mainstreamers** People who do not want to stand out from the crowd. They live a conventional life and buy established brands such as Thomson Holidays, McDonald's and Adidas.

○ **Aspirers** People who want success and to show it off. They buy designer brands, the latest gadgets, 'flash' cars and exotic products.

○ **Succeeders** People who have 'made it'. They do not need to show it. They buy quality products and can afford luxury and comfort. They may travel first-class.

○ **Reformers** This group want to make the world a better place. They tend to be educated professionals such as teachers and doctors. They may buy eco-friendly products and healthy foods and be interested in countryside recreation.

Grouping by ethnicity

For marketing purposes, it may be important to identify ethnic segments. People from different ethnic backgrounds may have different needs and may buy different products. Table 2 shows the different ethnic groups in the UK. There are over 4 million people from different ethnic backgrounds and this represents a large number of potential customers for the leisure and tourism industries. For example, the film industry may show Asian films in areas where there is an Asian community. Leisure centres may offer women-only swimming sessions for Muslim women. Hotels might decide to serve ethnic foods to cater for different ethnic groups. For example, some hotels near Niagara Falls provide Japanese breakfasts for the large number of tourists from Japan.

Table 2 *Ethnic groups in the UK 2002*

Ethnic group	thousands
White	52,956
Mixed	509
Indian	1,016
Pakistani	718
Bangladeshi	273
Other Asian	302
Black Caribbean	584
Black African	541
Black Other	59
Chinese	199
Other	458

Source: Annual Abstract of Statistics, 2004

Quick quiz

1 **True or false?**
   - Market segments contain people with similar characteristics.
   - Target marketing is used to aim products at particular groups of people.
   - A tour operator would not consider grouping people according to age.

2 Which of these groups is most likely buy a return coach ticket from Glasgow to London?
   (a) Class 7 **(b)** Aspirers **(c)** Class 1.1 **(d)** Succeeders

3 Which of these groups is most likely to buy designer sports wear?
   (a) Class 1.1 **(b)** Reformers **(c)** Mainstreamers **(d)** Aspirers

4 Which is the largest non-white ethnic group in the UK?
   (a) Black Caribbean **(b)** Chinese **(c)** Pakistani **(d)** Indian

5 According to lifestyle grouping, who is likely to buy eco-products?

Portfolio practice

British Airways

Serving drinks in First-Class

In October 2003, the supersonic jet Concorde was retired from service. This left a gap in the market for luxury air travel which many airlines have since tried to fill. For example, British Airways now offers a First-Class service between Heathrow and New York. The cost of the return flight is £3,675. The First-Class cabins are designed in blue, beige and deep reds, similar to the interior of a Rolls Royce car. Each seat is 57 centimetres wide with an extendable footrest and a 'buddy seat' so that travellers can sit together to chat and eat. At the touch of a button, the seat tilts and stretches out into a full sized flat bed. Passengers are given duvets, pillows and grey sleeper suits. The in-flight meals are planned and developed by several award-winning chefs including Sean Hill whose restaurant was voted one of the top twenty in the world by *Restaurant Magazine*. Passengers can also check into the Molten Brown Travel Spa at Heathrow for pre-flight pampering and be served free Piper-Heidsieck champagne during the flight.

Source: adapted from the Sunday Times 19.10.03

1. At which (i) social groups and (ii) lifestyle groups do you think British Airways is aiming this service? *(2 marks)*

2. Using British Airways as an example, explain what is meant by a market segment. *(4 marks)*

3. Is British Airways likely to group passengers according to gender? Explain your answer. *(4 marks)*

4. Would easyJet - the 'no-frills' airline - be interested in the same market segment that is being targeted by British Airways? Give reasons for your answer. *(6 marks)*

key terms

Market segments – part of a market that contains people with similar needs and wants.
Social class/socio-economic groups – people grouped according to their education, occupation and income.
Targeting – aiming products and services at a particular market segment.

Getting started...

Unit 26 showed that organisations in the leisure and tourism industries divide their markets into segments. They then target different products at different segments. Five methods of segmentation were discussed – age, gender, social class, lifestyle and ethnicity. This unit looks at other ways of grouping customers. Look at the case below.

Best Western Midland Hotel – Derby

The Best Western Midland Hotel in Derby has three main target markets.

- ✪ **Corporate customers** – visiting business people.
- ✪ **Conference delegates** – from national and international organisations.
- ✪ **Weekend breaks** – for families and couples.

The information below looks at the conference facilities provided by the hotel.

Garden Room conference room

24 hour conference delegate rate
(Monday-Friday)

£147.00 per person (minimum of 10 delegates)

This includes:

Conference room hire

Mid-morning coffee and biscuits

Finger buffet, fork buffet or a sit-down Restaurant lunch

Afternoon tea and biscuits

Overhead projector and screen

Flipchart and pens

3 course Table d'hôte dinner in the Wyvern Restaurant

Overnight stay in en-suite single room

Full English Breakfast

VAT at 17.5%

Best Western Midland Hotel

Conference facilities
The hotel provides seven conference rooms. Full secretarial facilities are available including direct telephones in each room. Word processing, fax and typing can be arranged with prior notice. A complete range of professional presentation equipment including microphone and sound systems, overhead projection, video, slides, back projection and LCD projection can all be arranged on your behalf.

(a) Who is being targeted in the above case?
(b) How much is the 24 hour conference delegate rate?
(c) Why do you think the Midland Hotel targets other market segments?

Geographic location

Many businesses in the leisure and tourism industries target groups of customers in particular geographic areas. The most obvious example is organisations such as restaurants, nightclubs, leisure centres, cinemas, theatres and fitness clubs targeting their own local areas. A leisure centre in Hartlepool is unlikely to attract customers from very far outside the town. The advert below was placed in a local newspaper and is designed to attract local customers.

Preston's most exclusive over 25's late night venue every Friday and Saturday

37 GLOVERS COURT PRESTON TEL 01772 202188
www.truthnightclub.com

New customers and existing customers

Distinguishing between new customers and existing customers may involve using different marketing methods when serving the two groups. New customers may need to be persuaded to buy a product for the first time. This can be done by using a powerful TV advert to suggest that they cannot do without the new product. For example, in July 2004, Heinz launched a £5 million TV advertising campaign to promote its new, healthier, salt-reduced baked beans.

Existing customers need to be rewarded for their loyalty. For example, by giving them preferential treatment such as a discount.

Distinguishing between these two groups is important because it costs about five times more to win a new customer than to keep an existing one. The advert below offers *Nuts* readers a free pint of Guinness.

Nuts FREE PINT OF GUINNESS COUPON

I claim my free pint of Guinness

Name ....

Walkabout redeemed at ....

Date ....

E-mail ....

Thanks to *Nuts* and Walkabout. See terms and conditions

VALID FROM 15–21 MARCH   WALKABOUT

Members and non-members

Some organisations in the leisure and tourism industry have membership schemes. For example, sports clubs such as golf, tennis, bowls and rugby as well as leisure centres, youth groups and zoos. Members and non-members may be treated slightly differently when it comes to marketing.

For example, at most golf clubs, members pay an annual fee and can play as often as they wish whereas non-members pay green fees every time they play. Many clubs operate in this way. Members use the facilities free but non-members have to pay. Members may receive other benefits as well such as discounts in the club bar. One of the main advantages to organisations of having members is that membership fees are paid in advance.

VALLEY GOLD

Most Premier League football clubs operate club membership schemes. Charlton Athletic has one for supporters over 16 called Valley Gold. Joining fees are £10 per month and the benefits include:

- entry into a match day lottery with cash prizes up to £750
- priority in the allocation of tickets for away matches
- £15 discount off season tickets 10% off all club merchandise.

Family circumstances or life cycle

This involves grouping people according to their family or household circumstances. The family life cycle refers to a person's stage in life. People's needs and spending patterns may be quite different depending on which stage they are at. For example, bachelors or spinsters may spend a lot of their income on leisure products such as night-life, music, computer games and package holidays. Full nest 3 may have less spare money to spend on leisure because of the cost of raising children. They may spend on home-based entertainment. The different categories are summarised below.

Stage in cycle	Description and leisure spending power
Bachelors/spinsters	Single people - reasonable spending power
Young couples	Newly weds or living together - higher spending power
Full nest 1	Young couple - youngest child under 6
Full nest 2	Young couple - youngest child 6 or over - lower spending power
Full nest 3	Older couple - older dependent children - lower spending power
Empty nest 1	Older couple - no children or children left home - higher spending power
Empty nest 2	Older couple - main earner retired - income restricted
Solitary survivor 1	Single/widowed and working - reasonable spending power
Solitary survivor 2	Single retired - restricted spending power

Corporate customer

Many organisations in the leisure and tourism industries provide services for businesses. These are CORPORATE CUSTOMERS. For example, organisations such as football clubs, hotels, even theme parks and zoos, provide conference facilities for businesses. These facilities include private rooms, equipment such as PowerPoint, overhead projectors, photocopiers and video conferencing, refreshments, meals and sometimes overnight accommodation. Many businesses spend money on CORPORATE HOSPITALITY by entertaining existing and potential business customers in the hope of making new contacts and new business opportunities. This has become an important part of the leisure industry. An example would be providing a private box at a stadium to watch a major sporting event. This would come with a TV, free programmes, drinks, meals and waiter service. Many hotels, pubs and restaurants provide special dining facilities for corporate customers. Special menus and reserved dining areas, for example.

Advantages of segmentation

Why might organisations in the leisure and tourism industries want to divide markets into segments?

- They can meet the needs of different customer groups more easily by finding out, in detail, what each specific group wants.

- Targeting products at the wrong customer group might be avoided. This will reduce waste in advertising costs, for example.

- A business might be able to offer different products in different segments. Like tour operators offering different types of holidays to different groups, for example. This will help to increase revenue and profit.

- Smaller organisations can survive by concentrating on one segment. Like a restaurant serving vegan food, for example. This is called NICHE MARKETING.

In practice, the same organisation may provide a number of different products for different market segments. It is also common for organisations to use more than one method of segmentation

Quick quiz

1 **True or false?**
- ☺ The leisure and tourism industries would not provide products for corporate customers.
- ☺ An advantage of an organisation having a membership scheme is that the membership fees are paid in advance.
- ☺ Grouping customers by geographic location may be used by a tour operator selling specialist adventure holidays.

2 Which of these groups is most likely to spend on home-based leisure activities?
(a) Young couples   **(b)** Full nest 3   **(c)** Bachelors   **(d)** Empty nest 1

3 Which of these leisure activities might be most enjoyed by the Full nest 2 group?
(a) Theme park **(b)** Hang-gliding **(c)** Play at a theatre **(d)** Gourmet meal at a restaurant

4 Why is it important to distinguish between existing customers and new customers?

Portfolio practice

Market segments

The adverts below have been placed in newspapers and magazines by businesses in the leisure and tourism industries.

Family Active

Family Active Holidays
UK and France
Free call for a brochure
0500 749147
www.pgl.co.uk

Road-Knight **Get Out and About**

Lets you go shopping, meet up with family and friends, in fact go anywhere, anytime.

- ■ Rental available
- ■ Motability
- ■ 4-8 mph scooters
- ■ Free home trial
- ■ Travel scooters
- ■ 3 and 4 wheels

AS SEEN ON T.V.

FREEPHONE
0800 1 690 600

The Most Awaited
SATURDAY
EASTER Weekend March 26th

9:00pm - 3:00am
£7 before 10pm, £10 after...
Dress Glam Smart funky

Levels 3 & 4:
R'n'B, Hip Hop, Ragga, Bashment Swing

Level 5:
Soul, funk, Swing Rare grooves, funky House Classics

£7 Pass each
admits two b4 11:30pm
valid only with this Ad

SupA baD
at the **marquee** club
(formerly HOME)
1 Leicester Sq London WC2
info
www.lumbrlous.co.uk

1. Which life cycle groups are the adverts aimed at? *(3 marks)*
2. Describe the characteristics of people in Empty nest 1 and suggest some leisure activities that they might enjoy. *(3 marks)*
3. Explain why the advert on the right is probably targeting a geographical market segment. *(4 marks)*
4. Using each of the three adverts, explain the advantages to organisations in the leisure and tourism industries of segmenting markets. *(7 marks)*

key terms

Corporate customers – businesses that buy products in the leisure and tourism industries.
Corporate hospitality – businesses spending money on entertaining existing and potential business clients.
Niche marketing – aiming a product at one small segment in the market.

Getting started...

Organisations in the leisure and tourism industry often collect information from people. This information is used to help them decide which products and services to provide and how they might be marketed. Look at the organisations in the cases below.

The Fairview Hotel

The Fairview Hotel is situated on a cliff top in Devon. It attracts holidaymakers and people taking weekend breaks. The owner recently placed suggestion boxes in the rooms to invite guests to comment on the services provided. A suggestion made by a recent guest is shown below.

Fairview Hotel - guest suggestions

The minibar contained a poor selection of beers. There were too many foreign lagers. I would have welcomed the opportunity to buy some bottled real ales such as Fullers' London Pride or Timothy Taylor's Landlord Bitter.

Tim Dobinson

International Sports Tours

International Sports Tours (IST) is a specialist tour operator. It organises trips abroad to major sporting events such as international football and rugby matches and Test Matches. Every year it invites about ten customers to join a lengthy group discussion about the trips they have been on. IST interviews the group and then records their comments for analysis. IST is interested in customer comments about:

- problems experienced
- highlights of each trip
- quality of accommodation
- quality of food
- efficiency of transport
- ticket distribution
- ideas for improvements
- ideas for other trips.

A customer discussion group

(a) How is information being collected in each case?
(b) How might the information be used?

What is market research?

MARKET RESEARCH is a process used to find out about customer needs and wants. It involves collecting information from people and using it to decide which products to produce and how to market them. For example, a theme park might ask its customers:

- where they travelled from
- how they travelled there
- who they came with
- their ages, likes, interests and lifestyles
- which rides they liked
- what entrance fees they would be prepared to pay
- which restaurants they liked.

The theme park might use this information to improve its services and marketing methods.

Primary research

PRIMARY RESEARCH involves collecting new information. This might be done by questioning people or watching their behaviour. The main advantage of primary research is that the data is original and up to date. PRIMARY DATA can also be collected according to the exact needs of the organisation. But collecting primary data is expensive and it takes time.

The market research process

1 The first step in the process is to identify the aim or purpose of the research. It might be to find out the type of person that might buy a product or how much they are prepared to pay.

2 It is important to plan research. For example, by deciding which methods of data collection will be used and who is going to be questioned.

3 The third stage involves collecting information. Perhaps by telephoning people at home or interviewing them in the street.

4 Collating the information involves organising the data so that it can be read and understood. Graphs and charts are often used.

5 Analysing information involves looking at the results and drawing conclusions. For example, a survey by a restaurant might show that people go there because they get good value for money.

6 The final stage is to present the findings to others such as managers and decision-makers.

Figure 1 *Stages in the market research process*

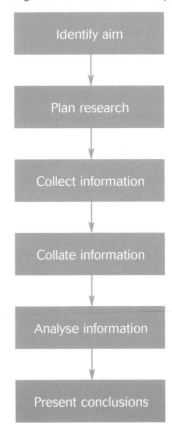

Identify aim

↓

Plan research

↓

Collect information

↓

Collate information

↓

Analyse information

↓

Present conclusions

Secondary or desk research

SECONDARY RESEARCH or DESK RESEARCH means collecting information that already exists. This SECONDARY DATA can be found in various places. The organisation itself might have some data such as sales figures, previous market research reports, a record of complaints or customer databases. Secondary data will also be found outside the organisation. The government publishes statistics that might be helpful such as the amount of money people spend on leisure and tourism. Data can be collected from other businesses, newspapers, the Internet, registers and directories such as *Yellow Pages*. There are also some specialist organisations that sell market research data. The main advantage of secondary research is that it is cheaper and quicker to gather data. But the information may not always be completely up to date and it can be difficult to find the exact information that is needed.

The purpose of market research

Market research can be used by an organisation in the leisure and tourism industry to find out a number of things.

The market
- ☻ How big is the market?
- ☻ Who are the customers?
- ☻ How much might customers spend?
- ☻ What are the market segments?

Competition
- ☻ What are the market shares?
- ☻ What products do competitors sell?
- ☻ What are the competitors' strengths and weaknesses?
- ☻ What prices are competitors charging?

The product
- ☻ Why do customers buy the product?
- ☻ How can the product be improved?
- ☻ What new products might be wanted?

Promotion
- ☻ How good are the organisation's promotions?
- ☻ Which are the best adverts?
- ☻ What promotions do competitors use?

Quantitative and qualitative research

QUANTITATIVE RESEARCH involves collecting data that is written as numbers. It is often presented in graphs, charts and tables. Figure 2 shows where Euro Disney's visitors came from in 2002. This is **quantitative data**.

Figure 2 *Geographical breakdown of Euro Disney's visitors.*

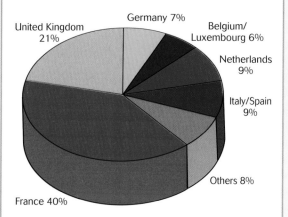

Source: Euro Disney Annual Report 2002

QUALITATIVE RESEARCH involves collecting data that is written in words. The idea is to find out what people think, their opinions, attitudes and beliefs. Some **qualitative data** is given in the box below. It shows a customer's response after dining at a new restaurant.

> 'I liked the Balham Bistro because the staff were friendly and had a sense of humour. The service was fast and the food was exquisite. The wine was served at the perfect temperature and the dining room was non-smoking.'

Businesses often collect both sorts of information. Quantitative data is quicker to collect and collate and easier to analyse. However, qualitative data is often very informative.

Quick quiz

1 **True or false?**

- ✪ One advantage of primary research is that data is up to date.
- ✪ Qualitative data is easier to analyse than quantitative data.
- ✪ Secondary data can only be found outside an organisation.

2 What is the difference between collecting and collating information?

3 What is meant by analysing information in the market research process?

4 How might market research be used to find out about competitors?

5 State two sources of secondary data that might exist outside the organisation.

Portfolio practice

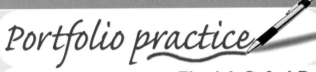

Elswick Safari Park

Elswick Safari Park carried out some research to try and find out why visitor numbers were falling. Visitors to the park had fallen from 56,400 in 1998 to 49,400 in 2004. A survey was carried out by interviewing people over the telephone. 1,000 telephone numbers were chosen from the local telephone directory. Table 1 shows the answers to five key questions from the survey and Table 2 shows a selection of comments made by the people interviewed.

Table 1 *Answers to 5 questions from the survey*

1. Have you ever been to Elswick Safari Park?
   YES 18% NO 82%
2. Have you ever been to any other safari park?
   YES 21% NO 79%
3. Would you visit Elswick Safari Park if it was cheaper?
   YES 44% NO 56%
4. Have you heard the radio advert for the Park?
   YES 7% NO 93%
5. Have you seen the newspaper advert for the Park?
   YES 29% NO 71%

Table 2 *Comments made by some of the people surveyed*

'There's no public transport to the Park since the bus service was withdrawn.'

'It's too expensive - it would cost me and my family over £60 to go for the day.'

'There aren't any tigers in the Park.'

'I didn't even know there was a Safari Park at Elswick.'

1. What is the aim of the research carried out by Elswick Safari Park? *(2 marks)*

2. Explain whether the research carried out by Elswick Safari Park is primary or secondary. *(4 marks)*

3. Using examples from the case, explain the difference between qualitative data and quantitative data. *(4 marks)*

4. Analyse the data for Elswick Safari Park and suggest reasons why visitor numbers have fallen in recent years. *(7 marks)*

key terms

Market research – how businesses find out about customers' needs.
Primary data – information collected for the first time.
Primary research – collecting new information.
Qualitative research – gathering written information, i.e. qualitative data.
Quantitative research – gathering numerical information, i.e. quantitative data.
Secondary data – information that already exists.
Secondary research or desk research – collecting information that already exists.

Getting started...

Organisations in the leisure and tourism industry can collect information using different methods. For example, a travel agent might use the Internet to gather information about holiday prices. When primary research is being carried out, organisations have to collect new information. Look at the methods being used below to collect new information.

Pershore Holidays

Pershore Holidays organises package holidays for disabled people. Most of its customers use wheelchairs so catering for their special needs is very important. The company is continually trying to improve its service. It collects information from customers by sending questionnaires to their homes when they return from holiday. Many of these questions are aimed at finding out whether their particular needs have been adequately met. Customers that return the completed questionnaires are entered into a monthly prize draw which offers a cash prize of £100.

Queueing for The London Eye

Ann and Lloyd Westwood

Ann and Lloyd Westwood want to open a new restaurant in Northampton. They decided to do some market research to find out what kind of food people wanted and what sort of price range people would be most interested in. They thought the best way to do this was to interview people in the town centre. Although a lot of people ignored their requests for an interview, they still managed to get 150 responses in one weekend. Ann and Lloyd discovered that a lot of people liked Italian food. It was a good job they carried out the research because Ann had wanted to serve mainly French food.

Market research

(a) What methods are being used to collect information in the two cases?
(b) In each case, explain briefly why the research is important.

Postal surveys

POSTAL SURVEYS are a popular method of research. They are simple and involve people returning QUESTIONNAIRES in the post. They have the following advantages:

- ✪ It is cheap because interviewers do not have to be trained.
- ✪ It is quick – questionnaires can be sent out and returned within a week or so.
- ✪ People can take their time and give thoughtful answers.
- ✪ People all over the country can be surveyed, if necessary.
- ✪ Honest answers may be more likely to be given because there is no interviewer.

But there are some disadvantages of sending questionnaires in the post.
- ✪ Only around 20% will be returned – most people just throw them away.
- ✪ Some questionnaires can take several weeks to be returned.
- ✪ They are impersonal and often, people do not have a good reason to spend time filling them in.
- ✪ Without help, people might leave sections blank or complete them incorrectly.

To persuade people to return questionnaires, they may be given an incentive. Usually, a prepaid envelope will be provided. Vouchers for goods or free entrance into a draw to win a holiday, for example, are also common.
Questionnaires can be distributed in several ways.

- ✪ Sent by post.
- ✪ Given out at the end of a holiday, visit or meal, for example.
- ✪ Given out on site. For example, at theme parks or hotels.

Telephone questionnaires

The number of organisations using telephone questionnaires is growing. This method involves ringing people at home and asking them questions over the telephone. The main advantages include:

- ✪ quicker than postal surveys – answers can be typed into a computer database as they are given
- ✪ the response rate is very high – most people will answer questions over the telephone 'on their own territory'
- ✪ people all over the country can be questioned, if necessary
- ✪ people can be given help if they need it.

Conducting a telephone questionnaire

But there are some disadvantages.
- ✪ They are more expensive than postal surveys because trained staff are used.
- ✪ Only short interviews can be conducted because people will complain about their time being taken up.
- ✪ Interviewers may rush the interview because they are under pressure to make a lot of calls. This may mean that people do not think properly about their answers.
- ✪ This type of activity is increasing and many people are becoming irritated by it. They see it as an invasion of their privacy and they often think that callers are trying to sell them something. Because of this, some people may not be willing to be interviewed.

Personal surveys

PERSONAL SURVEYS involve interviewing one person at a time, face to face. This may be done in the street, in a person's home or perhaps on an organisation's premises. Interviews are usually based on a written questionnaire with the interviewer recording answers on a sheet. If the interview is conducted in a room, the responses may be taped. The main advantages include the following.

✪ Good response rate once people have been stopped in the street.

✪ Help can be given if people do not understand the question.

✪ People have time to think about their answers.

✪ People may feel that their views are valued when they are interviewed personally.

Some disadvantages of personal interviews include the following.

✪ They are more expensive because trained staff are used and they may have to travel.

✪ It is more difficult to interview people from a wide geographical area.

✪ The information collected might not be accurate particularly if the interviewer is not very skilled or suggests certain answers to people.

✪ Some people will avoid interviewers because they may not have the time or may feel uncomfortable.

✪ It can take a long time to gather a fairly small amount of information.

Focus groups

A FOCUS GROUP is like a group interview. Several people are invited to attend a group discussion where they will be questioned and encouraged to talk in depth about products and services. The discussion may be video-recorded so that comments can be analysed later. Focus groups provide a lot of information and help get to the bottom of people's views. However, they are expensive and time-consuming. People are usually paid for taking part in focus groups.

Observation

It is possible to gather information by observing people. One way of doing this is to film customers. For example, it might be possible to film people in a theme park to find out how long they are prepared to wait for a ride. An organisation might also film the flow of customers around a store or visitor attraction to see what attracts their interest. Some organisations use MYSTERY SHOPPERS to gather information. These are people who pose as customers. For example, a travel agent might send mystery shoppers to some of its branches to observe the quality of service been given by its employees.

Internet

The Internet can be used to collect primary data and secondary data. For example, a hotel could use the Internet to find out what its competitors are charging for rooms. This is secondary data. Primary data can be collected using a questionnaire that people fill in on their computers. Many organisations have questionnaires on their websites which allow customers to express their views. Some organisations encourage customers to send emails. These may provide useful information for market research purposes.

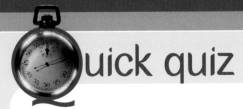

Quick quiz

1 **True or false?**

✪ One of the disadvantages of postal surveys is that they are impersonal.

✪ Running a focus group can be expensive and time-consuming.

✪ It is not possible to gather primary data using the Internet.

2 Match the correct research method in the box with the appropriate statement.

✪ A method that involves filming people as they move around a museum, for example.

✪ A method that does not allow guidance to be given to respondents.

✪ A method where people may feel that their views are more valued.

> Focus group   Observation
> Postal survey Personal survey

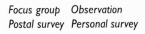

Portfolio practice

Bude Holiday Village and GoThere.com

Bude Holiday Village

Bude Holiday Village targets families with young children. Recently, it has upgraded its facilities and is trying to attract families with teenage children. For example, it has a modern disco, up-to-date computer games and Internet cafés. To check whether the new facilities were matching the needs of these families, questionnaires were posted to 1,000 customers. This cost £760 but unfortunately only 12% were returned.

GoThere.com

GoThere.com is an online business. It sells holidays, travel tickets and insurance from its website. During 2004, it received 320 voluntary emails from its customers giving feedback about the services they had been sold. Most of them were complaints or drew attention to weaknesses. Many of them were helpful but unfortunately,

✪ it was not always known who had sent them,

✪ many may have been stopped by filters, and

✪ there was no quantitative data.

1. How many responses did Bude Holiday Village get from its postal survey? *(2 marks)*
2. How might Bude Holiday Village have increased the number of responses? *(3 marks)*
3. Explain two advantages to Bude Holiday Village of using postal surveys. *(4 marks)*
4. For market research purposes, how useful are the emails that GoThere.com received? *(7 marks)*

key terms

Focus group – a group of people brought together to provide views and opinions about products and services.

Mystery shopper – someone who anonymously visits a business or organisation and reports back to the management on the quality of a product or service.

Personal surveys – a method of collecting data that involves a face-to-face interview.

Postal surveys – a method of collecting information that involves sending questionnaires to people through the post.

Questionnaires – a document used to collect data. It contains a list of questions for people to answer.

30 Questionnaires

Getting started...

A lot of market research involves the use of questionnaires. A questionnaire is a document which contains a set of questions. They are used mainly in postal surveys and personal surveys. They provide a very simple way of recording information. Look at the questionnaire below. It was used by a tour operator specialising in fly and drive holidays to Florida. It was given to 1,000 customers on the plane journey home and is designed to find out what sort of people buy their holidays. 950 questionnaires were returned.

Florida Fly & Drive – Questionnaire

1. Which age group do you belong to?

   18 – 25 ☐   26 – 35 ☐   36 – 45 ☐   46 – 55 ☐   Over 55 ☐

2. What is your marital status?

   Single ☐   Married ☐   Widowed ☐   Divorced ☐

3. How many children do you have? ....

4. What is your income group?

   0 – 15K ☐   16K – 25K ☐   26K – 35K ☐   36K – 45K ☐   Over 45K ☐

5. What is your occupation? ....

6. Which daily newspaper do you read?

   Mirror ☐   Sun ☐   Mail ☐   Star ☐   Times ☐   Guardian ☐

   Independent ☐   Telegraph ☐   Other (Please state)......................

7. Do you buy products or services online?   Yes ☐   No ☐

8. Which airport did you fly from?

   Heathrow ☐   Gatwick ☐   Birmingham ☐   Manchester ☐

9. How did you book your holiday?

   Travel agent ☐   Online ☐   Direct (brochure) ☐   Direct (independent) ☐

10. Will you return to Florida?   Yes ☐   No ☐

(a) The answers to question 8 were Heathrow 248, Gatwick 198, Birmingham 210 and Manchester 294. Draw a bar chart to represent the data.

(b) Explain whether this questionnaire is collecting mainly quantitative (information written as numbers) or qualitative (information written in words) data.

Designing questionnaires

The importance of good design

Why is it important to produce a well-designed questionnaire?

- ✪ It will be easier to complete and will therefore save time and money.
- ✪ People will find it easier to fill in and will be more willing to do so.
- ✪ People will answer all the questions.
- ✪ It will produce a lot of useful information that can be used to help make important decisions, such as what price to charge for a service.

Poorly designed questionnaires are likely to annoy people and lead to a low response rate. This is a waste.

Features of good design

The first step in producing a good questionnaire is to be clear about its aim or purpose. For example, the aim of the one used by Florida Fly & Drive was to find out who bought its holidays. The company was trying to build a CUSTOMER PROFILE.

These features will help improve the quality of a questionnaire.

- ✪ Keep it short. People are then more likely to complete it.
- ✪ Provide clear instructions on how to complete it.
- ✪ Use straightforward language.
- ✪ Do not ask unnecessary questions. Only ask those which help to achieve the aim of the questionnaire.
- ✪ Ask the most important questions first in case it is not fully completed.
- ✪ Use a balance of OPEN and CLOSED QUESTIONS. These are explained later.
- ✪ Leave plenty of space for responses to open questions.
- ✪ Divide questions into categories wherever possible.
- ✪ Think how the answers will be collated and analysed. Remember that quantitative data is easier to handle.
- ✪ Avoid questions that test someone's memory such as, 'When did you last have an Indian take-away?' This will save time.
- ✪ Use a high standard of presentation.

Closed questions

Closed questions are those that ask for a specific reply from a small selection of responses. People usually have to tick a box to give their answer like the one shown in the example here. Closed questions are useful when there is only a limited range of responses. They are simple to answer and they provide quantitative data which is easier to analyse. But this type of question is not suitable when there are many possible answers.

What type of holiday accommodation do you prefer?

Hotel	☐	Guest-house	☐
Chalet	☐	Villa	☐
Apartment	☐	Other	☐

Open questions

Open questions allow people to answer using their own words. They can be used to find out people's views and opinions and they can produce a lot of useful information. However, the data can be difficult to collate and analyse. For example, it is not usually possible to produce graphs and charts from answers to open questions. When asking open questions, it is important to leave enough space for the answer. Two examples of open questions are given here.

Why did you choose to go to Crete for your holiday?

....

....

....

What did you like about your tour guide when crossing the Sahara Desert?

....

....

....

Attitude scales

A common way of measuring how much people liked or disliked something is to use a statement with an ATTITUDE SCALE. In the example below, people are required to tick a box to show whether they agree or disagree with the statement regarding food quality. This is useful because these opinions can be expressed as numbers.

The food in the members' bar was good value for money.

Strongly Disagree	Disagree	Agree	Strongly Agree
☐	☐	☐	☐

Sampling

When an organisation wants to collect information from a particular market, it is impossible to question every single person who buys products in that market. There would be far too many – perhaps millions – so a SAMPLE is chosen. This means that a small part of the market is selected and questioned. Provided that the selection is statistically fair and accurate, the responses of those questioned are likely to reflect the views of the total market. For example, a survey of a travel agency's customers would involve giving each customer a number, e.g. from 1 to 5,000. A table of random numbers is then used to select members of the sample – say 10% of all customers. This is called RANDOM SAMPLING. It offers a good chance that the sample will represent the customers as a whole.

Using questionnaires

When using questionnaires to gather information, the following tips might be useful.

- ✪ The questionnaire should be tested first, perhaps on some work colleagues. If there are any problems, it can then be changed before it goes out to customers.

- ✪ When using postal surveys, it may be helpful to send a covering letter to explain what the questionnaire is all about. It is important to tell people that the information collected from them will be confidential.

- ✪ People are more likely to complete questionnaires if they are given some form of incentive. For example, free entry into a draw with a prize or a gift of some kind.

- ✪ When conducting personal interviews, it is important that the interviewer is presentable, professional and can prove their identity. This helps people to feel more comfortable.

Quick quiz

1 **True or false?**
- ✪ A good question is one that tests someone's memory.
- ✪ Well-designed questionnaires will save an organisation money.
- ✪ Using attitude scales helps to quantify people's opinions.

2 Which of these is a closed question?
   (a) What did you think of the Elizabethan display in the museum?
   (b) Did you use public transport to travel to the stadium? Yes……. No…….
   (c) How do you decide where to go on holiday?
   (d) Why do you enjoy ten-pin bowling?

3 State one disadvantage of using an open question.

4 State two reasons why questionnaire design is important.

5 State one advantage of using a closed question.

Portfolio practice

Airport survey

A busy European airport wants to find out what people do when they are waiting in the airport lounge for their flight. It wants to gather information on how they spend their time and money. For example, do they sit and read, go shopping, have a meal, go for a drink, play computer games or enjoy some other activity? The airport is also keen to know how early people arrive for their flight and whether they feel relaxed waiting around. Finally, it would also be useful to know how much money people spend in the airport.

An airport lounge

(a) Design a questionnaire that could be used to gather the information the airport wants. (Do not use more than eight questions.) *(10 marks)*

(b) What makes a good questionnaire? Explain your answer. *(7 marks)*

key terms

Attitude scale – people are asked to indicate whether they agree or disagree with a statement, usually by ticking a box.

Closed questions – those which have a small range of set responses, usually answered by ticking a box.

Customer profile – the various characteristics of a typical customer in a particular market.

Open questions – those which people can answer in their own words.

Random sampling – every member of a particular market has an equal chance of being selected in a survey.

Sample – a small part of the market that would be questioned in a survey to show what the whole market is like.

Getting started...

Different organisations in the leisure and tourism industries may market their products and services in different ways. For example, in the airline business, 'no frills' airlines such as easyJet rely on low prices to attract customers. British Airways uses extensive advertising to sell its services. Look at the methods used to sell products below.

Heathcotes — Longridge

Paul Heathcote is a well-known chef. He owns restaurants in Longridge, Preston, Liverpool, Manchester, Leeds and Wrightington. In 2004, the Longridge Restaurant regained its Michelin Star (an award for very high quality food). Longridge serves the very best of modern British cuisine in luxurious surroundings. It is recognised as the North's premier restaurant and has built a worldwide reputation for its fine food and service. This reputation has been spread mainly by word of mouth.

Heathcotes restaurant, Longridge

Tour operators

Most of the big tour operators advertise their holidays in glossy brochures. They are very colourful and eye-catching. They contain photos of accommodation, destinations and visitor attractions such as beautiful scenery and famous buildings.

Holiday Autos

Holiday Autos rents out cars to holidaymakers when they arrive at their destination. It claims to offer low prices and there are further discounts for booking online.

Part of the home page for holidayautos.co.uk

(a) What attracts customers in each of the cases?
(b) Do you think the prices charged by Paul Heathcote's Longridge restaurant would be high or low? Explain your answer.

The marketing mix

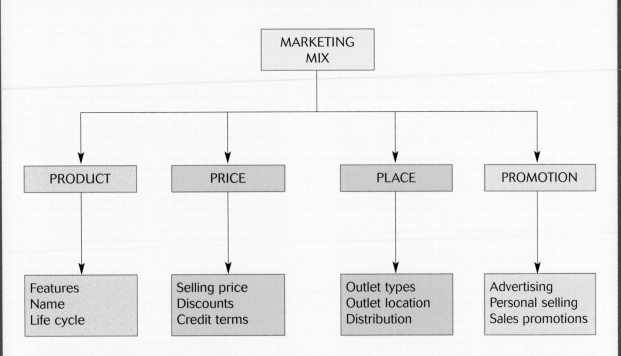

What is the marketing mix?

Marketing is about getting the right product, to the right people, at the right place, at the right price using the right promotion. The MARKETING MIX is the combination of marketing activities that an organisation uses to do this. It is a 'tool' made up of four parts as shown in the diagram above. The four parts are known as the 'four Ps' and they are:

- ✪ PRODUCT The goods and services supplied by organisations.

- ✪ PRICE The amount of money that customers pay for the goods and services.

- ✪ PLACE The outlets where goods and services can be bought by customers.

- ✪ PROMOTION The methods used to encourage customers to buy the goods and services.

Different organisations in the leisure and tourism industries will attach different importance to each part of the mix. Many companies now offer their services online – this is an example of 'place' being important. Some companies try to be the cheapest in the market – this is an example of 'price' being important. Organisations will try to get the 'right mix' when marketing their products.

The product

Products can be either goods or services. Some examples of goods in the leisure and tourism industries are books, computer games, CDs, sports equipment and gardening tools. Examples of services are restaurant meals, rail travel, a swimming lesson, package holidays and DVD rental.

Organisations have to provide products to satisfy people's wants and needs. This involves making sure that certain things are right such as:

- ✪ **features** – these are the things that help a product do what customers expect.

- ✪ **name** – a lot of customers buy products because they have a well-known name

- ✪ **appearance** – many people like products that look good.

Organisations generally develop products over time. This means that they modify them, improve them, or even change them, if they have come to the end of their life. Units 32 and 33 discuss the importance of the product in more detail.

Price

The selling price is the amount of money that customers pay for a product. It is important for organisations to get the price right. If it is too high, people will not buy the product and may buy those of the competitor. On the other hand, if it is too low, a business may not make any profit. Various methods or strategies can be used when setting prices. For example, a new Chinese take-away restaurant may set a price that is deliberately lower than that of other Chinese take-aways in the town. This strategy is designed to win customers from its competitors. Many organisations offer discounts or free credit (buying products and paying for them later at no extra cost).

Price is discussed in detail in Units 34 and 35.

Place

Organisations can choose where to make their products available. For example, a video rental business might locate its shop next to an off-licence or a take-away restaurant. Making products available in the right place can be very important for some products. Organisations generally attempt to supply products in places that are convenient for customers. Some hotels deliberately locate next to airports as this is convenient for their target market. These are people who have just arrived at the airport or those who plan to fly the next day.

Place is discussed in more detail in Unit 36.

An airport hotel, Manchester

Promotion

Organisations try very hard to encourage people to buy their products. They can choose from a wide range of methods to achieve this aim. The methods they use are all different types of promotion.
Examples include:

- ✪ advertising
- ✪ direct marketing
- ✪ public relations
- ✪ personal selling
- ✪ displays
- ✪ sponsorship
- ✪ demonstrations
- ✪ sales promotions.

Different organisations prefer different methods. For example, large tour operators can afford to advertise on television. Many pubs, bars and nightclubs rely on sales promotions such as 'All drinks for £1' or 'Two drinks for the price of one'. Restaurants often offer free wine or free children's meals. Promotion is discussed in more detail in Units 37 and 38.

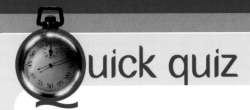

Quick quiz

1 **True or false?**

- ○ Renting a car on holiday is an example of a service.

- ○ Buying some fishing tackle from an angling shop is an example of a service.

- ○ The marketing mix is a tool used by organisations to help meet customers' needs and wants.

2 Complete this sentence using the words from the box.
Marketing is about getting the right ....
to the right people, at the right ...., at
the right ...., using the right ....

Place	*Promotion*
Price	*Product*

3 Which of these is **not** a promotion?
(a) Public relations **(b)** Advertising **(c)** Sales promotions **(d)** Brand name

4 Many organisations sell their products online. Which of the four Ps does this reflect?

5 What is meant by the selling price?

Portfolio practice

PC World

PC World is a computer superstore with branches in many towns and cities around the UK. It also has a website and customers can buy online. It sells computers, computer accessories, digital cameras, DV camcorders and computer software. One method used by PC World to promote its products is a free brochure. The information shown below is taken from a brochure distributed with a Sunday newspaper.

1. What is the selling price of the Epson Photo Printer? *(1 mark)*

2. Explain, using examples, whether PC World sells goods or services. *(2 marks)*

3. Using examples from the case, explain one method used by PC World to promote its products. *(3 marks)*

4. Explain why PC World makes its products available online. *(4 marks)*

5. Which of the four Ps do you think is the most important to PC World? Explain your answer. *(7 marks)*

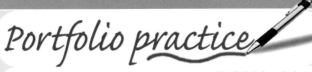

EPSON Stylus Photo R200

The new Stylus Photo R200 is a fully featured, photo-quality inkjet printer with benefits from six colour printing for natural colours. Other great features include separate ink tanks for easy replacement and the ability to print directly onto printable CDs and DVDs. With up to 5760 optimised dpi resolution, the R200 offers outstanding print quality with superb features.

- Up to 5760x1440 dpi resolution
- Up to 15ppm mono
- Up to 15ppm colour
- Direct CD printing

HALF PRICE*
£49.99
USUAL IN-STORE
PRICE £99.99
SKU 605694

PC WORLD
The Computer Superstore

PHOTO PRINTER
*When bought with any digital camera over £100

WE **WON'T BE** BEATEN ON PRICE!*

* We will give you 110% of the difference back if you can find a lower price for the same product on offer from another retail store. We will do this where the offer is available to purchase from stock at another retail store - either at the time of purchase, or within 7 days of your purchase from PC World. You will need to produce your receipt where you have already purchased. We will not do this for the opening, closing down, ex-display, clearance, special order, members only, internet, mail order or extended warranty prices.

key terms

Marketing mix – a tool used by organisations to meet customer needs and wants. It is made up of four parts – product, price, place and promotion.

Place – the outlets where organisations make their products available.

Price – the amount that customers pay for a product.

Product – goods or services provided by organisations.

Promotion – methods used by organisations to encourage people to buy products.

32 The product

Getting started...

Products are supplied to satisfy the customer's needs and wants. They can be physical goods like a powerboat or camping equipment. However, in the leisure and tourism industries, most products are services such as watching an international rugby match, coach transport, hotel accommodation or a golf lesson. But what makes a good product? This often depends on the customer. For some people, the appearance of the product is important. For others, the quality of the product, the level of after sales service, the packaging, its durability (how long it lasts) or its name is important. Look at the cases below.

The Richards family

Mr and Mrs Richards and their three young children went to Thorness Bay Holiday Park on the Isle of Wight for their annual holiday. They all had a terrific time. Mrs Richards said, 'The wide range of facilities was excellent. There was lots for the children to do. They loved the adventure playground, the Indoor Fun Pool and Sparky's Krew'. Mr Richards said, 'We stayed in a caravan. It was clean and there was plenty of space. There were lots of convenient facilities and my wife and I were able to relax knowing that the kids were safe and happy. It was one of the best holidays we've ever had.'

Thorness Bay Holiday Park

Hafza and Fatima

Hafza and Fatima were both 14 in the same week. They wanted to spend their birthday money on a new mobile phone. In the shop, they ended up looking at two particular handsets.

Hafza   They're both really cool aren't they?

Fatima   Yeh, they look wicked.

Hafza   I think the Sharp one's the best.

Fatima   Yeh. Me too. I love that flip screen. It's really smart.

Hafza   Cheryl's got one like that.

Fatima   Yeh, but it doesn't look as good as that does it?

Hafza   No, let's go for it.

Fatima   OK, we'll get that one.

In each case:
(a) Is the product a good or service?
(b) What is it about the product that the customers like?

Product features

Product features are the things about a good or service that makes it attractive to buy. When buying products, different features appeal to different people. For example, two couples might want to book a weekend break. One might choose a countryside hotel while the other might prefer a city break. They are similar products but have quite different features. Which features are important to people?

- Products should be **functional.** This means that a product should serve the purpose it was bought for. For example, waterproof walking boots mustn't let in water.

- For some people the **appearance** of products is important. They like products that look good. Examples might be sportswear and sports equipment.

- Some people buy products because of their **image**. They might go to certain fitness clubs, holiday destinations and nightclubs because they believe that their image says something about the type of people they are.

- Some people look at **health and safety** features. For example, some people might prefer to avoid burger bars because they believe their products are unhealthy. Parents may choose certain holiday destinations because they are particularly safe for children.

- **Affordability** might be important. For many people, their choice is restricted because they can only afford certain options.

The product mix

Many organisations provide a range of products. This is called the PRODUCT MIX. For example, JJB Sports sells a wide range of different products in its stores. These include sportswear such as training shoes, football boots, football shirts, swim-wear and track suits, and sports equipment such as golf clubs, cricket bats, rugby balls and squash racquets. Each of these products is part of JJB Sports' product mix.

Flamingo Land theme park in Malton, North Yorkshire has a number of key products in its product mix. These include:

- Zoo
- White Knuckle rides
- Kiddies' Kingdom
- Holiday Village
- Shows.

Part of the JJB product range

One reason why organisations offer more than one product is to cater for different market segments. They will also increase their revenue and may make more profit.

The brand name

Many organisations give their products BRAND NAMES. This is a unique name that makes a product stand out from that of its competitors. Examples of brand names in the leisure and tourism industries include Virgin, BA, Heineken, Going Places, Adidas and Pizza Hut. Most people will recognise all these brand names. A good brand name is likely to be short, easy to identify and remember. Brand names are used for several reasons.

○ **To help recognition** If customers recognise a brand, they may trust it and buy it.

○ **To make the product different** In some markets such as air travel, all suppliers provide the same product – a seat on an aircraft. However, people may believe that a flight to New York sold by Virgin is different from one sold by BA.

○ **To create brand loyalty** Once people start buying a particular brand, they may carry on buying it for a long time. They become loyal and it is difficult for other businesses to get them to change.

○ **To develop a brand image** People might believe that a brand name says something about a product or the kind of people that buy it. Consequently, they buy that brand to buy into that particular image.

After sales service

Many organisations provide AFTER SALES SERVICE. These are the back-up services provided after a product has been sold. This is very important to some customers. It provides them with security when buying a product. Examples might include:

○ **Servicing and repairs** When buying certain products such as technical products like a television or DVD player, a business might offer free servicing and repairs for a period of time. These services are often covered by a guarantee which promises that a product or service will meet certain standards and specifications.

○ **Helplines** Again, with some technical products like computers, a customer might have problems with setting it up or operating it. A business might offer a free helpline which can be contacted by telephone for guidance.

○ **Ensuring satisfaction** Many organisations check to see if their customers received a good service. For example, tour operators ask if their customers enjoyed their holiday. They might use a questionnaire to do this.

○ **Deal with complaints** An important part of after sales service is dealing with customer complaints. This might involve apologising for poor service or replacing a faulty product. These days, organisations are much better in compensating people who are not happy with the product or service they have bought.

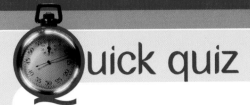

Quick quiz

1 True or false?

- ✪ Giving advice about a product before it is purchased is an example of after sales service.
- ✪ The RAC is an example of a brand name.
- ✪ A business might add to its product mix to cater for another market segment.

2 Which of these is not a product feature?
(a) Affordability (b) Functionality (c) Image (d) Brand loyalty

3 Which of these is not a brand name?
(a) Nokia (b) KFC (c) Manchester United (d) Highbury

4 Is image an important product feature for everyone?

Portfolio practice

Kuoni

The tour operator Kuoni has been trading for 98 years. It has been recognised as the best long haul tour operator in Britain for the last 21 years. Kuoni claims to be dedicated to quality, attention to detail and personal service. It provides package holidays in quality accommodation at the following destinations:

- ✪ Indian sub-continent
- ✪ The Americas
- ✪ Caribbean & Bermuda
- ✪ Africa & Indian Ocean
- ✪ North Africa & Middle East
- ✪ Far East & Pacific
- ✪ USA & Canada.

A World of Difference

Kuoni also sells cruises and organises weddings and safaris at the above destinations. Most of the packages provided by Kuoni sell at over £1,000 per person.

QUESTIONNAIRE We are committed to improving the standard of our holidays and it is only with the help of your feedback that we will be able to achieve our aim. We would therefore appreciate it if you would spend a few moments to complete and return the questionnaire which you will find in your document wallet. The Quality Control Manager at Kuoni Travel Limited, Kuoni House, Dorking, Surrey RH5 4AZ (email address CUSTOMER@KUONI.CO.UK) would also welcome and act upon any comments you would like to pass on to us.

IF YOU HAD A PROBLEM If a problem remains unresolved during your holiday, you should make a complaint in writing to Kuoni within 28 days of the completion of the holiday. Please remember to quote your holiday booking number. We will reply to you within 28 days of receipt of your letter, as laid down by the ABTA Tour Operator's Code of Conduct.

DEALING WITH COMPLAINTS We certainly hope that we can settle any holiday complaints amicably, however, should this prove not to be the case you may refer any dispute relating to this contract to an Arbitrator appointed by the Chartered Institute of Arbitrators. The scheme provides for a simple and inexpensive method of arbitration on documents alone with restricted liability for you in respect of costs. The scheme does not apply to claims for an amount greater than £5000 per person or £15000 per booking form.

1. What is the brand name in this case? *(1 mark)*
2. Give three reasons why businesses use brand names. *(3 marks)*
3. Using this case as an example, explain what is meant by the product mix. *(4 marks)*
4. Explain how Kuoni provides after sales service. *(6 marks)*

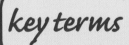

key terms

After sales service – back-up services provided by an organisation after a product has been sold.

Brand names – the name given to a particular product or service to distinguish it from other similar products.

Product mix – the range of different products supplied by an organisation.

33 The product life cycle

Getting started...

Products may pass through different stages during their time on the market. For example, when a product is first introduced its sales might be quite low. There is also the chance that people will not like it and that it will have to be withdrawn. Many products on the market, such as Club 18-30 holidays, are well-established and sell well every year. But some products get out of date and have to be replaced with newer ones. Look at the products below.

Arsenal FC

Arsenal FC, the North London Premiership football club, was formed in 1886. Since then it has won many trophies including the league and cup double three times. In 2003/04, Arsenal became the first club in modern history to go unbeaten for a whole season. For many years, Arsenal has attracted attendances of around 40,000. The club will be moving to a larger stadium which is scheduled to open in time for the start of the 2006/07 season.

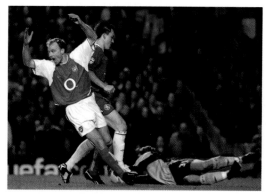

Arsenal v Chelsea

Rubik's cube

Rubik's cube was invented by the Hungarian, Erno Rubik, who was obsessed with 3-D geometry. The cube made its first public appearance in 1979 at the Nurenberg Toy Show but did not become popular until the 1980s. By 1982, around 100 million cubes had been sold. But sales fell quickly and in 1983 production of the cube stopped. In the early 1990s, it made a slight recovery but there is very little interest in the cube now.

Harry Potter and the Prisoner of Azkaban

A cinema film has a fairly short life – perhaps a couple of years. However, sequels are used to prolong the life of a good film idea. *Harry Potter and the Prisoner of Azkaban*, released in 2004, was the third Harry Potter film. It is Harry's third year at Hogwarts School of Witchcraft and Wizardry. He learns that a convicted murderer, Sirius Black, has escaped from Azkaban prison and could be coming after him next. It has been reported that six Harry Potter films might be made.

(a) State whether the products in the above cases are
   (i) new (ii) well established (iii) out of date.
(b) Which of these products is likely to be around in 25 years time? Explain your answer.

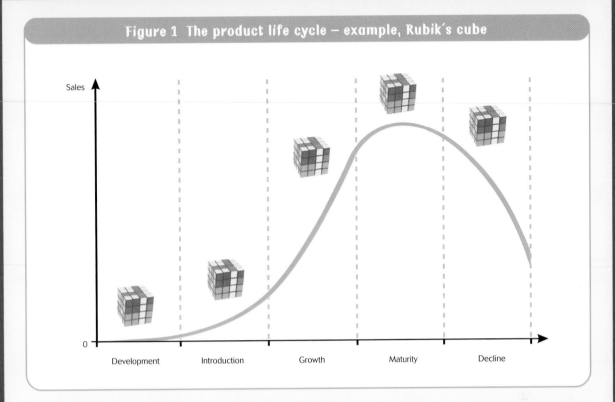

Figure 1 The product life cycle – example, Rubik's cube

What is the product life cycle?

The PRODUCT LIFE CYCLE is a concept which shows the sales of a product as it passes through the different stages in its life. The life of a product is the amount of time it is available on the market. The diagram in Figure 1 shows the various stages that most products pass through during their life. These are development, introduction, growth, maturity and decline. Understanding this cycle can be helpful to a business in developing its marketing strategy. For example, different types of promotion might be used in different stages.

Development

During this stage, the product is being researched, designed and tested. There are no sales and a business might be anxious because new product development is expensive and risky. Also, there is no certainty that the product will ever be launched. Many new products never get beyond the development stage.

Introduction

This is when the product is first launched. Some businesses introduce their products in stages. For example, the Sony PlayStation was introduced in Japan first, then the US and Europe later. Sales are likely to be low to start with and the product is not likely to be profitable. A lot of money will be spent on advertising or promotion to inform people about the product. At this stage, prices may be kept low to attract people's interest. However, if the product is unique, prices might be very high. For example, mobile phones, PCs and DVDs were expensive when they were first launched.

Growth

Once people get to know about a product and like it, sales will start to grow rapidly and the product may become profitable. A business may try to develop some brand loyalty by advertising. The growth in sales and the popularity of the product will eventually attract competitors into the market. This might force the business to lower its prices.

Maturity

There are two parts to the maturity stage. First of all, sales will reach a peak. This means that they will not grow any more. The business will usually be making a profit but competition could be quite fierce. Eventually, the market becomes saturated which means that sales will start to fall and some competitors may be forced out of the market. Prices will be lower now and businesses might be forced to spend more on advertising and promotion to keep their share of their market. This will lead to lower profits. During the saturation stage, people may not buy the product because they already have one or have tried it. For example, the sale of phone handsets has fallen in recent years as mobile phones have become increasingly popular.

Decline

Many products begin to lose their appeal. People are less interested in the product and sales start to decline rapidly. Perhaps there has been a change in consumer tastes or technology has resulted in brand-new products. This happened with sales of video players which fell in the 1990s when DVD players were launched. As profits fall, a business may have to consider withdrawing the product. Examples of products in the leisure and tourism industry that might be declining are holidays at traditional British seaside resorts and board games in favour of computer games.

Extending a product's life

Many businesses try to prolong the life of a product. They might do this by using EXTENSION STRATEGIES. Here are a number of examples.

- **Find new markets** Businesses could sell their products to new groups of customers. For example, sportswear is now being sold to people that do not play any sport.

- **Change the packaging** A change in the appearance of a product or its packaging might encourage people to buy a product again. For example, soft drinks manufacturers sell their products in cans, glass bottles, plastic bottles and mini-sized cans.

- **Increase the product range** For example, Lego is always bringing out new versions of its basic product. Crisp manufacturers are offering more and more flavours to choose from.

- **Modify the product** It is common to redesign old products and relaunch them as being new. For example, nightclubs and bars are often refurbished and renamed to keep customers interested.

Using the product life cycle

Why might organisations be interested in a product's life cycle?

- It will help to manage cash flow. For example, in the development stage a business knows that there will be no revenue. It might decide to borrow money to pay for the development.

- It helps to decide when a product needs to be withdrawn from the market. If a declining product is left on the market too long, it might damage the company's image.

- It will show when a business can expect to make a profit from a product.

- It will help to plan marketing activities. Different types of advertising are often needed at different stages. For example, when a product is launched, people need to be made aware of it. But when a product is mature, it may need an advert which is designed to maintain and reaffirm people's confidence in it.

- It helps a business set prices for the product. For example, higher prices might be charged in the growth stage.

Quick quiz

1 **True or false?**
- ○ All products have the same life span.
- ○ During the maturity stage, sales start to grow.
- ○ A product becomes profitable during the development stage.

2 In which stage of the product life cycle is the price likely to be lowest?
(a) Introduction (b) Growth (c) Maturity (d) Decline

3 In which stage of the product life cycle is there no revenue?
(a) Introduction (b) Growth (c) Maturity (d) Development

4 Which of these products is likely to have a short life span?
(a) Pop song (b) Long haul package holiday (c) Chicken Tikka Massala
(d) Foster's Lager

5 Name three extension strategies.

Portfolio practice

The Crawford Brewing Company

The Crawford Brewing Company has been brewing beer for 130 years. It has relied heavily on two good-selling brews – Crawford's Bitter and Crawford's Special Bitter. However, in the 1990s, the company's sales fell because of the increasing popularity of bottled lagers. The company responded by launching a new product in 1998 called Crawford's Golden – a smooth, light, golden, fruity bitter. The beer took twelve months to develop and cost the company £22,000. Sales of the beer are shown in Table 1.

1. Using the information in Table 1, draw a graph to show the product life cycle of Crawford's Golden. Label clearly the development, introduction, growth and maturity stages. *(8 marks)*
2. What happens to sales in the maturity stage of Crawford's Golden? *(1 mark)*
3. State one possible reason for this sales pattern. *(2 marks)*
4. Discuss how The Crawford Brewing Company might use the product life cycle to promote its new product. *(6 marks)*

Table 1 *Sales of Crawford's Golden*

Date	1997	1998	1999	2000	2001	2002	2003	2004
Sales (barrels)	0	200	600	2,000	4,000	7,000	7,500	7,500

key terms

Extension strategies – methods used to prolong the life of a product.

Product life cycle - the stages that a product goes through during its life on the market - from its development, through growth and maturity, to the stage where sales decline and it is withdrawn.

Getting started...

One important marketing decision that must be made is what price to charge. This is the amount of money that customers have to pay for the product. Pricing can be quite complex. It is common for organisations to have many different prices for the same product. GNER trains offers up to twelve different prices for a return train journey from Newcastle to London. For example, the cheapest ticket is £62 for a Super Advance Return and the dearest is £277 for a Special Executive Return (quoted for 7 June 2004). Look at the example below.

Aston Villa FC

Like most football clubs, Aston Villa FC sells tickets at different prices for the same match. Details of prices charged for the 2004/05 season are shown below.

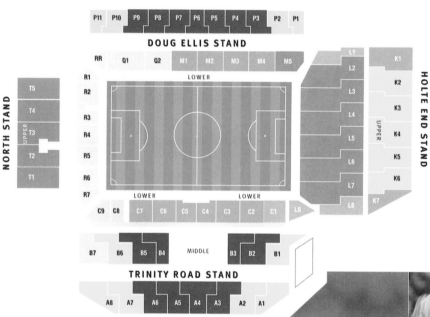

Plan of Aston Villa Stadium

Ticket Prices

Match Ticket Prices

Location	Adult	U16 **	Student ◊	Over 65 ‡
Trinity Road Upper Centre / Trinity Road Middle Centre / Doug Ellis Upper Centre	£29.00	£13.00	£22.00	£15.00
Trinity Road Upper Wings / Trinity Road Middle Wings / Doug Ellis Upper Wings / Holte End Upper Centre	£26.00	£13.00	£19.00	£14.00
Trinity Road Lower Centre / Doug Ellis Lower Centre / Holte End Upper Wings	£24.00	£13.00	£18.00	£13.00
Doug Ellis Lower Wings / Holte End Lower Centre / North Stand Upper Centre	£23.00	£13.00	£17.00	£13.00
Trinity Road Lower Wings / Holte End Lower Wings	£23.00	£13.00	£17.00	£13.00
North Stand Upper Wings	£17.00	£7.00	£17.00	£9.00
Family Area *	£17.00	£7.00	£17.00	£9.00

* Tickets in the Family Area are only sold to family parties, ie the group must contain at least one under 16 year old. See terms and conditions for details.

** Concessionary tickets are only available to juniors under the age of 16 as at 1st September 2004.

◊ On production of a valid NUS card.

† For students under the age of 19 as at 1st September 2004 and registered with the club scheme.

‡ For those over the age of 65 as at 1st September 2004.

For all the above conditions, documentary evidence must be produced at the time of purchase and may be checked by the Club from time to time during the season.

(a) What is the price of (i) a student ticket in the Holte End Lower Wing (ii) an adult in the P6 area of the stadium?

(b) Why do you think Aston Villa charges different prices for match tickets?

Actual selling price

The amount of money paid by customers for goods or services is called the ACTUAL SELLING PRICE. Many customers look at the actual selling price when deciding whether to buy something. For example, a family going on a package holiday is unlikely to choose a particular package without first checking the price. For some people, price is the most important factor when choosing to buy a product. This may be because they have limited income.

For organisations, price is the most flexible part of the marketing mix because it can be changed so easily. Price might be reduced for a short time to get people interested in a product or it might be increased if there is huge demand. Many organisations use price to attract customers by suggesting that their products are cheap. The adverts shown below are examples of organisations suggesting that their prices are cheap.

Special offers

Credit terms

Some organisations offer their customers CREDIT. This means that they can buy a product now and pay for it later. This type of arrangement is more likely when the price of a product is high – for example, a summer holiday. Customers might book their holiday in January and pay a small deposit, perhaps 5% of the total price. Then, a few weeks before the date of the holiday, the outstanding amount is paid. Season tickets can often be bought on credit. For example, many football clubs allow their supporters to pay for season tickets by instalments throughout the season. But they may be charged extra for this arrangement.

Credit cards

Customers in the leisure and tourism industries can also enjoy credit if they use credit cards to pay for products. However, with credit cards the credit is given by a bank. Credit is actually free for a certain amount of time – up to six weeks – but if a customer does not pay what is owed by a specified date, the extra charges made by the bank are very high. Credit cards are likely to be accepted by most of the organisations in the leisure and tourism industries, such as restaurants, travel agents, train operators and theme parks. When buying products online, credit cards are one of the few ways in which customers can pay.

Profitability

Most organisations in the leisure and tourism industries need to make a profit. This is because they are businesses and are owned by people who want to make money. This means that they have to charge a price that more than covers costs.

For example, an ice cream vendor might expect to sell 500 ice creams on a good day. If it costs 70p to provide the ice cream and they are sold to customers for £1, how much profit will be made?

The vendor will receive £500 in revenue (£1 x 500) when selling 500 ice creams. However, to supply 500 ice creams will cost £350 (70p x 500). If these costs are subtracted from revenue, the vendor will be left with a profit of £150. This is summarised below.

Profit = revenue – costs

= 500 x £1 – 500 x 70p

= £500 – £350

Profit = £150

By charging a price of £1, the vendor makes a profit.

Quick quiz

1 **True or false?**
- ✪ Price is the most flexible part of the marketing mix.
- ✪ Credit is likely to be given if the price of a product is low.
- ✪ Some organisations charge different prices for the same product.

2 Which of these is not likely to be paid with a credit card?
(a) Package holiday **(b)** Train ticket **(c)** Taxi fare **(d)** DVD player

3 What might a tour operator do if it cannot sell some of its holidays?
(a) Lower price **(b)** Raise price **(c)** Double price **(d)** None of these

4 Why might the tour operator choose this strategy?

5 Explain briefly why it is important for a business to charge a high enough price to make a profit.

Portfolio practice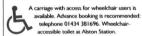

South Tynedale Railway

The South Tynedale Railway is a charitable organisation. It operates narrow gauge passenger trains along a two mile line along the scenic South Tyne valley between Alston in Cumbria and Kirkhaugh in Northumberland. Train services operate on certain dates between Easter and October and Santa Special trains on certain dates in December each year. The Railway is run by volunteers of the South Tynedale Railway Preservation Society. The Society is responsible for the operation and maintenance of the railway, organising special events, publicity and fundraising.

Fares to Kirkhaugh

RETURN:	Adult	£5.00
	Child(3-15)	£2.00
	Dog	£0.50
SINGLE:	Adult	£3.00
	Child(3-15)	£1.50
	Dog	£0.50
ALL DAY:	Adult	£12.50
	Child(3-15)	£5.00

Children under 3 years travel free, except during some special events. Discounts for pre-booked parties of ten or more passengers. Different fares may apply during some special events- please enquire for details.

♿ A carriage with access for wheelchair users is available. Advance booking is recommended: telephone 01434 381696. Wheelchair-accessible toilet at Alston Station.

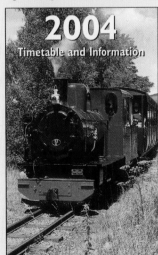

SOUTH TYNEDALE RAILWAY

Alston, Cumbria
England's Highest Narrow-Gauge Railway

2004
Timetable and Information

TALKING TIMETABLE: 01434 382828
OTHER INFORMATION: 01434 381696
www.strps.org.uk
South Tynedale Railway,
The Railway Station, Alston, Cumbria CA9 3JB
Registered Charity No. 514939

1. What is the actual selling price of a return ticket to Kirkhaugh for a (i) 17 year old (ii) a two year old? *(2 marks)*

2. What provision is made for wheelchair users by South Tynedale Railway? *(3 marks)*

3. Do you think that South Tynedale Railway offers credit? Explain your answer. *(4 marks)*

4. Discuss whether you think the prices charged by the organisation are designed to make a profit. *(6 marks)*

key terms
Actual selling price – the amount of money paid by customers when they buy a product.
Credit – buying products and paying for them at a later date.

Getting started...

Charging the right price for products is often difficult. Organisations need to cover costs and many want to make a profit. However, they do not want to charge too much in case they lose customers. Different methods might be used to arrive at the actual selling price. For example, some organisations just charge the same as their competitors. Others look at their costs and then add something on for profit. Look at the methods used below.

Kelso Sports

Kevin Jackson owns Kelso Sports, a sports shop in the centre of Kelso. It sells a range of sports equipment and sportswear. He has a simple pricing method – he adds 40% to the cost of the stock he buys. For example, some training shoes he purchased from a supplier for £20 were sold for £28. He works out 40% of £20 (which is £8) and adds it to £20. Kevin likes this method because he is sure to cover the cost of the stock he buys.

Cheap as Chips

Cheap as Chips is a fish and chip shop which opened in 2003. When it opened, the owner wanted it to be the cheapest chippy in town. He looked at the prices of chips charged by all the other shops and undercut them by 20p. He thought this would get people coming into the shop.

Cheap as Chips
The cheapest chips in Town

The Norfolk Bus Company

The Norfolk Bus Company provides bus services between Norwich and outlying villages. It is owned by Gillian Saggers. She charges two different prices for bus services on each route. For example, between 8.00 am and 9.00 am and 4.30 pm and 6.00 pm, the single fare from Strumpshaw to Norwich is £1.50. However, the rest of the day it is 90p. She charges lower prices during the middle of the day and the evenings to encourage more people to use the bus service.

(a) Describe how prices are set in each of the above cases.
(b) What might be the reasons for using the methods described in (a)?

Pricing methods

When an organisation decides what the actual selling price should be, a number of factors may be taken into account.

- **The cost of products** An organisation must cover its costs because if it doesn't, it will not be able to carry on trading. Therefore, some pricing methods are based on costs.
- **Competitors** Many organisations set prices after they have looked at what their rivals are charging. For example, it is common to copy competitors' prices. This helps to avoid 'price wars' where businesses undercut each other.
- **Customers** It is important to take into account what customers are prepared to pay. Customers want value for money. Generally, an organisation will charge as much as it can without losing its customers to rivals. But choosing the right price is difficult. Some of the methods used to set prices are explained below.

Cost plus pricing

One of the simplest methods of pricing is COST PLUS PRICING. This is done by adding a MARK-UP to sales. The mark-up (which is usually a percentage) is the amount of profit an organisation wants to make on each unit sold. For example, a hot dog vendor outside a sports stadium might calculate that each hot dog costs 80p to supply. If the price charged by the vendor is £1.20, the mark-up is 40p or 50% (50% x 80p = 40p).

Mark-up 40p		
	=	Price £1.20
Cost 80p		

This method is popular where the cost of the product sold is easily calculated. For example, it might be used by sports retailers, tour operators or souvenir shops. The problem with this method is that it does not take into account what customers are willing to pay or what rivals are charging.

Competition based pricing

COMPETITION BASED PRICING means that organisations are influenced by their rivals when setting prices. This method is often used when competition in the market is fierce. One approach is to set a price that is about the same as every other organisation. This helps to avoid a 'price war' in the market. Price wars involve businesses under-cutting each other which, in turn, reduces their revenue.

Another approach is to use DESTROYER PRICING to eliminate a competitor. This is done by charging a very low price for a long enough period to drive a rival out of business. For example, US Airways is expected to go bankrupt in 2005 because of rising fuel costs and stiff competition from American budget airlines such as SouthWest Airlines and JetBlue.

Market orientated pricing

Most organisations look at what is happening in the market when they set their prices. This is called MARKET ORIENTATED PRICING which is concerned with looking at what customers might be prepared to pay at certain times and in certain situations. For example, a large group of people would expect to pay less for entry into a theme park than a single family. Also, senior citizens often expect discounts when paying for certain products such as bus travel. There are a number of different approaches to market orientated pricing.

Peak and off-peak pricing

Prices for the same product often vary according to the time they are bought. Generally, organisations charge higher prices when they are busy and lower prices when they are quiet. For example, many rail and bus companies charge more at peak times when people are traveling to and from work. They reduce prices off-peak to encourage more customers to use their services. Higher prices help to increase revenue when demand is high.

Tour operators charge different prices for the same holiday taken at different times of the year. Higher prices are charged during the high season (usually during the school holidays) and lower prices the rest of the time.

Accommodation	1/4 – 15/5	16/5 – 11/9	12/9 – 4/10
Single room	£51	£62	£52
Double room	£46	£56	£47

Hotels also vary charges according to the time of the booking. For example, many London hotels charge more during the week when they have a lot of business guests but reduce prices at weekends to encourage tourists to use their facilities. Hotels might also vary their charges at different times of the year. The prices in the table above are those charged by the Scourie Hotel, Scotland in 2004. They are per person for dinner, bed and breakfast.

Discounts

Many organisations offer some customers discounts on their normal prices. They are usually offered to the following customers.

- ☺ Large groups
- ☺ Students
- ☺ Senior citizens
- ☺ The unemployed
- ☺ School parties

One reason why discounts are offered to these groups is to attract a wider range of customers. Without discounts, some of these customers might not buy the product. Discounts also help to increase revenue and make better use of facilities, such as leisure centres. Finally, discounts are usually given to customers shopping online. This is because it is cheaper to sell products this way and customers are sharing the benefit of lower costs.

Special offers

Sometimes products are offered to all customers at a special low price. The main purpose of special offers is to encourage sales of products. Tour operators often use special offers to sell holidays a few days before they are due to go out of date.

Quick quiz

1 **True or false?**

- Cost plus pricing does not take into account the amount that customers are prepared to pay.
- Destroyer pricing is designed to eliminate rivals in the market.
- Low prices are charged during peak times.

2 A business charges £25 for a product that cost £20 to supply. What is the mark-up?
(a) £5 **(b)** £25 **(c)** £10 **(d)** £20

3 Which of these is **not** likely to be offered a discount?
(a) Senior citizens **(b)** Adults **(c)** The unemployed **(d)** Students

4 Which of these pricing methods is based on the prices that rivals charge?
(a) Cost plus **(b)** Competition based **(c)** Peak **(d)** Market orientated

5 How much would the Scourie Hotel charge for a double room per person on 12 June 2004?

Portfolio practice

Pricing methods

OUR LATEST PRICES	OFF PEAK Weekdays only (exc. Bank holidays & school holidays	STANDARD Weekends /Bank holidays & school holidays
Admission & Rides		
Age 12+	£16.00	£18.00
Age 4-11	£12.00	£14.00
Grandee (60 years+)	£8.00	£8.50
Disabled Visitor & Helper (each)	£9.00	£10.50
Under 4 years	Free	Free
Family Supersavers		
Family ticket (2 adults/2 children age 4-11 years	£50.00	£59.00
Xtra Family Ticket (2 adults/3 children age 4-11 years	£60.00	£71.00
Family Plus 4 ticket (2 adults/2 children age 12+)	£59.00	£67.00

Drayton Manor Theme Park and Zoo

Or choose...
Set of 5 Special Episodes VHS DVD
(from the Complete Collection) Save £15
VHS RRP £49.99 Now £34.99
DVD RRP £44.99 Now £29.99
Enjoy five Special Edition Morse mysteries, including the moving farewell episode, *The Remorseful Day*. Also includes: *The Way Through The Woods*, *The Daughters of Cain*, *Death is Now My Neighbour* and *The Wench is Dead*. Screened 1995 - 2000. Choose from 5 DVDs or 5 VHS tapes. Cert. 15.
VHS comes in 5 boxes; DVD in 3 boxes.

Morse VHS/DVDs

Kuoni – Sri Lanka

Bentota Beach Hotel, Sri Lanka

Holiday Ref	Holiday	Meals	No. of Nights	01 Jan- 31 Jan	01 Feb- 28 Feb	01 Mar- 01 Apr	02 Apr- 30 Apr	01 Msy- 30 Jun	01 Jul- 08 Jul	09 Jul- 26 Jul	27 Jul- 17 Aug	18 Aug- 13 Sep	14 Sep- 26 Oct	27 Oct- 25 Nov	26 Nov- 31 Dec
CY637	Club Bentota (STD)	ALL	5	745	776	750	657	639	669	967	997	725	695	699	735
CY638	Club Bentota (DLX)	ALL	5	785	799	780	687	667	699	987	1032	760	719	745	770
CY636	Club Bentota (JV)	ALL	5	948	969	943	810	810	815	1110	1155	898	863	948	958
CY639	Bayroo (STD)	ALL	5	730	751	735	647	629	659	957	997	725	695	675	690
CY640	Bayroo (SUP)	ALL	5	740	761	745	662	643	674	972	1010	735	709	690	699
CY641	Bentota Beach (STD)	RB	5	795	819	799	627	599	639	937	967	695	650	660	675
CY642	Bentota Beach (SUP)	RB	5	855	876	859	672	647	684	982	1012	740	695	720	735

Holiday prices (£)

1. What is the price of (i) 5 nights at Club Bentota (CY638) arriving on 1 July (ii) a set of Morse DVDs (iii) standard entrance for an adult at Drayton Manor? *(3 marks)*
2. State two groups of customers that get discounts at Drayton Manor. *(2 marks)*
3. Explain why some customers are given discounts for products. *(4 marks)*
4. Using examples from the case, discuss why peak and off-peak pricing is used by organisations. *(7 marks)*

key terms

Competition based pricing – where price is set according to what competitors are charging.

Cost plus pricing – where price is set by working out the cost of a product and then adding a profit margin.

Destroyer pricing – where price is set very low for a period of time to try and drive a rival out of business.

Market orientated pricing – where prices are set according to what is happening in the market.

Mark-up – the amount added to the cost of a product to arrive at the selling price.

36 Place

Getting started...

Organisations have to make their products available to customers in the right place at the right time. This means that customers should be able to buy products at times and places that are convenient to them. In recent years, the number of places where people can buy products in the leisure and tourist industries has increased. For example, holidays, air tickets, rail tickets, theatre tickets and sports equipment can all be purchased on the Internet. Many organisations sell their products from several different places. Look at the example below.

Pontin's

Pontin's owns eight holiday centres in places like Blackpool, Prestatyn and Hemsby. Each centre offers a variety of self-catering accommodation, entertainment for the whole family, restaurants and other leisure facilities. Holidays can be purchased in different places.

 You can now book online just click on

www.pontins.com

and fill in the booking form online.

 Ring us direct on:
08705 33 11 99

Lines open: Monday to Friday   8.30am to 8.30pm
Saturdays (February - October)   8.30am to 8.30pm
(November - January)   9.00am to 6.00pm
Sundays and Public Holidays   10.00am to 5.00pm
Our friendly holiday advisors will:
• Check availability • Take your details • Take a reservation
edit/debit card
ite)
I for training purposes only.
y be extended.

Visit Visit your local travel agent where they can confirm availability instantly. You will be required to complete a booking form and pay a deposit or the full payment to your travel agent. You will be given a receipt and sent your holiday and travel documents shortly after full payment has been received.

(a) Describe briefly how customers might book a Pontin's holiday.
(b) Why do you think Pontin's has three different methods of booking?

What is meant by place?

Place is one of the four Ps in the marketing mix. It is important for organisations to make their products easy for customers to buy. It does not matter how good a product is – if customers cannot buy it, it will not sell. Place is all about convenience. This might explain why an increasing number of organisations such as supermarkets, take-away restaurants and retailers, deliver products right to the front door.

The types of outlet or facility used

Some of the common places where organisations in the leisure and tourism industries sell their products are shown in Figure 1.

Figure 1 *Types of outlet or facility used to sell products in the leisure and tourism industries.*

Airports and stations	Travel agents	Leisure centres	Restaurants and cafés
Sports shops	PLACE		Cinemas and theatres
Theme parks	Video shops	The Internet	Hotels

The locations of outlets or facilities

Organisations have to think about the best place to locate their outlets and facilities. For example, there is little point in locating a large leisure centre in a small, rural village. There would not be enough customers to make it worthwhile. Many factors might influence the location of outlets and facilities.

- ○ **The market** Many outlets in the leisure and tourism industries are located near to their markets. This means that outlets are near to customers. For example, cinemas and theatres are located in towns and cities where a lot of people live.

- ○ **Transport networks** Some organisations expect their customers to travel a long way so they may locate outlets close to good transport links such as motorways or airports. For example, the NEC is located close to Birmingham Airport, the M6, the M45 and it also has its own mainline railway station.

- ○ **Geography** Some leisure activities need particular geographical features. For example, ski centres have to be built in mountains where snow is guaranteed.

- ○ **Staff availability** If an organisation is going to employ a lot of staff in one of its outlets, it will have to make sure that there are enough people to recruit in the area. If outlets are located in areas where there are worker shortages, wages are likely to be higher and there may be staffing problems.

- ○ **Near to other facilities** Different types of outlets are often located near to each other. For example, restaurants might be located near to a multiplex cinema. Video rental shops may be sited near off-licenses and take-away restaurants. Catering outlets are usually found near tourist attractions such as the Tower of London.

- ○ **Existing sites** In some cases, locations cannot be chosen because they already exist. Historic sites, like Hadrian's Wall, cannot be changed.

Distribution channels

The path taken to get products from organisations to customers is called a DISTRIBUTION CHANNEL. For example, the channel in Figure 2 shows that tour operators use travel agents to sell their package holidays to customers.

Figure 2 *A distribution channel for package holidays*

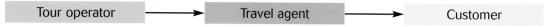

It is common for some organisations to use several channels of distribution. For example, a hotel may use some or all of the channels shown in Figure 3 to sell accommodation. Direct channels, such as telephone or Internet bookings, are often less expensive because commission does not have to be paid to an agent. When products are sold direct to customers, this is called DIRECT SELLING.

Figure 3 *Channels of distribution that a hotel might use*

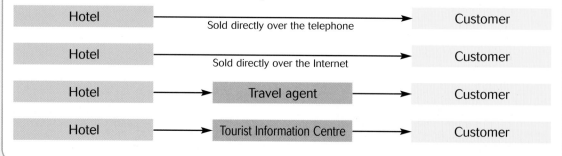

Quick quiz

1. **True or false?**
   - A video rental shop is likely to be located near to an off-licence.
   - A theatre is likely to be located in a rural area.
   - A Tourist Information Centre may be used to book hotel accommodation.

2. Which of these is **not** likely to be used to sell a theatre ticket?
   (a) Internet **(b)** Ticketmaster **(c)** Telephone **(d)** Supermarket

3. Which of these facilities would be influenced by geographical features in its location?
   (a) Canoe slalom **(b)** Take-away restaurant **(c)** Cinema **(d)** Sports shop

4. Which of these facilities is most likely to be located near to its market?
   (a) Theme park **(b)** Holiday destination **(c)** Sports shop **(d)** Historical site

5. State one important factor that would have to be taken into account when locating a new leisure centre.

Portfolio practice

Balmoral

Balmoral, originally a sixteenth century tower-house, was visited by Queen Victoria and Prince Albert in 1848. They liked it so much that Prince Albert bought it in 1852. Every year since, the Royal Family has returned to Balmoral for summer and early autumn to enjoy the scenery and tranquility.

1. What has influenced the location of this attraction? Explain your answer briefly. *(2 marks)*

2. What facilities are provided for people with special needs? *(2 marks)*

3. It is common to locate leisure facilities near to other attractions. What examples are there in this case and why are they provided? *(4 marks)*

4. Identify and compare the two methods used by Balmoral to sell souvenirs. *(7 marks)*

key terms

Direct selling – selling products directly to customers without using an agent.
Distribution channel – the path taken to get products from organisations to customers.

Getting started...

Organisations in the leisure and tourism industries have to tell their customers about their products. People need information about what products are available, what they are like, how much they are and how they can be bought. There are many different ways of doing this. For example, many organisations have websites where people can find out about goods and services. Look at the methods being used below.

Black Isle Wildlife Park

The Black Isle Wildlife Park is near Inverness in Scotland. In addition to some unusual animals such as wallabies, raccoons, meerkat, maras, alpaca and llamas, people can also watch chicks hatch in incubators. The leaflet below is used to tell people about the park.

Warwickshire County Cricket Club

Warwickshire County Cricket Club is based at Edgbaston in Birmingham. It plays cricket in the national first division and hosts a Test Match each year. A lot of information about fixtures, tickets and other club information is available on its website.

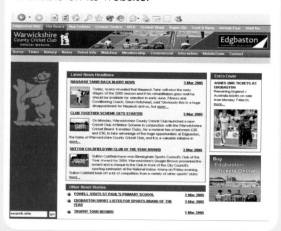

Tour operators

Most tour operators produce glossy brochures to give people information about their holidays. Some examples are shown below.

(a) Briefly describe the methods that are being used by each of these organisations to tell people about their products.

(b) Which of these methods do you think is the most popular today?

What is promotion?

PROMOTION is one of the four Ps in the marketing mix. It involves communicating with customers and aims to:

- ○ make them aware that products are available
- ○ give out important information about products
- ○ persuade them to buy products for the first time
- ○ encourage them to carry on buying products.

Promotion is probably the most recognised activity in the marketing process. Various techniques can be used to promote products.

Advertising

ADVERTISING involves paying media owners (newspapers or TV companies, for example) for publishing, displaying or broadcasting information about products and services. It is one of the most common promotional techniques and can be carried out using a variety of different media such as:

- ○ television
- ○ radio
- ○ cinema
- ○ posters
- ○ magazines
- ○ newspapers
- ○ Internet
- ○ public transport.

Advantages and disadvantages of different advertising media

	Advantages	Disadvantages		Advantages	Disadvantages
Television	Big impact	Expensive	Cinema	Sound & movement	Limited audience
	Entertaining	Ads might be ignored		Big impact	Message short-lived
	Vast audience	Message short-lived		Targeting possible	
	Sound and movement		Radio	Sound	Not visual
Newspapers & magazines	National or regional coverage	No movement or sound		Targeting possible	Interrupts music - can be irritating
		Individual ads may be		Relatively cheap	
	Relatively cheap	lost among many others	Posters	Seen repeatedly	Limited information
	Ads linked to features	Delays between ad		National coverage	Difficult to measure
	Can refer back to ad	design and printing		Good for short	effectiveness
	Groups can be targeted			messages	Can deteriorate
Internet	Cheap	Limited audience			
	Hits can be monitored	Technical problems			

Direct marketing

DIRECT MARKETING involves sending information direct to customers' homes. The information tells people about products and also encourages them to buy. There are three main approaches to direct marketing.

- ○ **Direct mail** is very popular. It involves sending letters or leaflets to people through the post. For example, a football club might send information about club merchandise to a supporter that has a record of buying tickets. Sometimes an organisation may obtain names and addresses of people from a database. This enables personalised letters to be sent to potential customers.

- ○ **Telemarketing** is a type of direct selling over the phone where an organisation contacts a member of the public with the intention of making a sale. For example, British Telecom uses telemarketing to sell Internet packages and system upgrades.

- ○ **Door-to-door distribution** is similar to direct mail but it is not personalised and does not use the postal system. It involves delivering leaflets, perhaps with local newspapers, to provide information.

The main advantage of direct marketing is that organisations can target those customers that are most likely to buy products. This reduces waste in marketing. For example, there is no point in direct mailing a Manchester City supporter inviting them to buy a season ticket for Old Trafford (the home of Manchester United).

The main disadvantage of direct marketing is that many people ignore telephone sellers and 'junk mail'. Direct mail is often thrown away unopened.

Public relations

Most organisations try to create a favourable image with the public. This is called PUBLIC RELATIONS (PR). It is done by providing the media with information about the organisation. This might include interesting stories about the organisation and its activities or details of events that are taking place. It can also involve providing hospitality to VIPs and keeping local communities happy by minimising noise and pollution, for example. PR is popular because much of it is free. The article below is taken from a local newspaper. It provides information about forthcoming activities at a youth centre.

WELCOME TO CENTRE FUNDAY

MEOLS Cop Youth Centre is hosting a fun activity day called Sex, Drugs and Rock and Roll on Saturday, June 5.

All young people are welcome to come down, from noon to 4pm.

Workshops will be based around the following: Breakdance with Danny (Rapid), Street Art, Creative Art, The Climbing Wall, Football, Art Mosaic, Beauty, Drugs Info and Sexual Health Info.

Throughout the afternoon there will be live bands and a DJ mixing tunes, with refreshment in the form of alcohol-free cocktails.

Personal selling

PERSONAL SELLING involves using a sales team to promote and sell products through personal contact. It may be carried out face-to-face or over the telephone. Personal selling is most likely to be used when products are complex and expensive. It is often used by travel agents to sell holidays, for example. The main aim of a sales person is to make a sale. But it is important that the product sold matches the needs of the customer, otherwise they will be dissatisfied. The main advantage of personal selling is that the sales person can discuss with the customer which products are most likely to be suitable. A disadvantage is that employing a sales team is expensive. Personal selling may also be used by:

- ○ waiting staff in restaurants to sell items on the menu
- ○ time-share companies to sell shares in apartments and villas
- ○ retailers when selling sports equipment
- ○ cabin crew to sell duty-free goods
- ○ holiday resort representatives to sell excursions.

Quick quiz

1   **True or false?**

   ☺ An organisation making a donation to a local hospital is an example of PR.

   ☺ Door-to-door distribution is an example of PR.

   ☺ Promotion might be used to encourage repeat purchases.

2   Which of these is **not** an advantage of using posters to place adverts?
   (a) Big impact   **(b)** Good for short messages   **(c)** Seen repeatedly
   (d) National coverage

3   Which of these types of media is most likely to be used to advertise an Italian
   restaurant in Swindon?   **(a)** Television   **(b)** Local newspaper   **(c)** Internet
   (d) National newspaper

4   Which of these is **not** an example of direct marketing?
   (a) Telemarketing **(b)** Sponsorship **(c)** Direct mailing **(d)** Door-to-door distribution

5   State one advantage and one disadvantage of personal selling.

Portfolio practice

Warner Breaks

1.   Describe briefly what Warner Breaks is promoting. *(2 marks)*

2.   Which method of promotion is the company using? Explain your answer. *(3 marks)*

3.   Explain the main advantage and disadvantage to Warner Breaks of using this method of promotion. *(4 marks)*

4.   Explain why a company like Warner Breaks might not use television to advertise its products. *(7 marks)*

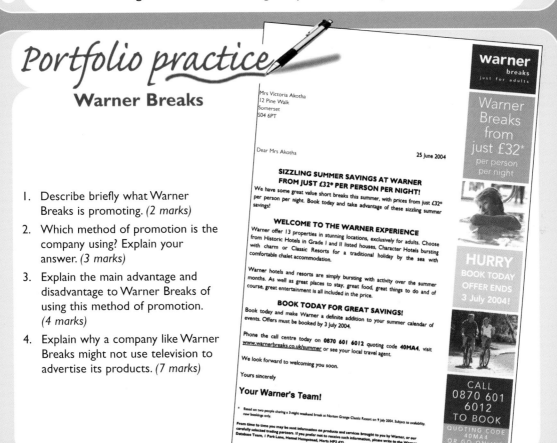

key terms

Advertising – paying media owners (newspapers or TV companies, for example) for publishing, displaying or broadcasting information about products and services.

Direct marketing – sending out information about products direct to a person's home.

Personal selling – promotion which involves face-to-face contact between the buyer and seller.

Promotion – trying to obtain or retain customers by drawing attention to products.

Public relations – promoting a good image about an organisation or its products.

Getting started...

The type of promotion used by an organisation often depends on the sort of product that it sells. For example, some products, such as sportswear, can often be displayed attractively to draw customers. But products that cannot be displayed have to be promoted in a different way. For example, a restaurant might offer a free bottle of wine to attract customers. Look at the methods being used below.

Westbrook Fitness Centre

In 2004, the Westbrook Fitness Centre decided to have a special promotion to boost its membership. It placed the advert below in a local newspaper.

WESTBROOK FITNESS CENTRE

SPECIAL PROMOTION

During June 2004, Westbrook will be open to non-members for £1. Guests will have access to all the club's facilities and anyone taking out a membership during June will receive a free pair of training shoes from the club shop. The offer is open to all adults over the age of 18.

Vodafone

Vodafone promotes its organisation by paying the England cricket team to wear its name and logo on the team's cricket shirts and other cricket wear.

Travel agents

The windows of all travel agents are packed with information about holidays. Most of the information is about destinations and prices.

(a) Describe the promotional methods used in each of the above cases.

(b) In each of the above cases, distinguish between the methods that promote the product and those that promote the organisation. Briefly explain your answer.

Displays

Some organisations promote their products by displaying samples in prominent places. Displays help to create interest in products which may lead to a sale. Some products form part of a POINT-OF-SALE DISPLAY. This is where products are displayed at the point where they will be sold to a customer – in a sports shop, for example. Travel agents use window displays where maps, photographs of destinations and details of holidays form displays. In some cases, displays at exhibitions for example, there will be staff on hand to give further information to customers and perhaps encourage them to buy.

A window display

Displays can be:

- ⚽ flexible – they can be changed regularly, for example
- ⚽ cheap – the materials used are either products that will be sold or inexpensive posters
- ⚽ interactive – some displays allow customers to touch and test products.

Sponsorship

SPONSORSHIP is a very important promotional method. Between 1990 and 2000, the value of world sponsorship deals grew from about $8 billion to $25 billion. Sponsorship involves one organisation paying another organisation to be associated with an event or product. This usually means that the sponsor's name (the organisation that pays the money) appears somewhere prominently. For example, the Rugby Union European Cup is sponsored by Heineken and is called the Heineken Cup. The test series between England and the West Indies in 2004 was sponsored by N Power. Most professional sports teams, such as Premier League football clubs, are sponsored by a variety of businesses. Sports, arts and entertainment events are popular targets for sponsors because they usually get a lot of TV coverage. This means that the sponsor's name appears on TV. Therefore, sponsorship may be regarded as a cheap form of TV advertising. The table below illustrates the importance of football around the world to sponsors.

Table 1 *Major football sponsorship deals*

League/cup	Sponsor	Type of sponsor	Amount
FAPL	Barclays	Title sponsor	$30m
Champions League	Amstel/Ford/Mastercard/Sony	Partners	$30m each
La Championnal	Orange	Title sponsors	$16.2m
Euro 2004	T-Mobile	Partner	$15m
Serie A	TIM	Title sponsor	$11.2m
Primera Liga	Toyota	Title sponsor	$8m
Champions League	Vodafone	Mobile rights	$4m
Copa Libertadores	Toyota	Title sponsor	$3m
Chinese League	Siemens	Title sponsor	$2m
African Nations Cup	Nokia	Title sponsor	$500,000

Source: Octagon Marketing

Demonstrations

Most products sold by the leisure and tourist industries are services. Because of this, a potential customer may not be able to easily appreciate the characteristics of the product. This makes it difficult for the customer when deciding what to buy. For example, an opera house might find it difficult to explain the enjoyment of seeing an opera. Someone who has never been to an opera might think they would not enjoy it. To overcome this problem some organisations use demonstrations to promote their services. This allows people to try out products before deciding whether to buy them. For example, a business hiring out bouncy castles for children's parties might invite children to try out different inflatables before their parents decide which one to hire. Demonstrations and visits are popular with sports clubs, sports centres, fitness centres, time-shares and conference centres.

Sales promotions

SALES PROMOTIONS are often used to encourage people to buy products. They aim to give a short-term boost to sales. Lots of different methods might be used by organisations in the travel and tourism industries. These include:

- **Money-off vouchers** These might be cut out from local newspapers or could be sent to previous customers by direct mail.

- **Discounts** These might be given for buying large quantities of a product. For example, discounts are given to large groups at theme parks and other visitor attractions.

- **Competitions** Buying a certain product might entitle the customer to free entry into a competition. There is likely to be a substantial prize such as a holiday abroad.

- **Free gifts** For example, a travel agent might give free travel insurance to a customer booking a holiday.

- **Combination offers** This is where two organisations join together and share the costs of a sales promotion. For example, a daily newspaper and a train operator might encourage people to collect a series of vouchers from five editions of the newspaper. The full series of vouchers would then entitle the reader to cheaper fares on a train journey. The combination offer would help to boost the sales of two products – newspapers and rail travel.

- **PR promotions** An example might be where an organisation promises to donate a percentage of its sales to charity.

- **Loyalty schemes** This is where regular customers are rewarded for repeat purchases. One very popular loyalty scheme in the travel and tourism industry is Air Miles. Points are awarded according to the distance traveled with a particular airline. Free flights are given to passengers when they have accumulated enough air miles.

Quick quiz

1. **True or false?**
   - ✪ Barclays Bank pays $30m to the FA Premier League in a sponsorship deal.
   - ✪ Advertising is a method of sales promotion.
   - ✪ Demonstrations are often used to promote services.

2. Which of these is **not** a method of sales promotion?
   (a) Free gifts **(b)** Sponsorship **(c)** Competitions **(d)** PR promotions

3. Which of these is **not** an advantage of displays?
   (a) Can be interactive **(b)** Cheap **(c)** Flexible **(d)** Have a huge impact

4. State two places where money off vouchers might be found.

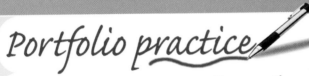

Portfolio practice

Promotion

1. What method of sales promotion is being used by Knowsley Safari Park? *(1 mark)*

2. What benefits is the holder of the voucher entitled to? *(2 marks)*

3. Explain the purpose of this promotion. *(2 marks)*

4. Use the bar graph to explain the importance of sponsorship to organisations in the leisure and tourism industries. *(3 marks)*

5. Use the previous table of recent major football sponsorship deals to explain the possible benefits to Amstel, Ford, MasterCard and Sony in sponsoring The Champions League. *(7 marks)*

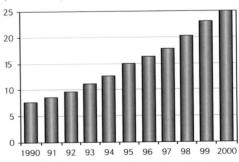

Figure 1 *Value of world sponsorship rights ($ billion)*

Source: Financial Times 27.5.03

---

key terms

Point-of-sale display – promoting products where they are sold using special displays of products or notices in windows.

Sales promotions – methods used to boost short-term sales.

Sponsorship – where one organisation pays another organisation in exchange for its name being associated with a product or event.

39 Promotional materials 1

Getting started...

A wide range of different promotional materials are used by organisations. These are what the customer actually sees. For example, organisations that advertise their products might use posters on billboards, small ads in newspapers or 'glossy' ads in magazines. Most tour operators publish colourful brochures to promote their holidays. Look at the materials being used below.

The Bartons Arms

The Bartons Arms is one of the few remaining authentic Victorian pubs in Birmingham. Built in 1901, it contains all the original features such as rich mahogany woodworkings, stained and engraved glass windows and mirrors, snob-screens for privacy and Minton-Hollins tiles. The leaflet below is available inside the pub and in prominent places around the local area.

THE BARTONS ARMS
Birmingham's Finest Victorian Pub
Oakham ales FREE HOUSE
144 High Street
Aston
Birmingham
B6 4UP
0121 - 333 - 5988

In addition to our extensive range of real ales listed below, Seasonal beers and One-Off brews are also often available.

J.H.B. 3.8% A.B.V.
A golden beer whose aroma is dominated by hops that give characteristic citrus notes. Hops and fruit on the palate are balanced by malt and a bitter base. Dry hoppy finish with soft fruit flavours.

WHITE DWARF 4.3% A.B.V.
Piercing bitterness in this 'brite' English style wheat beer, mellows to reveal fruit overtones amidst a dry as bone finish. A real thirst quencher.

BISHOPS FAREWELL 4.6% A.B.V.
A strong premium beer of structured quality dominated by elaborate fruity hop notes, with a grainy background and dry finish.

BLACK HOLE PORTER 5.5% A.B.V.
Big, dark malt flavours in this almost black beer combine with a sweet fruity hop taste to make this strong porter exceedingly drinkable for it's strength.

HELTERSKELTER 5.0% A.B.V.
A strong, golden ale with an intense hop aroma and character, hops and fruit oscillate above a refined bitterness.

Gecko's

Gecko's specialise in adventure holidays. This advert appeared in the travel magazine *Wanderlust* in April 2005.

CHINA · LATIN AMERICA · EGYPT · TURKEY · MOROCCO
Gecko's
Grassroots Adventures
● Small group adventure holidays
● Committed to responsible tourism
● Local leaders using local transport
For more information log on to our website or call:
01635 872 040
geckosadventures.co.uk
AFRICA · NEPAL · INDIA · SOUTH EAST ASIA

(a) Describe briefly the promotional materials being used in each of the above cases.
(b) In each case, state three pieces of information which the promotional materials provide.

Effectiveness of advertisements

Organisations have to give careful thought to the type of adverts they use. They have to compare how effective an advert is likely to be against its cost. Effective adverts are those that catch the attention of a large part of the target audience. For example, an advert designed to sell gardening accessories might be best placed in a gardening magazine.

Different organisations use different types of adverts. For example, British Airways is a large airline and can afford to advertise on TV. In contrast, easyJet, the 'no-frills' airline, advertises in national newspapers. Generally, smaller companies use cheaper methods of advertising.

One of the problems with advertising is that it is often difficult to evaluate how effective a particular advert has been. This is especially so when more than one promotional method is being used at the same time. Sometimes, when customers buy a product, they are asked by sales staff where they heard about it. Keeping records like this helps to evaluate the effectiveness of adverts.

Adverts need to attract the attention of potential customers. For example, adverts in newspapers and magazines tend to be effective if they:

- are colourful
- contain concise information
- have an illustration
- contain a catchy headline
- contain a lot of white space (this helps to make the advert stand out).

The advert shown here was placed in *Blues and Soul* magazine in April 2005.

Welcome to the Soul Lounge

SOUL LOUNGE

3 CD SET

INCOGNITO
OMAR
MAYSA
ANGIE STONE
ROSIE GAINES
BRENDA RUSSELL
D-INFLUENCE
RAPHAEL SAADIQ
ANGELA JOHNSON
TORTURED SOUL
RAHSAAN PATTERSON

More than 3 hours of soulful grooves
40 tracks on 3 CDs at a special price

The effectiveness of advertising can be summarised by **AIDA** which stands for **A**ttention, **I**nterest, **D**esire and **A**ction. An advertisement must grab attention (e.g. by using bold headlines); it must attract interest (e.g. by featuring a famous personality); it must create desire (e.g. by offering incentives such as a discount voucher); and it must lead to action (e.g. by giving contact details such as a phone number or website for further information).

Advertising agencies

ADVERTISING AGENCIES might be used by large companies. Agencies will:

- carry out research into the best type of promotion to use
- design materials such as TV, radio, cinema or magazine adverts
- organise production such as artwork, printing or filming
- book the selected media such as TV, radio, magazines or newspapers.

Controls on advertising

When organisations are designing advertising material they must not mislead customers. To help organisations avoid misleading their customers, **The British Code of Advertising and Sales Promotion** provides guidelines about the content of adverts. For example:

- All prices should be inclusive of taxes and other charges. Extras, such as insurance, should be stated.
- Conditions, such as the need to travel as a couple and share a room, should be clear.
- Travel dates and itineraries must be accurate.
- Any amenities advertised, such as those for people with special needs, should be available.
- Photographs in brochures should show accurately the nature of the location. For example, disadvantages must not be hidden.

The ADVERTISING STANDARDS AUTHORITY is responsible for monitoring adverts and investigating any complaints.

Brochures

Brochures are an essential promotional tool in the holiday industry. Even though some tour operators can afford to advertise on television, they also use brochures. The following are some features of brochures.

- ✪ They are colourful with photos of holiday destinations and accommodation.
- ✪ Each one will focus on a particular type of holiday, price range or region.
- ✪ They are divided into sections – by country, for example.
- ✪ Each section contains information about specific resorts such as types and quality of accommodation, details of facilities, prices and conditions.
- ✪ They usually contain a booking form at the back.
- ✪ They are quite bulky and expensive to produce.
- ✪ They are distributed through travel agents.

Holiday brochures

Leaflets

Leaflets are probably the most popular form of promotional material in the leisure and tourism industries. They are cheaper to produce than brochures, less bulky and generally quite effective. Their main purpose is to give brief information about facilities or an attraction. They are usually colourful and most of them contain photographs. They are distributed through Tourist Information Centres, hotels, at the attraction itself and in other public places such as libraries. Most leaflets are distributed in local areas because they are designed to attract local people or visitors to the area. The advert shown here is for a company that specialises in the production and distribution of leaflets for organisations.

Posters

The purpose of most posters is to attract people's attention and give some brief information. They are designed for impact. Some posters are very large and are displayed on billboards and transport such as buses. Posters are also used in shop windows to encourage people to stop, look and go in. It is particularly difficult to evaluate the effectiveness of posters but because they are cheap, it matters less.

Poster in a travel agent's window

Quick quiz

1 **True or false?**
- The Advertising Standards Authority is responsible for dealing with customer complaints about package holidays.
- Leaflets usually contain a booking form at the back.
- Posters usually contain detailed information about products.

2 At which time of day might a Harry Potter film be best advertised on TV?
(a) 1.00pm – 3.00pm **(b)** 4.00pm – 6.00pm **(c)** 9.00pm – 11.00pm **(d)** After midnight

3 Which of the following is **not** a feature of an effective newspaper advert?
(a) Small **(b)** Colourful **(c)** Illustrated **(d)** Catchy headline

4 Which promotional material is designed to have a big impact?
(a) Billboard poster **(b)** Leaflet **(c)** Small ad in a newspaper **(d)** Brochure

5 State three functions of an advertising agency.

Portfolio practice

Comparing adverts and leaflets

Lastminute.com is an online travel agent that sells holidays, weekend breaks. travel insurance, flights, ferry tickets, accommodation and many other products in the tourist industry. The advert below was placed in the *Sunday Times* in July 2004.

summer on sale

greece	from £119	portugal	from £189
ibiza	from £149	cyprus	from £189
turkey	from £149	majorca	from £195

more beaches. better deals.

book these & other amazing holiday deals   **lastminute.com**

1. What is the main purpose of the Lastminute.com advert? *(2 marks)*

2. State two possible reasons why the advert might be effective. *(2 marks)*

3. Where might the leaflets shown here be distributed? *(2 marks)*

4. Explain the advantages to Kendal Golf Club and Blair Drummond Safari Park of using leaflets as promotional material. *(4 marks)*

5. Give reasons why the materials shown here might have been chosen by each of the organisations. *(7 marks)*

key terms

Advertising agency – a business that handles all aspects of promotion for other organisations.
Advertising Standards Authority (ASA) – an independent body that monitors advertising in the UK.
AIDA – an advertising principle that stands for attention, interest, desire and action.

Getting started...

Some promotional materials have become more popular in recent years as organisations have developed increasingly sophisticated ways of promoting their products. Look at the examples used below.

Artweeks

Local artists in North Oxfordshire are organising an event known as Artweeks. The public are invited to visit their studios to view their work. Samples of their work will be hung in Witney Museum so that people can decide which studios they would like to visit. Organiser Maureen Wilsker said, 'We are convinced that by seeing samples of artists' work in advance, people will plan their Artweeks visits with more confidence.' Free Artweeks guides will be available in public libraries, tourist offices and at the artists' studios. Outside the museum and the studios, bold yellow and blue signs will state: ARTWORK ON VIEW.

Source: Witney & West Oxfordshire Gazette 26 May 2004

Shrek 2

Film distributors spend millions of pounds promoting new films. One of the many methods they use is to sell products such as pens, mugs, T-shirts, books, models and posters associated with the film and its characters.

Naturally Morocco

Naturally Morocco organises ecotourism holidays in Morocco. It provides reasonably priced, clean and comfortable accommodation that gives customers a taste of Moroccan culture. The aim is to provide holidays with the lowest cost to the environment and to local culture. For example, water is mainly heated by solar power and unbleached sheets are used on guests' beds.

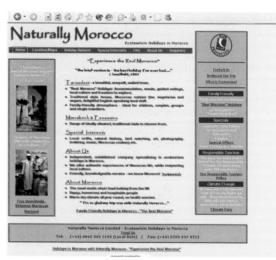

Naturally Morocco's website

(a) Describe briefly the promotional materials being used in each of the above cases.
(b) Which of the above do you think is the cheapest method? Explain your answer.

Merchandising materials

A David Beckham England Football shirt, a Harrod's carrier bag, a Wigan Warriors' RLFC team poster, a Harry Potter T-shirt, an Alton Towers mug and a London Eye calendar are all examples of MERCHANDISING materials. They may be sold by organisations or given away as free gifts. Their purpose is to promote the organisation or the products it sells. But many organisations sell merchandising materials to increase their revenue. For example, football clubs sell a huge range of merchandising materials at club shops in, or near to, their stadiums.

Preston North End football team's merchandising shop

Visitor attractions such as Madame Tussauds, Blackpool Tower, Windsor Castle, London Zoo, museums and many others also have shops or kiosks on site where merchandising is sold. In some cases, merchandising is given away to people who might influence others to become customers. For example, in 2004 Nike launched a campaign to raise awareness of the European Football Cup and, at the same time, promote its range of football products by giving them to famous football players such as Thierry Henry and Ronaldo. Merchandising also helps to raise the public profile of organisations.

Videos and DVDs

Some organisations use videos and DVDs to help promote their products. For example, Disney sends out free promotional videos and DVDs to people who are thinking of visiting its theme parks in Los Angeles, Florida or Paris. Videos and DVD's help organisations to show potential customers what their services are like by giving them a flavour of what to expect. They are particularly helpful when selling services because it is difficult to promote products like holidays and large visitor attractions by using newspapers, magazines and TV, for example. The advantage of videos and DVDs is that they can communicate a lot of information. They also use sound and action which makes the promotion more interesting and appealing. However, they are expensive to produce and distribute to customers.

Videos and DVDs are also sold by some organisations as a product. For example, football clubs put together packages of highlights or memorable matches which they then sell to supporters. There is also a very wide range of keep-fit, aerobics, yoga and dieting videos and DVDs on the market.

EXPO 2005 Aichi, Japan

At EXPO 2005, the international community will meet to discuss global issues such as global warming and the shortage of natural resources. The organisers produced a five minute video to promote the event. It features the official theme song 'I'll Be Your Love' and shows the various sites, facilities and themes that will make up the exhibition. The video won third place at a U.S. International Film and Video Festival in the 'Presentations Created for Visitor Centres, Museums, Theme Parks, Plant Tours, Fairs, etc.' category.

Source: adapted from the EXPO 2005 website

Press releases

Many organisations provide the media with reports and stories about their activities. This helps to raise the profile of the organisations and gives potential customers information about forthcoming events. The media tends to be interested in publishing press releases if they are interesting and have a personal angle. Some organisations have frequent contact with the media and provide information regularly. The main advantage of press releases is that they cost very little. The public relations department may spend time collecting and presenting information to the media, but the publication is free. Also, people are more likely to read press releases because they are not adverts. The article on the right about the German low-cost airline, Hapag-Lloyd Express, appeared in the *Observer* on 7 March 2004.

'Pick a price' on Germany flights

German low-cost airline Hapag-Lloyd Express is offering travellers the chance to pick their own price for tickets booked on the inaugural flights of three new routes from the UK and Ireland.

The 'pick a price' seats are being offered on a first-come, first-served basis for the new services from Manchester to Stuttgart on 21 April, Newcastle to Hanover on 2 May and Dublin to Stuttgart on 17 April. To register, passengers can log on to www.hlx.com and select the route they want, or call 0870 606 0519 between now and 13 March. Passengers must fly back by 13 May and pay the price they pick for their return tickets on board the 148-seater outbound flight. A maximum of two tickets is allowed per bid.

Internet

The Internet is a relatively new, but extremely powerful, promotional tool. Many organisations in the leisure and tourism industries have their own web sites which contain promotional materials. Airlines, holiday companies, restaurants, visitor attractions, travel agents, leisure centres, libraries and hotels are just some examples. There are various advantages to organisations of using the Internet to display promotional materials.

Sandals' home page

- There is no limit to the amount of information that can be made available.
- It is quick and convenient for users.
- It is very cost-effective.
- Promotional videos can be accessed.
- It has booking facilities.
- It is available globally.
- It is available 24 hours a day, every day.
- It can be used to collect data about customers if they complete an online questionnaire.

Quick quiz

1. **True or false?**
   - On the Internet, promotional materials are only available during office hours.
   - Press releases are an expensive form of promotion.
   - Some organisations provide merchandising materials free of charge.

2. State two examples of merchandising materials that a Premier League football club might sell.

3. State one advantage to a tour operator of producing a promotional video.

4. State one disadvantage to a tour operator of producing a promotional video.

Portfolio practice

Benny's Bistro

Benny Petrocolis owns Benny's Bistro, a continental style restaurant in Balham, London. The restaurant is popular and Benny is a well-known character in the area. He also has a reputation for employing local people and training them to a high standard. In 2001, Benny recruited two local teenagers, Anita Roberts and Shameer Patel, who had

recently spent 12 months in a young offender's institution. No one else would employ them because of their criminal records. But Benny wanted to give them a second chance by training them up as chefs. After three years, both of them won a 'Young Chef of the Year' award. They had benefited from the training at Benny's Bistro and they had also completed a catering course at a local college. In 2004, Anita was offered a job at a top hotel in London while Shameer was promoted to second chef at Benny's Bistro.

Student waiters and chefs training

1. State briefly why Benny is not likely to use a video to promote his business. *(2 marks)*
2. Benny is thinking of producing a website to promote his business. Discuss two possible advantages to the Bistro. *(4 marks)*
3. Benny often uses press releases to promote his restaurant. State briefly why the information given in the case might make a good press release. *(2 marks)*
4. Write a simple press release for a local newspaper using the information in the case. *(7 marks)*

key terms   Merchandising – products that might be sold or given away to customers to help promote an organisation or its products.

Getting started...

It is important for organisations to assess their performance. If they are not performing very well, they may decide that they need to take action to improve. To look at how well they are doing, they might identify things that they are good at and others where there is room for improvement. Consider the case below.

Westone High School

Westone High School in Carlisle runs a number of evening leisure courses for adults such as fine art, languages, local history, archery and fencing. The courses provide some extra revenue for the school but recently, the number of people attending has dropped. Peter Walker, the Director of Leisure Courses at Westone, arranged a meeting with the Head Teacher to discuss the performance of the department. During the meeting, they identified the things they do well and others that need improvement.

Things they do well

- Good quality teaching staff.
- Wide range of courses.
- Well-equipped and spacious teaching rooms.
- Competitive prices for courses.

Areas for improvement

- Poor marketing – no regular advertising.
- Poor communication – for example, when courses change or staff are absent.
- Poor refreshment facilities.

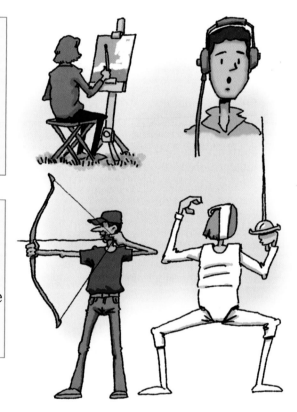

(a) Briefly describe the benefits to Westone High School of the meeting between Peter Walker and the Head Teacher.

(b) State two ways in which the school could improve its marketing of leisure courses.

What is SWOT analysis?

Organisations can analyse their performance by using the SWOT ANALYSIS. This involves identifying the factors that affect the performance of the organisation. These factors are put into four categories:

- **S**trengths
- **W**eaknesses
- **O**pportunities
- **T**hreats.

The strengths and weaknesses are internal forces. These are the things that the organisation can control like staff recruitment or marketing activities.

The opportunities and threats are external forces. They are the things that the organisation cannot control such as changes in market conditions, the weather or interest rates.

Strengths

An organisation's strengths are the things it does well and that help to improve its performance. They might be recognised by customers. They are internal factors because they can be controlled by the organisation. For example, a restaurant may consider that it has the following strengths:

- fast service
- friendly service
- interesting and varied menu
- good location
- high profile chef.

Weaknesses

An organisation's weaknesses are the things that it does badly. They cause poor performance and hold the organisation back. They might result in customer complaints or staff dissatisfaction. They are internal factors because they can be controlled by the organisation. For example, a cinema might consider that its weaknesses are:

- insufficient facilities for those with special needs
- inadequate heating during the winter
- poor selection of refreshments
- high staff turnover, i.e. staff who don't stay very long.

Opportunities

External factors might provide an organisation with new opportunities. These are the things that could be done to improve performance in response to changes outside the organisation's control. For example, a theme park might identify the following opportunities:

- an exciting new ride becomes available because of developments in technology
- some land next to the park has come on to the market
- a new motorway link is planned nearby.

Threats

External forces can also threaten an organisation's performance. These are things outside the control of the organisation that could be damaging in the future. For example, a long haul tour operator might identify the following as possible threats:

- an increase in interest rates
- a fall in the exchange rate
- higher fuel costs
- an increased threat of terrorist attacks.

How might an organisation use SWOT analysis?

If an organisation decides to use SWOT analysis, it may gather together a small team of staff to carry it out. People from different parts of the organisation might be involved. For example, The Grand Hotel in Cheltenham carried out a SWOT analysis. The owner was disappointed with recent profit levels so he asked the Manager, the Head Chef and one of the housekeepers to attend a meeting. They spent the morning identifying the hotel's strengths, weaknesses, opportunities and threats. Briefly, they were as follows:

A business meeting

Strengths
- competitive prices
- good town-centre location
- excellent reputation for food (residents only)
- high-class chef.

Weaknesses
- insufficient parking area
- 12 of the rooms need refurbishing
- high staff turnover
- low income from the public bar.

Opportunities
- open the restaurant to the public
- visitors to the town are increasing
- people are taking weekend breaks more often.

Threats
- competition from a new town-centre hotel that is due to open next year
- interest rates are likely to increase (the owner of the hotel has a large bank loan).

Once the **S**trengths, **W**eaknesses, **O**pportunities and **T**hreats have been identified, an organisation may put together an ACTION PLAN. The plan will set out the actions it is going to take to improve performance within a certain period of time. Generally, this involves building on the strengths, getting rid of or reducing weaknesses, seizing opportunities and minimising threats. After the meeting, the Grand Hotel's team mapped out the following action plan for the next two months:
- Emphasise pricing, location and food on the hotel website and all other marketing materials.
- Place some ads in the local newspaper to promote the public bar. Emphasise that there is real ale, a log fire and a buffet between 5.30 and 7.30 pm.
- Register with the TIC.

In the next six months:
- Refurbish six of the rooms.
- Open up the restaurant to the public and emphasise the gourmet menu.
- Improve recruitment and induction methods for staff.

In the next 12 months:
- Reduce the loan by cutting the owner's salary.
- Arrange a meeting with the new hotel competitor to discuss some joint marketing.
- Refurbish the remaining six rooms.

This is how a SWOT analysis might be used. It is also important to evaluate an action plan by finding out what effect the plan has had on the performance of the organisation.

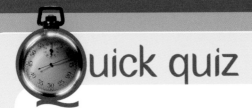

Quick quiz

1   **True or false?**

  ✪ A SWOT analysis is used to calculate the profit that an organisation makes.

  ✪ An organisation must seize any opportunities it identifies.

  ✪ Threats are an internal force that could affect the performance of an organisation.

2   Which of these would a tour operator consider to be a threat?
  (a) High staff turnover **(b)** Rising cost of accommodation
  (c) A competitor goes bankrupt **(d)** An increase in people travelling abroad

3   Which of these would be a weakness for a theme park?
  (a) Rising interest rates **(b)** Competitive prices **(c)** Very long queues **(d)** Bad weather

4   Which of these would be strength for a leisure centre?
  (a) Isolated location **(b)** Increased interest in sport
  (c) Highly trained staff **(d)** Increase in the local population

5   What should an organisation do after a SWOT analysis has been carried out?

Portfolio practice

Sutherland Cottages

Annie McPherson owns four holiday cottages in Sutherland, Scotland. The income from the cottages has supported Annie and her family for 10 years but recently, two of her three children have left home and the work needed to maintain and clean the cottages has got too much for her. Two months ago, a visitor from England offered Annie £120,000 for one of the cottages. She  bought it nine years ago for £23,500. She decided that she was not ready to sell. The cottages have beautiful coastal locations, are well-equipped, modern and well-maintained. However, they are isolated and the nearest shop and pub are about 15 miles away. The rent charged by Annie is quite low but the cottages are fully booked in the summer and there is often a long waiting list for cancellations. Her children used to say that Annie was soft and that she should raise the rent.

  During the winter, the cottages are often empty and locals complain because there is a housing shortage for young people in the area. Unfortunately, because of this, the cottages are vandalised occasionally. There is also a problem with flooding in two of the cottages. Annie wants to build the business up to get the best possible price before she sells the cottages in five years time. To do this, she carries out a SWOT analysis.

1. What is the difference between a strength and an opportunity in a SWOT analysis? *(2 marks)*

2. Identify two of each of the following (i) strengths (ii) weaknesses (iii) opportunities (iv) threats, in Annie's holiday letting business. *(8 marks)*

3. What action could Annie take in the next few years to build the business? *(7 marks)*

key terms

Action plan – a written statement setting out a series of actions to be taken to improve performance within a certain period of time.

SWOT analysis – an analysis of the internal strengths and weaknesses and the external threats and opportunities facing an organisation.

Promotional campaigns

Getting started...

Marketing is important to organisations in the leisure and tourism industries because they usually have to compete for customers. To do this, they often put together a package of marketing activities to promote their products. For example, a national fast-food restaurant, such as KFC, might cut its prices for a month to increase sales. This price cut might be supported by a TV advertising campaign and some full page ads in national newspapers. The organisation would hope that this package would have a big impact on sales. Look at the example below.

The Butcher's Arms – Dinosaur Den

The Butcher's Arms is an old country pub in the Peak District, Derbyshire. Jenny Nolan, the landlady, wanted to attract more families with young children so she planned the following marketing activities.

✪ She organised the building of a children's play area, called the Dinosaur Den, in the pub's garden. It was in the shape of a giant dinosaur and children could get inside the dinosaur by crawling into its mouth.

✪ She changed the lunch time menus to include special children's meals such as Brontosaurus Burgers, Gorgosaurus and chips and Pyroraptor nuggets.

✪ A full-page colour advert, featuring the Dinosaur Den and the children's menu, was placed in a local newspaper.

✪ An article about the Dinosaur Den was published by a journalist in the local newspaper.

(a) Who is the target market in this case?
(b) What promotional materials are being used by Jenny?

What is a promotional campaign?

An organisation can choose from a wide range of different promotional techniques and materials when marketing its products. Organisations often use a PROMOTIONAL CAMPAIGN. This is a well-planned period of promotion which involves using a number of techniques and materials to achieve a particular marketing aim. For example, in 2004, three of Cheshire's main tourist attractions – Chester Zoo, The Blue Planet Aquarium and Cheshire Oaks – got together to attract more families from Birmingham. They spent £78,000 on a promotional campaign which involved:

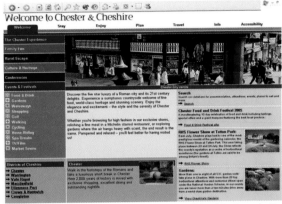

Cheshire's website

- sending leaflets promoting the World-of-Wonder themed campaign to more than 500,000 Birmingham homes
- using radio and newspaper advertising
- setting up a special website to provide information - www.wowcheshire.co.uk
- opening an information telephone line to deal with enquiries
- providing incentives, such as vouchers and a competition, to encourage families to visit all three attractions.

What does a promotional campaign try to achieve?

The diagram in Figure 1 shows the different stages involved when using a promotional campaign. The first step is to identify the aim of the campaign. Examples could include:

- increase sales
- improve image
- launch a new product
- inject some life into an old product
- raise awareness of products
- target a new market segment.

In the example above, the aim of the World-of-Wonder campaign was to attract more customers from Birmingham and encourage them to visit all three Cheshire attractions.

Clear objectives will help the organisation to focus. The success of the campaign will depend on whether the objectives have been met.

What is the target market?

Promotional campaigns are aimed at a particular target market so it is important to clearly identify the target market. This avoids wasting promotional materials on people who are not likely to buy the product. Also, different target markets are likely to respond to different types of promotional materials. For example, low-income families might respond well to a promotion that uses money-off vouchers. In the example above, the target market is families in the Birmingham area.

Which promotional techniques should be used?

Organisations have a wide range of promotional techniques to choose from such as advertising, sponsorship, direct mail, displays and leaflets. These have been discussed in previous units. The choice of technique will depend on the:

- size of the organisation
- nature of the product being promoted
- amount of money available for promotion
- type of target market.

For example, a big theme park can afford to use TV advertising aimed at a national target market. But a small nightclub might rely on ads in a local newspaper to attract local residents. In a promotional campaign, several different techniques are likely to be used to support each other. These should have a bigger impact.

What promotional materials should be used?

When choosing materials for a promotional campaign, the nature of the target market is very important. This is because people of different ages, genders and social groups may not respond in the same way to words, images, ideas and sounds. For example, young children may respond to colourful images with few, if any, words in a poster campaign.

Promotional campaigns are likely to use a range of different materials all at the same time. In the Cheshire example above, leaflets, radio ads, newspaper ads, incentives and the Internet were all materials used to encourage more families from Birmingham to visit attractions. Whichever materials are selected, it is important that they create a big impact.

Figure 1 *Stages in a promotional campaign*

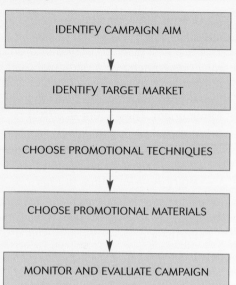

```
IDENTIFY CAMPAIGN AIM
        ↓
IDENTIFY TARGET MARKET
        ↓
CHOOSE PROMOTIONAL TECHNIQUES
        ↓
CHOOSE PROMOTIONAL MATERIALS
        ↓
MONITOR AND EVALUATE CAMPAIGN
```

AIDA

One approach when choosing or designing materials for a promotional campaign is to use AIDA. This stands for:

☺ **A**ttention
☺ **I**nterest
☺ **D**esire
☺ **A**ction.

Attention The first thing promotional material must do is grab people's attention. This might involve using a lot of colour, a famous celebrity, an original idea or offering a bargain.

Interest Once people's attention has been caught, their interest has to be maintained. They must be persuaded to carry on reading or watching an advert, for example. This might be done by showing that the product is relevant – for example, an advert for a nightclub aimed at single people which shows that they are likely to have lots of fun and meet members of the opposite sex.

Desire Promotional materials must make people want the product. This is done by emphasising its attractive features. For example, a theme park might describe its new white-knuckle ride as 'chilling', 'frightening', 'scary' or 'mind-blowing'.

Action The final stage is to show people how to buy the product. Ideally, people will be given the chance to contact the seller immediately. For example, a telephone number might be given at the end of a TV advert.

How can campaigns be monitored and evaluated?

This final stage in the campaign must not be overlooked. Whilst the campaign is running, it will have to be monitored. This involves checking that everything is going according to plan. Vodafone, the sponsor for the England cricket team, sends a rep with the team when they are touring to make sure that the company gets the agreed coverage from the deal. For example, the rep will make sure that the Vodafone logos are prominently displayed during interviews with the players.

It is important to evaluate the campaign to see if it was worth the expense. This might be done by asking people where they heard about the organisation when they buy a product. Market research might be used to ask people specific questions about the campaign. The information obtained might be used to help in planning future campaigns. The success of the campaign will depend on whether the aims have been met.

Quick quiz

1. **True or false?**
   - ✪ A promotional campaign often involves using several different promotional techniques at the same time.
   - ✪ Monitoring a promotional campaign involves checking to see whether the aims have been met.
   - ✪ Promotional campaigns tend to last for a long period of time.

2. Which of these is the first stage when planning a promotional campaign?
   - **(a)** Monitor the campaign
   - **(b)** Identify the aim
   - **(c)** Identify target market
   - **(d)** Choose some promotional materials

3. Which of these is **not** likely to be an aim of a promotional campaign?
   - **(a)** Raise awareness
   - **(b)** Target a new market
   - **(c)** Increase sales
   - **(d)** Reduce costs

4. Which of these will **not** affect the choice of promotional techniques?
   - **(a)** Size of the organisation
   - **(b)** Amount of money available
   - **(c)** Location of the organisation
   - **(d)** Nature of the product

5. What is AIDA used for?

Portfolio practice

Ordnance Survey

In 2001, Ordnance Survey, the national mapping agency, launched the first stage of its biggest ever marketing campaign for its world famous paper maps. 'Your Passport to Great Britain' was designed to encourage day-trippers and holiday-makers to rediscover the British countryside. The campaign involved:

- ✪ a four-week promotion using large colour ads in national newspapers and full-page colour ads in walking magazines
- ✪ supporting point-of-sale material and promotional events
- ✪ competitions which offered the chance to win weekend breaks in Britain, and many other prizes.

Ordnance Survey maps

Some new maps were launched as part of the campaign. Explorer maps, for example, show footpaths and other rights of way very clearly along with other tourist and leisure facilities such as camping and caravan sites, viewpoints, rural car parks, museums, nature reserves, craft centres and public gardens.

1. What is the aim of the Ordnance Survey campaign? *(2 marks)*
2. State three promotional techniques being used in the campaign. *(3 marks)*
3. Explain why several different promotional techniques have been used in the campaign. *(4 marks)*
4. How could Ordnance Survey evaluate the success of its campaign? *(7 marks)*

key terms

AIDA – an approach to designing or choosing appropriate promotional materials. It stands for Attention, Interest, Desire and Action.

Promotional campaign – a plan which involves using a range of promotional techniques and materials over a period of time to achieve a particular aim.

Getting started...

In the leisure and tourism industries, it is very important to make sure that customers are happy with the products they buy and that they enjoy themselves. Consequently, organisations have to look after their customers. For example, tour operators employ reps to look after customers during their holiday. Look at the examples below where customers are receiving careful attention from staff.

Tourist Information Centres (TICs)

One of the main purposes of TICs is to provide people with information. The staff working in the TIC will have a good knowledge of the local area. For example, they will know about local attractions, accommodation, transport links, restaurants and many other local facilities.

TOURIST INFORMATION

Sutton Travel Ltd

Shelly Thomas works at Sutton Travel Ltd. Two months ago, she sold a holiday to a couple who wanted to honeymoon in Mauritius. But the time of the outgoing flight has changed slightly so she has sent out the letter shown below to the customer.

Tel: 0121 555 6599

Sutton Travel Ltd
4 High Street
Sutton Coldfield
West Midlands
WM9 ER2

Dear Ms Harding,

I am writing to let you know that the time of your flight from Birmingham Airport on 23.7.04 has been changed slightly. Flight KLM 1200 will now depart at 12.40. I do hope this won't inconvenience you. If you have any further queries, you are welcome to contact me.

Yours sincerely

Shelly Thomas

Andre's

Andre's is a restaurant in Basingstoke specialising in vegetarian and vegan cuisine. It has an excellent reputation for high-quality food and first-class service. The restaurant employs a sommelier (a wine waiter who is an expert on wines). He takes the wine order from diners and often gives them advice about which wines go best with particular types of food.

In each of the above cases:
(a) State whether staff are sending a message, giving advice or providing information.
(b) State why it is important for staff to look after customers.

What is customer service?

CUSTOMER SERVICE is about looking after customers and giving them what they want and need. Most organisations in the leisure and tourism industries are MARKET ORIENTATED. This means that they focus on the customer – they believe that the customer is the most important person of all. If people experience good customer service, they are likely to return and buy more products. They may also tell their friends and relatives who might also buy products. Some organisations aim to exceed customer expectations. This approach will go a long way to help keep customers satisfied. Features of good customer service might include:

- making sure that people are sold the right products
- always being courteous, friendly and helpful to customers
- dealing with complaints and problems sensitively and in a practical way
- reassuring customers when they have doubts
- making sure customers feel important and cared for.

Air New Zealand inflight food

Providing information

Part of customer service involves providing information. For example, when people are choosing a holiday destination they might want to know about a particular country, its people, the culture, the resort, the accommodation, prices, weather, attractions, hazards, currency and so on. Such information can be provided in three main ways.

Paper-based information Most organisations provide information in leaflets, booklets, brochures, adverts or guidebooks, for example. Tour operators, visitor attractions, cinemas, theatres, museums, restaurants, bus and train operators, leisure centres, sports clubs and hotels are all likely to provide printed information about their products. It is presented in an attractive way to attract customers. Printed information also has to be clear, accurate and easy to understand.

Oral information People often prefer to get information directly from staff. They may wish to ask specific questions or need clarification about something written in a brochure, for example. If a member of staff is unable to provide the information, it may be necessary to ask a colleague or carry out some research. This might involve contacting the customer later.

Computer-based information Increasingly, organisations have websites where a wide range of information is available. The advantage of providing information this way is that it is available 24 hours a day, 365 days a year. It is also easy to update and customers can make bookings.

Alton Towers' website

Giving advice

Giving advice should not be confused with providing information. Some people may need guidance or help when making decisions. In the leisure and tourism industries, people are often doing things or going to places for the first time so they may need reassurance. Customers often expect staff in organisations to be experts. Staff may be asked for their opinions by customers. For example:

- Which airline do you think provides the best food?

- Is it advisable to take US dollars or sterling to Bangladesh?

- Which brand of skis would you recommend?

- Do you think it will be safe for my children to swim in the sea?

- Where is the best place for nightlife, Magaluf or Santa Ponca?

Customers often trust staff when asking for advice. It is therefore important for an organisation to train its staff well so that they are knowledgeable and confident. Giving sound advice is important in customer service. Staff training is discussed in Unit 45.

Information desk at Luton Airport

Receiving and passing on messages

Providing customer service requires good communication skills. This means that staff should be competent at both receiving and passing on messages. Messages have to be passed on swiftly and accurately. The consequences of passing on information incorrectly can be very serious. For example, what might happen if a holiday-maker thinks they have been told that the airport bus will pick them up at 5.00 pm when it is actually 5.00 am?

Many organisations have systems to ensure that messages are passed on accurately to the right person. For example, they might use a simple form. The one below is used to pass on telephone messages.

Telephone message

To:................. Mr. Banks ....

Caller:.............. Zoe Larcombe.......................

Time:.............. 11.25 ....

Date:.............. 3.8.04 ....

Tel. No .... 01774 299900.......................

Taken by:.......... Julie Ward..............................

Message:......*I will have to cancel tomorrow's appointment due to an air traffic control strike. Please ring back this afternoon if possible*. ....

Communication is discussed in more detail in Units 51 and 52.

Keeping records

Most organisations in the leisure and tourist industries hold information about their customers. Part of customer service involves collecting this information and making sure it is up to date. The most common customer details are such things as the name, address and telephone number.

However, the records kept will depend on the type of organisation. For example, a fitness club might keep records of their members' basic health. This might be required for health and safety reasons.

Keeping records helps organisations to provide a better customer service. Keeping customer records is discussed in more detail in Unit 55.

Quick quiz

1 Look at the telephone message in the section above.
   - ✪ Who took the telephone call?
   - ✪ Who was the call made to?
   - ✪ Who was the caller?

2 Which of these questions is a request for advice?
   (a) What is the time of the first train to London?
   (b) Do you think the Hotel Du Paris is better than the Montparnasse?
   (c) What time does the museum open?
   (d) Which is the nearest airport to Gijon?

3 Which of these items of customer information is **not** likely to be recorded by a travel agent?
   (a) Car registration number **(b)** Name **(c)** Address **(d)** Telephone number

4 Which of these is **not** part of customer service?
   (a) Giving advice **(c)** Providing information
   (b) Keeping records **(d)** Ordering brochures from a tour operator

5 State three features of good customer service.

Portfolio practice

Lanka.com

John and Ali are students and have booked a holiday in Sri Lanka. It is their first trip outside Europe. They booked the holiday with Lanka.com after searching online for a cheap deal. They paid £489 each for flights from London Heathrow to Colombo Airport. They plan to backpack around the country travelling by bus and train. Ali is looking forward to seeing elephants for the first time and John wants to visit some of the historical sites. After the bookings were made, Ali sent an email to Lanka.com asking for advice on protection against mosquitoes. Nevinka Wijesinghe, one of Lanka.com's employees, is going to send him some advice. She has found the information shown above.

To minimise any contact with mosquitoes:
- Wear light-coloured clothing.
- Wear long trousers and long-sleeved shirts.
- Use mosquito repellents containing DEET on exposed areas (prolonged overuse of DEET may be harmful).
- When sleeping, use a mosquito net treated with mosquito repellent (permethrin) — it may be worth taking your own.
- Treat clothes with permethrin.
- Consult your GP for advice on malaria tablets.

Stilt fishermen in Sri Lanka

1. How might Nevinka send the advice on mosquito protection to Ali? *(1 mark)*
2. State three advantages of providing computer-based information. *(3 marks)*
3. Explain what is meant by good customer service and why it is important to Lanka.com. *(4 marks)*
4. Draft a letter for Nevinka containing the advice that Ali has asked for. *(7 marks)*

key terms Customer service – looking after customers by giving them what they want and need.
Market orientated – focusing on the wants and needs of the customer.

Getting started...

Much of the work in customer service involves giving advice and information to people and receiving and passing on messages. This requires good communication skills and quite a lot of specialised knowledge. But some aspects of customer service can be more demanding and will require quite different skills. For example, a park ranger may have to look after a distressed child while the parents are found. Look at the different types of customer service being delivered below.

The Rawlins family

The Rawlins family went on a package holiday to Torremolinos. When they arrived at Malaga airport, they were held up at customs for three hours and this meant that they missed their coach to the hotel. Fortunately, the rep was still at the airport. She knew the family were somewhere in the airport complex and anticipated a problem. She found the family and arranged for a taxi to take them to the hotel.

Ski West

Ski West organises skiing holidays in the French Alps. Unfortunately, one week in November, one of their parties arrived at a resort called St Martin to find that there was no snow. After two days, they complained angrily that there was nothing to do and the drinks at the resort were outrageously expensive. The Ski West rep dealt with the complaint by apologising and organising a coach trip to a nearby town where drinks were cheaper.

Kristijan Karadov

Kristijan Karadov has just moved to Warwick from Croatia. His father has a job at a local university. Kristijan wants to join a leisure centre to meet new people and play badminton. He can speak English a little bit but struggles to read and write it. Jenny is the receptionist at the leisure centre and she helps Kristijan to fill in the application form.

(a) Describe the type of customer service work being carried out by the staff in each of the above cases.
(b) Suggest two skills that customer services staff might need to help them do the above jobs.

Providing assistance

Some customers may require assistance when enjoying activities in the leisure and tourism industries. This might be because they cannot cope on their own or because they are in unfamiliar situations. For example, someone might be new to a leisure class and not be sure of the systems or procedures. The following are examples of situations where assistance might be provided.

- Elderly people may require physical assistance such as help climbing down the steps from a coach or an aircraft.
- A single parent might need support when struggling with toddlers.
- A non-English speaker may require guidance when following some instructions.
- Some backpackers at a hostel might need to use a telephone to send an urgent message home.
- A football supporter may need help find to find her seat in the stadium.

People employed in the leisure and tourism industries need to understand the importance of providing this sort of assistance. They should recognise that it is good practice to offer assistance rather than assume that a customer needs it. Some people prefer to manage on their own. Others may not want their disabilities, special needs or vulnerabilities exposed. Customer service is all about making people feel comfortable and welcome.

Dealing with problems

Another part of customer service is dealing with people's problems. The types of problem that might arise will depend on where in the industry it occurs. For example, in a restaurant, common problems might include double-booking, coping with a kitchen fire, trying to fit people in that have not booked and running out of ingredients. At a swimming pool, problems might include lost locker keys, faulty vending machines, theft of property and swimmers with cramp. Many problems can be anticipated and staff can be trained to deal with them. For example, nearly all staff will be trained in basic first aid but their training is likely to go further than this. When customers encounter problems they may be frustrated, worried, in pain, anxious or agitated. Customer services staff may be trained to deal with people in these circumstances. A general approach might involve:

- Calming and reassuring people by suggesting that the problem will soon be solved.

- Putting into action company procedures for dealing with the particular problem.

- Seeking the help of a supervisor or manager if necessary.

- Completing any necessary documentation such as filling in an accident book.

- For serious problems, it may be necessary to call the emergency services.

Dealing with dissatisfied customers

One of the more difficult jobs in customer services is handling customer complaints. It is unlikely that the complaint will arise because of the actions of customer services staff – it is usually about the organisation that these staff work for. Consequently, customer services staff have to deal with complaints effectively. If a customer is still dissatisfied after a complaint has been dealt with, it is unlikely that he or she will return. The image of the organisation might also be damaged. In some respects, complaints are inevitable and staff are trained to deal with them. Some organisations provide clear opportunities for customers to complain – for example, in questionnaires. They use this customer feedback to improve services in the future. Again, the type of complaints received by organisations will depend on where in the industry it is made. For example, at a theme park, customers might complain about the:

- length of the queues
- state of the toilets
- lack of facilities for babies.

At a pop concert, people might complain about:

- not being able to see properly
- a lack of refreshment facilities
- one of the bands not turning up.

Complaints can be received in writing, over the telephone or in person. The most difficult to deal with are those made in person. This is because a customer might become abusive. Handling complaints in the leisure and tourism industries is covered in detail in Unit 54.

Offering extra services

As well as the standard services offered by organisations, such as package holidays by tour operators, exhibitions by an art gallery and accommodation by hotels, a range of extra services might be provided.
For example:

- An airline might offer free drinks and a free buffet between meals on a long flight.
- A hotel might provide laundry services.
- A tour operator might provide free champagne, flowers and a bowl of fruit for honeymooners.
- Premier League football clubs often organise tours of their stadiums.
- Visitor attractions may allow customers to pay for tickets online or over the telephone which they can pick up on arrival.

Honeymooners in Mauritius

Generally, these extra services help to make life more comfortable and convenient for customers and they may also help an organisation to exceed customer expectations. The provision of extra services has grown in recent years as businesses in the leisure and tourism industries compete for customers.

Quick quiz

1 **True or false?**

☼ Customer services staff should not attempt to handle complaints.

☼ Extra services are often provided to compete against other organisations.

☼ Some organisations provide opportunities for customers to complain.

2 Which of these is an example of extra services provided by a tour operator?

(a) Transfer from the airport to the resort

(b) Self-catering apartment

(c) Free welcome pack in an apartment (e.g. tea, coffee, milk, bread etc.)

(d) Flight to the destination

3 State three ways in which a customer might make a complaint.

4 State three groups of customers that might need assistance.

5 State three problems that could occur on a long haul flight.

Portfolio practice

The Bullen Hotel

Eileen McDonald is a trainee manager at the Bullen Hotel, Stow-on-the-Wold, Gloucestershire. One afternoon, a hotel guest – Monique Raux from France – arrived at reception in a very distressed state. Monique's handbag, containing her passport, driving licence, credit cards, cash and travellers cheques, had been stolen. Monique could not speak very good English and Eileen's French was weak. The chef at the hotel could speak some French but he was not on duty for another two hours. The manager of the hotel would not be on duty for another six hours. Eileen felt that she would have to deal with the problem herself.

1. What might be the first thing that Eileen should do in the above case? *(2 marks)*
2. State three extra services that the Bullen Hotel might provide for its customers. *(3 marks)*
3. Explain how the extra services, listed in question 2, might benefit the Bullen Hotel. *(4 marks)*
4. Explain how you think Eileen should deal with the problem in the case. *(7 marks)*

Getting started...

Most organisations in the leisure and tourism industries train their staff in customer services. This helps to improve the quality of customer service and enables staff to do their jobs more effectively. Look at the cases below where staff are giving customer service.

Cheryl Bradley

Cheryl works in a leisure centre. One of the customers has fallen and injured her ankle. They are waiting for an ambulance.

Graham Turner

Graham works for a train operator. He is dealing with a very angry customer who has missed a business appointment because the train was two and a half hours late.

Emmanuel Asare

Emmanuel is a tennis coach. He works for a tennis club in Sussex. He organises coaching sessions for small groups and also gives one-to-one coaching.

Nelson Bravo

Nelson works in a Tourist Information Centre (TIC) at a seaside resort on the south coast. He spends all day giving out information and answering visitors' questions.

(a) What training might be needed by the staff in the cases above?

(b) What might happen if the staff in the above cases are not trained in customer service? Use Cheryl's case as an example.

Why do organisations train employees?

Training in customer services can help an organisation to provide a better service. Training will benefit employees as well by improving their skills.

Improve competence Training in customer services will help staff do their job more effectively. Staff need to learn the skills that are used in the job. For example, employees may need to learn how to calm a distressed child.

Motivation If staff are not trained, they may become frustrated because they cannot do their job. Also, if an organisation spends money training staff, they may feel more valued and work harder.

Technology Changes in technology may mean that staff have to learn how to use new equipment. For example, staff might need training after a new computer system has been installed to deal with customer records.

Legislation Changes in the law may mean staff have to be brought up to date with new practices. For example, new CONSUMER PROTECTION LAWS may require staff to learn a new procedure for dealing with customer complaints.

Promotion If staff receive training they might feel more confident and qualified to try for promotion in the organisation. They may feel capable of doing more complex work or taking on extra responsibility.

Flexibility By training staff in different jobs they will be able to do more in the organisation. For example, if someone working in customer services is off sick, another employee working elsewhere in the organisation will be able to cover if they have been trained.

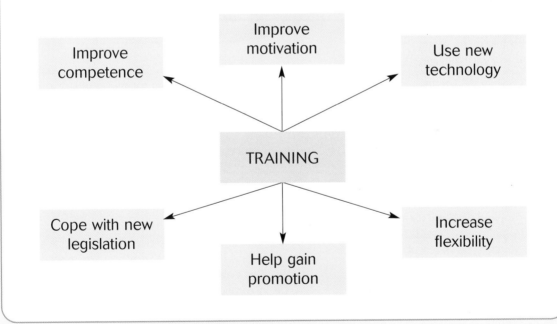

Induction training

Employees might receive INDUCTION TRAINING when they start a new job. It is designed to help staff overcome the anxiety of starting a new job and to settle in quickly. It might involve:

- ✪ Being introduced to new colleagues.
- ✪ A tour of the organisation.
- ✪ Learning about the history and structure of the organisation.
- ✪ Learning about the organisation's objectives and policies.
- ✪ Health and safety training and workplace rules.

On-the-job training

ON-THE-JOB TRAINING involves training staff in the work place. The main advantage of this is that the trainee will gain some real 'hands on' experience. It is also cheap and staff can contribute to the running of the organisation straightaway. However, trainees might make mistakes until they are fully trained and this could affect the quality of customer service. There are several methods of on-the-job training.

Learning from others In a travel agency, a new member of staff might sit next to an experienced worker to see how the job is done. After a while, they will be given the chance to copy the good practice of the experienced worker.

Coaching This is where a qualified teacher demonstrates the skills needed to do the job and then helps the trainee to acquire the skills.

Mentoring This involves an experienced worker supervising the training and development of a new worker. The mentor gives guidance, advice and answers questions.

Apprenticeship This is a formal training arrangement which might last for two years or more. Apprentices might receive different types of training which could include regular attendance at college.

Off-the-job training

OFF-THE-JOB TRAINING involves training staff away from the work place. It could be given at an organisation's own training centre, a college, a university or by a training provider such as ProEdge Skills, a specialist provider of customer services training. Training courses are also available online. A range of training methods might be used such as lectures, videos, role plays and simulations. The main advantage of this type of training is that it is provided by qualified trainers. It might also be less stressful for trainees. But it is expensive and employees do not make any contribution to the running of the organisation.

Training and qualifications in leisure and tourism

It is possible to gain qualifications in leisure and tourism and in customer services. For example, at school or college, students can do a GCSE and a GCE in Applied Leisure and Tourism. At university, it is possible to get a degree in hospitality, hotel and restaurant management, leisure, sport, and tourism. Employees can also get vocational qualifications. These are awarded to staff that can provide evidence of attainment in the workplace. There are four levels of qualification in areas such as customer services, administration, travel services or sport and recreation. Staff might also get training and qualifications in areas such as first aid and foreign languages to help them improve their customer service skills.

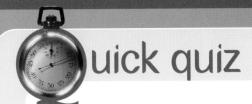

Quick quiz

1 **True or false?**
- One of the disadvantages of training is that it is expensive.
- Vocational qualifications can be gained at work.
- Mentoring is a method of off-the-job training.

2 Match the statements with the training methods in the box.
- Training given to a new employee that has just started.
- Pairing a trainee with an experienced worker who acts as a supervisor and advisor.
- Training that takes place while doing a job.

Induction training
On-the-job training
Off-the-job training
Coaching

3 How can training be used to improve flexibility in an organisation?

Portfolio practice

Welcome Host

Welcome Host is a one-day training programme designed to improve customer care skills. It is part of a national initiative that can help an organisation to:
- increase sales and profitability
- build repeat business
- provide higher standards of service for visitors and locals
- enhance customer satisfaction
- reduce complaint levels
- improve staff understanding of customer value.

A group training activity

   The training is aligned to the NVQ Level 2 in Customer Service. The courses will benefit both new and experienced staff working in areas such as accommodation and catering, travel and transport, leisure and entertainment and public sector and voluntary organisations. Welcome Host provides open courses (arranged by Regional Tourist Boards), where any employee can attend for £77 per day, or in-house courses tailored to the needs of the organisation for £695 per day. The Welcome Host programme involves group work and discussion and covers areas such as dealing with difficult situations, meeting specific needs, providing information and advice, communication, welcoming and understanding customers.

1. Explain why Welcome Host open courses are an example of off-the-job training. *(2 marks)*
2. State three ways that Welcome Host might be able to help an organisation. *(3 marks)*
3. Explain one advantage and one disadvantage to a business of sending seven staff to a Welcome Host open course rather than using their own in-house option. *(4 marks)*
4. Explain why an organisation might decide to train its staff and why it might decide to use a training provider like Welcome Host. *(7 marks)*

key terms

Consumer protection laws – laws which prevent organisations from exploiting their customers.
Induction training – training which provides a new employee with a structured introduction to the organisation.
Off-the-job training – training carried out away from the workplace.
On-the-job training – training in the workplace.

Getting started...

Not all customers will require the same type of service in the leisure and tourism industries. This is because the market is made up of different types of customer. For example, in a leisure centre, children will need more supervision, help and attention than adults. Also, some customers are businesses. For example, a hotel offering conference facilities might be providing customer service to an engineering company. Look at the different types of customer below.

Saga

The Saga Group Ltd is a business that caters especially for the needs of the over 50s. It sells holidays to worldwide destinations including cruises on its own ship. It owns an award-winning magazine, sells insurance and financial products and has several radio stations.

Compton Primary School

The Head Teacher of Compton Primary School is planning the annual summer excursion for a group of 40 pupils. They have decided to visit London Zoo. £350 is available to pay for the entrance fees. London Zoo offers cheap rates for group bookings. For groups of 20 or more, the rate per child is £7.80.

Anita Rawal

Anita Rawal is planning a trip to Australia on her own. She has booked a flight with a local travel agent and is now looking at different types of accommodation along the east coast of Australia. The agent is helping her to choose accommodation which is most suitable for single people. Anita has travelled independently before and knows that choosing the right type of accommodation is important.

(a) Identify the type of customers in the above cases.
(b) Will the £350 budget be enough to pay for the group's entrance into the zoo?

Individuals

One group of customers in the leisure and tourism industries is individuals. These are people that buy products on their own. They are dealt with on a one-to-one basis. Many individuals are single people but they could also be married men or women who are travelling alone or enjoying a leisure activity on their own. One advantage of serving individuals is that their needs are more easily met. This is because there is only one person to please. The needs of individuals might include:

- single rooms in a hotel
- the opportunity to meet other people
- partners in squash, golf, badminton and tennis or a special fitness programme.

Many individuals are young with a lot of disposable income. Organisations will be keen to attract these people because they may become long-term customers.

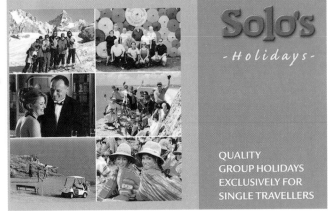

QUALITY
GROUP HOLIDAYS
EXCLUSIVELY FOR
SINGLE TRAVELLERS

Solo's – a holiday company specialising in singles

Groups

Sometimes, products or services are offered to groups of people. Examples might be a party of school children, a family group, a golf society, a hen-party or a hockey team. Groups usually have a leader or an organiser. This makes communication with the group easier. When dealing with groups, it has to be remembered that although each group is enjoying the same leisure activity, it is made up of individuals who might have different needs. For example:

- A guide showing a group of tourists around a museum may find that one of the group members has a special interest in some of the exhibits. This might mean that the guide has to answer more demanding questions from that person.

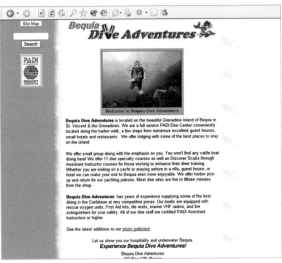

Bequia Dive Adventures – a company specialising in group holidays

- In a family group, the needs of small children will be different to those of the parents. For example, small children will not be able to consume alcohol in a pub.

Many organisations are very welcoming towards groups. For example, they may offer reduced rates or provide exclusive use of facilities. Some groups have ongoing bookings with leisure centres. For example, they might have exclusive use of a sports hall or a swimming pool at a particular time. Sometimes groups are not quite so welcome. For example, some pubs do not welcome coach parties using their facilities. The company pictured above provides special adventure holidays for groups of divers.

People of different ages

Customer services staff will have to deal with people of different ages. This may mean adapting to the needs of toddlers, teenagers, young adults and the elderly, for example. The bar graph in Figure 1 shows the projected age distribution of the UK population in 2006. Nearly half of the population lies in the 30-59 year old age range.

How might the needs of these different age groups differ?

Figure 1 *Projected age distribution of the UK population 2006*

○ The older generation might prefer to be addressed formerly as Mr and Mrs.

○ Teenagers and young adults may prefer holiday destinations with a lively night-life.

○ Young children may need to be occupied (with toys, books and games, for example) when flying – especially on long haul flights.

○ Some adult swimmers may prefer to use the pool when there are no children around.

○ Senior citizens may prefer different meal times – an early breakfast, for example.

○ Retired people and children often expect discounts or concessions for certain facilities and attractions.

Although different age groups may have different needs, customer services staff must not always assume that the same age groups want the same thing. For example, a 12 year old might be upset if offered a children's sized portion in a restaurant.

People from different cultures

It is common in the leisure and tourism industries to serve people from different cultural backgrounds. For example, Britain gets a lot of tourists from all over the world. People from different countries have different traditions, tastes, opinions and behaviour and their needs have to be met. And the UK itself is a mixture of different cultures. Examples of different cultural needs might include:

○ Italian tourists might prefer a continental breakfast at their hotel accommodation.

○ Jewish people do not eat pork.

○ Australians like the outdoor life.

○ Americans enjoy larger portions.

○ Elderly people have considerably more respect in Asia than in the UK.

○ Muslims must pray at certain times of the day.

○ A Buddhist needs time for meditation.

Prayer room for all faiths at Manchester Airport

When serving people from different cultural backgrounds, it is very important to respect their beliefs and behaviours. Staff must also avoid making assumptions about people.

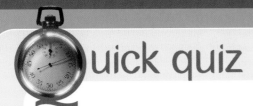

Quick quiz

1. **True or false?**
   - Individual customers will only be single people.
   - Customers in groups often expect discounts.
   - People living in Manchester might have different cultural backgrounds.

2. Some leisure centres provide a crèche. Which age group would this serve?
   (a) 75+ **(b)** 15 – 19 **(c)** 0 – 4 **(d)** 10 – 14

3. Which age group is least likely to enjoy the facilities at a theme park?
   (a) 75+ **(b)** 15 – 19 **(c)** 10 – 14 **(d)** 5 – 9

4. Which age groups are customer services staff in a travel agents most likely to deal with?
   (a) 75+ **(b)** 0 – 4 **(c)** 15 – 19 **(d)** 20 – 29

5. State three needs that the 75+ age group might have at a country hotel.

Portfolio practice

Blackpool hen-parties

Blackpool welcomes single-sex groups of women for hen-parties. The resort provides themed and specialist accommodation packages for hen-nights with deals that often include discounts for clubs, attractions and entertainment.

A girls' night out

What to expect

- Package deals and discounts for groups with 10 plus members, where the organiser goes free.
- Rooms which accommodate 3 or 4 people.
- Free or discount tickets to Blackpool's best nightclubs and cabaret venues such as Funny Girls and other activities such as ten pin bowling.
- Late night bars and cabaret entertainment.
- Late keys.
- Located within walking distance of pubs and clubs.
- Extended breakfast times.
- Restaurant recommendations.
- Extra support such as transport to the chosen entertainment.
- Information on local beauty therapists, massage therapists, nail decoration and treatments.

1. Using this case as an example, suggest why organisations are happy to accommodate groups of customers. *(2 marks)*
2. Give three examples of how an individual's needs might be different from the rest of the group in a hen-party. *(3 marks)*
3. Explain why it might be easier to deal with a hen-party if there is a leader. *(4 marks)*
4. Discuss the customer services that are being provided in Blackpool for hen-parties. *(7 marks)*

Getting started...

Some types of customers in the leisure and tourism industries have very specific needs. They may need rather more care and assistance than other customers and, in some cases, staff might need specialist training to deal with them. There may be special health and safety issues to consider, for example. Look at the types of customers below and the customer care needed.

Wacky Warehouse

Wacky Warehouse pubs are designed with children in mind. On average 6,760,000 children visit a Wacky Warehouse every year which is more than Alton Towers! Youngsters under 4' 9", supervised by an adult, can explore the giant indoor playbarn packed full of wobble bars, rope ladders, ball pools and slides. They are bigger than most play areas and have a tiny tots' soft play area for toddlers and a big fun adventure challenge with three levels of fun play equipment for older children. They are monitored by 'Wacky staff' many of whom hold formal child-care qualifications. However, parents or guardians must remain in the Wacky Warehouse.

Part of the play area in a Wacky Warehouse

Grand Theatre - Swansea

The Grand Theatre presents over 500 performances a year. It is also the base for Ballet Russe, the only Russian classically-trained ballet company in the UK. The Grand Theatre also has conference facilities, a School of Dance and Theatre of Arts, a Youth Theatre Group and a variety of education projects.

Access

The lift in the Arts Wing provides access to all floors of the theatre including the grand circle in the main auditorium. There is level access for wheelchair users into the stalls and also into the Footlights Bar. There are five positions available in the stalls for wheelchair users which can be requested when tickets are booked. To enhance sound reception for the hearing impaired, the loop system is available and sign language interpreted performances are provided for certain shows.

The reception area in the Grand Theatre, Swansea. The perspex dome over the customer's head enhances sound reception for the hearing impaired.

(a) *What types of customers are being catered for by the organisations in the above cases?*
(b) *Briefly describe the sort of care that these types of customers need.*

Non-English speakers

It is very common for customers in the leisure and tourism industries not to speak English. Many tourists in the UK are from overseas and there are also many ethnic groups living in the UK for whom English is not their first language. Organisations have to provide specific customer services for these groups so that they do not feel left out. But this can be difficult in the UK because very few English people can speak another language. Some provisions that are made for non-English speaking people include:

- information about facilities printed in different languages

- directions, such as those at airports, written in different languages

- symbols can be used on signs instead of words

- employing translators and guides that can speak more than one language

- training customer services staff to speak a little of another language

- providing headphones and tapes in different languages, on guided tours.

A bed and breakfast sign in English and Japanese

It is still possible to communicate with people even if they cannot speak English. For example, gestures and signs can be used. This might be a way of making non-English speaking people feel more welcome and comfortable.

People with specific needs

Some people need special customer services because they have specific needs. For example:

- Wheelchair users need lifts, ramps, reserved and wider car parking spaces, wider entrances to buildings and assistance with mobility.

- The visually impaired need spoken information, information in Braille, enlarged printed information, guidance around facilities and special or adapted equipment.

- The hearing impaired need staff to face them directly and speak very clearly (but not shout) so that they can lip-read. They need visual aids, information in sign language and special telephones.

- People who are dyslexic or who suffer from dyscalculia (literacy and numeracy difficulties respectively) may need help with reading, writing and recognising numbers.

Generally, these groups need staff to give them a little more time, respect and patience. It is particularly important not to patronise them by offering help if it is not needed. In some organisations, staff with specialised training may be used to provide expert customer service. Finally, customers with special needs may find it helpful to receive recommendations of places that cater for them particularly well.

> **abletogo.com**
>
> abletogo.com is a service designed to meet the needs of disabled and elderly travelers, and those with poor mobility. abletogo.com is a website containing information about holiday destinations that are suitable for people with mobility difficulties. The site provides listings of places that cater specifically for this group.

Young children

Families are often drawn to organisations that cater specifically for the needs of young children under five. Parents are unlikely to enjoy leisure activities if their young children are not safely supervised. This means that facilities for youngsters must be provided in places like holiday resorts, leisure centres, pubs, theme parks and restaurants. Many organisations cater very well for this type of customer. For example:

- ✪ Tour operators provide holidays in resorts where there are plenty of things for young children to do such as paddling pools, play areas and play groups.

- ✪ Pubs may provide special rooms, a box of toys, play areas and children's soft drinks and sweets.

- ✪ Restaurants may provide special children's menus, high chairs and reserved areas.

- ✪ Leisure centres may provide crèches while parents enjoy other activities.

A crèche

It is important that staff supervising young children are trained, qualified and that they satisfy the legal requirements for looking after young children.

Business people

Some organisations in the leisure and tourism industries deal with business customers. For example, many airline and train operators carry large numbers of business people. Business people go to conferences, meetings, exhibitions, trade fairs and presentations. Whilst away from home, they stay in hotels, eat in restaurants and may enjoy other leisure facilities such as theatres, cinemas, museums and pubs. Some organisations provide special customer services for business people. For example, West Bromwich Albion, the West Midlands football club, has a wide range of conference facilities for businesses. It has a number of specialist function rooms including The Platinum Suite in the East Stand which has the following facilities:

- ✪ up to 300 capacity (theatre style)
- ✪ natural daylight
- ✪ blackout facilities
- ✪ own bar
- ✪ own toilet facilities
- ✪ disabled access and toilet
- ✪ three lifts for access
- ✪ phone lines which allow Internet access and video conferencing.
- ✪ PA system and CD player.

It is important to remember that business people are often entertaining their clients when using the facilities in the leisure and tourism industries. This means that the style of customer service has to be highly polished and professional.

West Bromwich Albion function rooms – the Platinum Suite (top) and the Pennington Suite

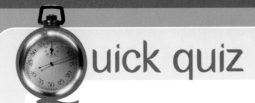

Quick quiz

1 **True or false?**
   - Pubs do not cater for young children.
   - Customer services staff may have to be qualified and trained to supervise young children.
   - Transport operators provide services for business people.

2 State three possible needs of the visually impaired.

3 State three possible needs of wheelchair users.

4 How might people with dyslexia and dyscalculia need extra help?

5 Why do you think sports clubs such as West Bromwich Albion provide services and facilities for business people?

Portfolio practice

DR Yachting

DR Yachting is a Greek company that provides sailing holidays for people with specific needs such as wheelchair users and the visually impaired. Their yachts are specially adapted with the following features.

- Easy access on widened catwalks with heightened borders.
- 4-point safety belts in the lounge to keep passengers stable and safe.
- The lounge roof can slide open for sunbathing.
- Tables in the lounge can seat eight people and a board fits between them for easy access by wheelchair.
- Handrails surround the yachts and all its areas, which allow safe and easy movement.
- There are two aisle-chairs which give easy access to the cabins and restroom where normal wheelchairs do not fit. There is also a special lift to help people to transfer from their own chairs to the aisle ones. These specially made chairs go to the lower level cabins via an electronically operated platform.
- The restrooms have special handrails to improve mobility.

Preparing to go sailing

For the visually impaired, the yacht is designed so that there are no obstacles or inclined decks. The living room, kitchen area, refrigerators and chart table are all open and on the same level. As a result, movement is easy, comfortable and safe. On the company's website, information is provided in Greek, English and German.

1. Which types of customer does DR Yachting cater for? *(1 mark)*
2. Why does DR Yachting provide information in three languages on its website? *(2 marks)*
3. Explain briefly, two important qualities that would be needed by staff working with DR Yachting's customers. *(4 marks)*
4. Explain how DR Yachting is meeting its customers' needs. *(7 marks)*

Getting started...

For most organisations, customers are people who use services or buy products. They may be members of the public or business people. But inside organisations there are other types of customers. These are work colleagues. For example, someone working for a tour operator in a London office might email a rep in Cyprus to notify her of some changes to a passenger list. The rep is the office worker's customer because she is going to provide a service to her. Look at the different types of customers below.

Swinton Tennis Club

Swinton Tennis Club has 186 members. 124 of these are tennis players and 62 are social members who are usually friends or relatives of the players.

Players and social members relax in the bar

JJB Sports

JJB Sports operates from around 430 stores in all the major towns and cities of the UK. The company's principal aim is to 'supply high quality, branded sports and leisure products to our customers at competitive prices'.

Personnel department – KerryTours

KerryTours is a tour operator based in Dublin. Three people work in the personnel department which is responsible for staff recruitment and selection, induction, training, processing wages, staff records and dealing with staff queries.

Glenmore Lodge - Aviemore

Glenmore Lodge is one of the premier mountain training centres in the world. It provides training courses for instructors in outdoor activities such as climbing, mountaineering, skiing and canoeing.

Ski instructor with young beginners

(a) In each case, identify the customers.
(b) In each case, state whether the customers are from outside or inside the organisation.

Who are external customers?

EXTERNAL CUSTOMERS are the people who buy products and services from organisations. They include people who buy a magazine from a newsagent and people who visit a theme park. One thing that they have in common is that they are all people from outside the organisation. Units 46 and 47 looked at the different types of external customers such as individuals, groups, customers with specific needs and business people. The people in the photograph are relaxing by the pool at their holiday destination. They are all external customers.

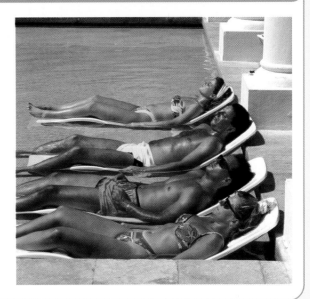

Why are external customers important?

External customers are very important because without them, organisations in the leisure and tourism industries would not exist. External customers buy the products and services which generate the revenue needed by these organisations. Most of the organisations in the leisure and tourism industries are businesses. The revenue from customers is used to meet the costs of running the business such as raw materials, wages, administration, marketing and other costs. Any money left over after these costs have been met is profit. This belongs to the owners of the business (although some tax will have to be paid). The boxes below show the revenue and profit (before tax) made by some businesses in the leisure and tourism industries in 2003 – Domino's Pizza (pizza delivery outlets), Eidos (software producer for computer games) and JD Wetherspoon (pub chain).

Domino's Pizza	Revenue	Profit
	£61.56m	£6.54m

Eidos	Revenue	Profit
	£151.5m	£17.35m

JD Wetherspoon	Revenue	Profit
	£730.9m	£56.14m

Organisations have to compete for external customers. For example, Domino's Pizza will compete with other pizza outlets such as Pizza Express and other take-away options such as Chinese, Indian and fish and chips. One way of competing is to try and provide the best service in the market.

Who are internal customers?

Many organisations in the leisure and tourism industries are large and may employ thousands of staff. For example, British Airways employs about 50,000 staff and JD Wetherspoon, 14,300. All these staff will have work colleagues who can be regarded as INTERNAL CUSTOMERS. This is because the work done by a member of staff is often for a work colleague. For example, an employee working in a call centre dealing with customer complaints might write a short report each week for a manager. In this case, the manager is an internal customer of the employee. It is important that the report is completed on time and gives the manager the information that is required.

Many large organisations are divided into departments such as marketing, finance and personnel. When dealing with people in another department, it is common to treat them like customers, i.e. to give them a good service. In smaller organisations where there are perhaps just three or four staff, work colleagues are still regarded as internal customers. This is because they will often do work for each other.

Work colleagues – internal customers

Why are internal customers important?

Although internal customers do not provide an organisation with money, they are still very important. An organisation would not function properly if employees did not do their jobs well. This involves working effectively with internal customers and providing them with the same high quality of service that they would for external customers. Many organisations use TEAM WORKING where staff are organised into small groups and take responsibility for a particular section of work. For example, a tour operator might have a team of 10 reps working at a particular holiday destination. The advantages of team working are that staff are more likely to help and support each other, come up with more ideas, operate flexibly and develop a team spirit. Teams might also plan their own work schedules, choose the way they work and solve problems. But sometimes there can be conflict between team members and they may not enjoy the extra responsibility given to them.

Part of a Eurocamp rep team

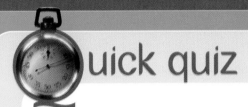

uick quiz

1 **True or false?**

- Internal customers buy products from an organisation.
- External customers are work colleagues.
- Stelios Haji-Ioannou, the owner of easyJet, is an example of an internal customer.

2 Which of these is an example of an external customer?
(a) A Tour rep
(b) A Park ranger
(c) A teenager buying a computer game from Blockbuster
(d) Swimming pool attendant

3 Which of these is an example of an internal customer?
(a) A hotel receptionist
(b) A hotel resident
(c) A visitor to Windsor Castle
(d) A couple enjoying a bar meal in a hotel

4 Which of these is **not** an example of an internal customer for a leisure centre?
(a) An aerobics instructor
(b) A badminton player
(c) The centre manager
(d) A lifeguard

5 State three advantages of team working.

Portfolio practice

Yates Group PLC

Yates Group PLC owns two pub chains - Yates and Ha! Ha! In 2003, the group employed 4,084 staff. It has spent a lot of money in recent years improving customer facilities. For example, 47 of its outlets have been converted into a new modern format. Most have benefited from the installation of Yates's TV, a multi-media entertainment package. It broadcasts a range of music videos and music CDs supported by eye-catching promotional activity and 'lifestyle' videos. It also allows lighting effects, music style, tempo and volume to track the varying numbers and types of customer at different times of the day.

Figure 1 *Yates's revenue*

£ million

Year	Revenue
1999	~120
2000	~144
2001	~156
2002	~162
2003	~154

1. How has Yates's revenue changed in recent years? *(2 marks)*
2. How does Yates's cater for different types of customers during the day? *(3 marks)*
3. (a) Using examples from the case, explain the difference between external and internal customers. *(4 marks)*
   (b) How many internal customers does Yates's have? *(1 mark)*
4. Explain the importance to Yates's of external and internal customers. *(7 marks)*

---

key terms

External customers – people who buy goods and services from organisations.
Internal customers – work colleagues.
Team working – employees working in groups with a common aim.

Getting started...

Organisations provide good quality customer service to help satisfy the needs and wants of external customers. But the organisations themselves will also benefit if they provide excellent customer service. Look at the benefits in the cases below.

Godiva Travel Ltd

Godiva Travel Ltd is a small travel agent in Coventry. In recent years, the owner, Ivan Lukic, has been worried about the decline in sales. He was fairly sure that the quality of customer service his staff was giving was not up to scratch. So in 2003, he sent all six of them on a three-day training course in order to improve their customer service skills.

Figure 1 *Godiva Travel sales*

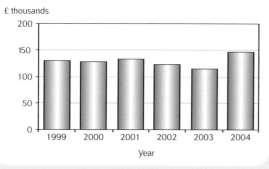

£ thousands

The Koh I Noor

The Koh I Noor, a value-for-money Indian restaurant, was opened near Leeds University in 2003. Its aim was to provide wholesome and inexpensive food for the student market. Within two weeks of opening, everybody in the student bar was talking about it. Sometimes, during the busy lunch-time period, people queued outside for a table. People liked the atmosphere and student-friendly service.

Corrington Library

Corrington Library was on the verge of closure. It had a poor image and local people said it was dull and unfriendly. When the local council appointed a new Head Librarian to manage the library, she was given strict instructions to improve its image. She did this by training staff in good customer service, putting up attractive posters, developing a new children's section, buying some computers to provide Internet access, starting a book club and opening a crèche. Twelve months later, an article appeared in the local newspaper praising the library's new image.

(a) How are the organisations in each of the above cases benefiting from good customer service?
(b) Which of the above organisations is likely to want to make a profit?

Benefits of customer service

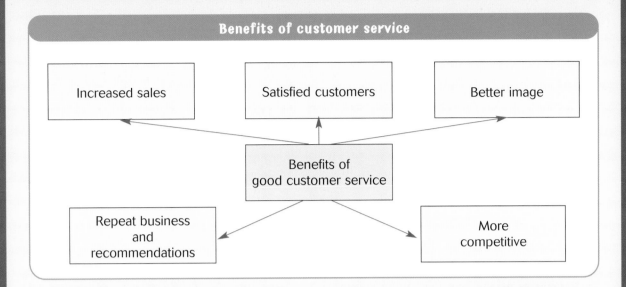

Increased sales

Satisfied customers

Better image

Benefits of good customer service

Repeat business and recommendations

More competitive

Satisfied customers

Organisations in the leisure and tourism industries provide products and services to satisfy the needs and wants of customers. Organisations may be able to meet their aim of making a profit if they satisfy customers. Customers are likely to be satisfied if:

- ✪ they are sold the correct product
- ✪ they are charged a fair price
- ✪ they are made to feel welcome and comfortable
- ✪ they are treated as special individuals
- ✪ their expectations are fulfilled.

Many organisations go out of their way to satisfy customers by trying to exceed their expectations. Look at the case below.

Muffin Break

Muffin Break, one of Australia's leading retailers of muffins and gourmet espresso coffee, is opening new shops in the UK. The company is committed to making customer service a priority. One of the directors, Hugh McCulloch says, 'Australian companies are famous for their hospitality and customer service, so we have an advantage, but we work very hard to live up to that reputation. If a customer walks into one of our shops at 6pm, just as it is about to close, they will be served. We do run loyalty schemes and special offers, but what really attracts and keeps customers is good service.'

Increased sales

If organisations provide good customer service they are likely to benefit financially. This means that they will get more customers and more sales. Most organisations in the leisure and tourism industries are businesses and they need sales revenue to survive and make a profit.

For example, by providing good customer service, a travel agent can increase sales revenue. If a family books a holiday and the sales assistant meets all their needs and makes them feel comfortable, they may be persuaded to buy other products from the same agent. For example, they may buy travel insurance, foreign currency and excursions.

The quality of customer service can make all the difference to a customer's experience. People like to be treated with respect by friendly staff and made to feel comfortable. Organisations that can provide customers with this sort of service will tend to get more sales.

Repeat business and recommendations

Market research suggests that it costs six times more to attract a new customer than it does to keep an existing one. To attract new customers, organisations have to spend money on market research, advertising and promotion, for example. To avoid or reduce these costs, many organisations provide excellent customer service in the hope that customers will remain loyal and come back again. The return of previous customers is called REPEAT BUSINESS.

Organisations also hope that by providing excellent customer service they will be recommended to the customer's friends and relatives. This is important because when people buy products they often ask friends or relatives for advice.

Organisations must also remember that if they give a poor service, people will tell their friends and relatives and they could lose potential customers.

Customer charters

Many organisations produce a CUSTOMER CHARTER. This tells a customer what sort of service can be expected from an organisation. For example, TSO, the online booking shop, has a customer charter. It covers such areas as the security of purchasing online, delivery charges, despatch, damaged goods, goods lost in transit, cancellations and complaints.

An extract from TSO's customer charter

Despatch

- We aim to despatch every order as quickly as possible.
- If we receive your order before 12pm and the item is in stock, we aim to despatch that day.
- If we receive an order after 12pm we still aim to despatch on the same day but, if this is not possible, on the following day.
- For items that are not in stock, we will notify you, ask if you wish to place an order and despatch the item as soon as we receive it.

Customer charters help to clarify customers' rights and provide guidelines for staff when providing customer service.

A better public image

Organisations are concerned about their reputation or image. Image can be improved by showing responsibility to various groups such as employees, customers, suppliers and the local community. If an organisation has a good public image this may reassure customers and encourage them to buy its products. An organisation's image will be improved if it provides excellent customer service. However, other ways are used to promote a positive image. Examples include:

- making donations to local charities
- sponsoring local sports teams and local events
- using effective public relations
- providing quality training and good working conditions for staff
- caring for the environment by using recycled materials, for example.

An edge over the competition

Organisations in the leisure and tourism industries compete with each other in a number of ways. For example, they charge different prices, use different advertising and promotion techniques and sell different types of products. Another way is to provide excellent customer care. This is becoming increasingly important. People are influenced by the quality of customer care and will prefer to buy products from organisations that meet their needs and exceed their expectations. Providing good customer service is particularly important when the prices and types of goods are the same, or very similar, to those of competitors.

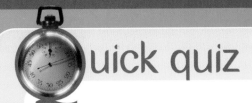

Quick quiz

1 **True or false?**
- ✿ It costs about six times more to keep a customer than it does to attract a new one.
- ✿ Advertising is one of the costs incurred when attracting new customers.
- ✿ It is cheap to rely on recommendations to gain new customers.

2 State three features that will make customers satisfied.

3 Why is customer service important to two travel agents selling exactly the same package holiday for exactly the same price?

4 In addition to providing excellent customer service, state two other ways in which an organisation can improve its image.

5 Organisations that provide good customer service are likely to benefit financially. What does this mean?

Portfolio practice

RAF Museum Customer Charter

A Lancaster bomber at the RAF Museum

The Royal Air Force Museum in Hendon is situated on the historic site of the original London Aerodrome. It is Britain's only national air museum dedicated to aviation and has over 200 aircraft. The collection includes some very early airplane designs and war planes such as the legendary Battle of Britain Spitfire airplanes and the Lancaster Bombers of World War II. It also has some of the latest modern jets and military aircraft. It is funded mainly by the RAF but also gets revenue from its souvenir shop, conferencing facilities and donations. The museum takes customer care seriously and has a customer charter. An extract is shown below.

1. Using this case as an example, explain what is meant by a customer charter. *(2 marks)*

2. State three guarantees that the RAF Museum makes in its charter. *(3 marks)*

3. Explain how the RAF Museum might benefit from having a customer charter. *(4 marks)*

4. Explain three benefits to the RAF Museum of good customer care. *(7 marks)*

Customer Care Policy (extract)
- The Museum will be open for 100% of the advertised opening hours.
- Telephone calls to the Museum switchboard will always be answered in person by a member of staff.
- Responses to business letters, faxes and emails and offers of donations will normally be within five working days.
- Enquiries about the collection and matters requiring research will normally be replied to within 20 working days.
- Complaints will be given the highest priority for investigation and written response.
- All areas accessible to the public will be maintained in a clean, presentable and safe condition at all times. Toilet facilities will be inspected regularly. Advice is given to the public on how to bring to notice matters requiring attention.

key terms

Customer charter – a list of promises or guarantees made to customers about the quality of customer services.
Repeat business – customers who return to buy more products.

Getting started...

Providing excellent customer service benefits an organisation in various ways. For example, external customers will be satisfied and more customers will be gained through repeat business and recommendations. The organisation will also benefit from increased sales, a better image and by being able to compete against its rivals. But there are also benefits if internal customers receive excellent service. Look at the internal customers below.

Gina Loria

Gina works for an airline company as a member of the cabin crew. She has spent the last twelve months on long haul flights between Manchester and Thailand. Since working with a new team, she has been more motivated. The support, encouragement and quality of service from her work colleagues has meant that Gina is much more satisfied in her job.

Li Ming Wu

Li Ming has worked for the Royal Hotel in Reading for two months. The hotel employs 130 staff and Li Ming reckons that this is the best place she has ever worked. She says that her work colleagues, supervisors and the manager all treat her with respect. She is delighted to be employed in such a pleasant environment.

Mike Whitehouse

Mike works for a large tour company and has just been promoted from Team Leader to Area Manager. In his farewell speech, he thanked his work colleagues for helping him in his achievement. He said that the quality of service from his team members was second to none and that he could not have won promotion without their hard work and support. Mike has a good reputation for giving high quality service to his internal customers.

(a) Describe the benefits of good quality customer service to each of the internal customers above.

(b) Describe the benefits of good quality internal customer service to each of the companies above.

The needs of internal customers

People go to work to satisfy certain needs such as:

- ☼ money to live on
- ☼ security and protection
- ☼ friendship and a feeling of belonging
- ☼ respect, recognition and status
- ☼ a chance to fulfil their potential.

These needs can be satisfied in the workplace. For example, people are paid so that they can buy food, clothes and somewhere to live. They will also make friends and perhaps work in a team where they will have a sense of belonging. The quality of service people receive from their work colleagues can also help to satisfy these needs. For example, a manager might praise an employee for doing a good job. The employee will regard this as recognition and respect. If the needs of internal customers are met, they will be happier in their jobs and this will help the organisation to satisfy the needs of its external customers more effectively.

How might workers provide a good service to internal customers?

Workers can provide a good service to internal customers by:

- ☼ completing work tasks to the best of their ability
- ☼ completing work tasks on time
- ☼ communicating information effectively
- ☼ being courteous to colleagues
- ☼ helping a colleague who is having difficulties
- ☼ covering for absent colleagues
- ☼ being open and honest.

What are the benefits of satisfying internal customers?

A more pleasant place to work

One of the main benefits of providing internal customers with excellent service is that the workplace environment will be more pleasant. A good working atmosphere, where people respect each other and are courteous to colleagues, will be appreciated by everyone. It will help to reduce stress, avoid arguments and improve everyone's working conditions. A pleasant working environment will also help people to make friends. This is one of the needs of internal customers mentioned above. Finally, it is also likely to benefit external customers because they often find themselves in other people's workplaces – for example, hotels, visitor attractions and holiday resorts.

A happier and more efficient workforce

If people are happy at work as a result of receiving excellent customer service from their colleagues, they are likely to be more efficient in the way that they do their jobs. For example, if a waiter in a restaurant has a good working relationship with the people in the kitchen, the restaurant manager, bar staff and other waiting staff, the restaurant will run more efficiently. Communication will be better, the correct orders will be placed, prompt service will be given, the food will be served hot and the atmosphere in the dining area will be relaxed and friendly. As a result, external customers will receive a better all-round service.

Customers enjoying a meal in a pleasant restaurant

Improved job satisfaction

It is important that people have JOB SATISFACTION. This is the extent to which a job provides an employee with satisfaction and fulfilment. Many people believe that job satisfaction is one of the things that motivates people at work. If people are well motivated, they will work more effectively.

People may get job satisfaction if:

- ✪ their work is interesting
- ✪ their work is challenging
- ✪ they are valued at work
- ✪ they are trained properly
- ✪ they have good managers
- ✪ they enjoy good working relationships with their colleagues.

Providing excellent service to internal customers also improves job satisfaction. This is because staff will be treated with respect, will be valued and will enjoy good working relationships. Again, people who have job satisfaction are likely to provide external customers with a good standard of service.

Improved chances of promotion

Most people working for an organisation hope to get promoted. This means that they will get a better job with increased responsibility and more pay. To earn promotion, workers have to show that they are good at their jobs. This involves providing excellent service to internal customers. For example, a manager might recommend one of her team for promotion after receiving several years of excellent service from that team member.

Many employees receive a formal APPRAISAL at work. This means that their performance is reviewed, evaluated and recorded. Details of the appraisal, part of which is likely to focus on internal customer service, may be taken into account when people are being considered for promotion. The chance of getting promotion in the future helps to motivate staff. This means that they will work harder and external customers will also benefit.

Quick quiz

1 **True or false?**

- An advantage of written communication is that it can be presented attractively to create a good impression.

- Body language cannot be used when communicating on the telephone.

- Call centres are used for face-to-face communication.

2 Which of these is **not** an example of electronic communication?
(a) Fax machine (b) Email (c) Letter (d) Pager device

3 Which method of communication would be used by a tour rep to contact a team leader in an emergency? (a) Mobile phone (b) Letter (c) The Internet (d) Fax machine

4 State two advantages of face-to-face communication.

5 State one disadvantage of written communication.

Portfolio practice

Yarnton Cars

Yarnton Cars is a successful car hire company. It specialises in leasing performance cars and also provides a limousine service for parties, stag-nights, hen-nights and special trips. Desislav works in the main office dealing with customers when they collect and return cars. He also takes bookings on the telephone.
One morning, he is asked by his boss to carry out the following communication tasks.

1. Explain to a new employee how to process a booking.

2. Confirm with a customer 15 miles away that the limousine she ordered for that evening would arrive at 8.30 and not 8.45.

2. Inform a customer that the company cannot take responsibility for property left in one of the cars.

1. Using an example from the case, explain what is meant by communication. *(2 marks)*
2. State three ways in which information can be sent electronically. *(3 marks)*
3. Which method of communication is most likely to be used for the tasks described above? *(3 marks)*
4. Explain why you have chosen the methods in question 3. *(9 marks)*

---

key terms

Call centre – a large office where employees, equipped with a telephone and a computer, deal with telephone calls from customers.
Communication – passing information from a sender to a receiver.

Getting started...

The methods used by staff when communicating with customers require certain skills. Staff can give better customer service if they have developed and practised these skills. To be a good communicator, a range of communication skills have to be learnt. Look at the communication skills being used in the cases below.

Sonia Choo

Sonia works for a travel agent. A customer has returned from holiday and has had a particularly bad time. She and her family got sunstroke and spent five days recovering. The travel agent is not to blame but Sonia must treat the customer sympathetically. She sits and listens to her for 20 minutes.

Chuck Clinton

Chuck is a rep for a tour operator specialising in holidays to Africa. He is based in the Gambia at the moment. One of his jobs is to brief new groups of holiday-makers when they arrive. He tells them about the local people and their customs and gives information about health and safety.

Karen Petit

Karen has just got a job at a call centre working for a travel insurance company. She is on a training course learning how to speak to customers on the telephone. When she starts work, all her calls will be recorded so that her telephone performance can be evaluated.

Jack O'Connelly

Jack spends a lot of his time at work writing to customers. He deals with complaints at a theme park. Many of the complaints are about the length of time people have to queue for the rides. Jack always writes a personal letter to the customer apologising on behalf of the company.

(a) What communication skills are being used in each of the above cases?
(b) Which of these skills is probably the most difficult?

Communication skills

In leisure and tourism, different communication skills will be required depending on what sort of job an employee does. These skills might include talking to groups, listening, asking questions, talking on the telephone, writing, and speaking face-to-face. When communicating with customers, it is necessary to use appropriate:

- language
- pitch and tone of voice
- pauses and silences
- body language.

Language

More formal language is needed when talking to customers because the employee does not usually know them personally. However, in some cases informal language is acceptable – when talking to regular and familiar customers, for example. It may also be necessary to adjust the language level – when talking to children, for example. These tips might be helpful.

Do not use:

- swear words or slang
- jargon (language used only in the industry)
- colloquialisms (language used only in the locality)
- bland statements.

Do:

- use simple and clear language
- speak professionally and courteously
- use people's surnames when addressing them.

Pitch and tone of voice

It is possible to make an impression by varying the tone and pitch of the voice. To make a good impression, the voice must sound positive and interesting. This can be done by speaking in a cheerful and enthusiastic way. The voice should put the customer at ease. Customers will have a bad impression if the voice sounds tired, bored, uninterested, aggressive, impatient or nervous. Using a flat, monotonous voice should be avoided.

Pauses and silences

To keep the customer's attention, pauses and silences should be used in the right places. This gives customers the chance to think about the information being provided and to ask questions. It also gives the employee time to think about what to say next.

Body language

More than 50% of face-to-face communication is done with body language. This is because sight is a more developed sense than hearing. It is possible to show emotions such as pleasure, enthusiasm, anger, surprise, disgust and fear without saying a single word.

Facial expressions such as smiles, frowns, eye, eyebrow and lip movements, and eye contact can be used to show how we feel. For example, raised eyebrows can be used to express surprise or anger.

Gestures such as nodding, or finger, hand, arm and shoulder movements, can be used to get messages across. For example, a thumbs-up gesture tells someone that things are OK. Folded arms usually suggest that a person is not interested.

Posture is to do with body positions and how close one person gets to another. Most people have invisible boundaries which must not be crossed. Getting too close to someone is often a sign of over-familiarity or aggression. Body language can be **open**, which shows that you are relaxed, confident, interested and friendly. If it is **closed**, it shows that you are uninterested, ill at ease, unfriendly or even hostile. Giving good customer service involves being able to use and read body language.

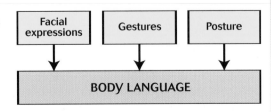

Talking to groups

Some jobs in leisure and tourism require employees to talk to groups. Tour reps, guides and managers, for example. Most people find this form of communication difficult and stressful. Some tips might be:

- always plan what you are going to say
- use some brief notes
- use visual aids to direct attention away from yourself
- be prepared for questions
- look at all members of the group
- remember to speak slightly louder than usual.

Writing skills

Written communication might involve using letters, emails, memos or preparing reports. It should be presented formally with no errors. Letters to customers that contain spelling mistakes, poor grammar and inappropriate language can give a bad and lasting impression. Word processors can be used which help to improve presentation, layout and accuracy. Inexperienced employees may get a colleague to check written communications before sending them out.

Listening and responding to customers

It is easy to underestimate the importance of listening skills. Employees have to be interested and attentive when customers are talking. If customers think that employees are not listening, this gives a bad impression. It is unprofessional and rude. Good listening skills involve:

- maintaining eye contact all the time
- concentrating on what is being said
- avoiding distractions
- not interrupting
- using pauses to make a meaningful contribution
- being ready with a response when the customer has finished speaking.

Customer needs can be satisfied more effectively if employees listen to what they are saying.

Telephone skills

When communicating over the telephone, body language cannot be used. This means that the tone and pitch of the voice becomes much more important. Good telephone technique involves:

- answering the phone promptly
- greeting the caller and giving the name of the organisation followed by your name
- locating the correct person quickly if the call is for someone else
- speaking clearly (do not eat or chew food)
- paying attention and keeping the voice interesting and enthusiastic
- making brief notes when the information is lengthy or important.

Working accurately

When communicating information to customers, it must be done accurately. Giving inaccurate information could easily lose a customer. For example, what might happen if you told a customer that the price of a holiday was £999, when in fact it was $999?

Asking appropriate questions

To provide excellent customer service, it is important to find out exactly what customers want. This might involve asking appropriate questions which customers understand. A combination of open and closed questions can be used. Open questions give customers the chance to say more. They can be used to get more detailed information and make the customer feel important. Closed questions require a simple 'yes' or 'no' answer. They are used to get simple information very quickly. They can also be used to eliminate options. Questions should be asked in a polite manner. It should not sound as though customers are being interviewed or cross-examined because this can be an unpleasant experience.

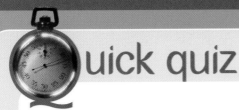

Quick quiz

1 **True or false?**
   - Body language is more important than words used when communicating face-to-face.
   - Using a flat, monotonous voice will capture the customer's interest.
   - Avoiding eye contact and nervous fidgeting would be an example of open body language.

2 Which of these is **not** a type of body language?
   (a) Gesturing (b) Shouting (c) Facial expression (d) Posture

3 Which of these is an open question?
   (a) How can I help you? (b) Did you have a pleasant flight?
   (c) Would you like ice in your drink? (d) Would you like to fly first class?

4 Which of the following is **not** a gesture?
   (a) Waving (b) Raising eyebrows (c) Handshake (d) Nodding

5 State three tips that might be given to someone talking to a group.

Portfolio practice

The Hertford Fitness Club

Malcolm Wright was disciplined by his manager for giving poor customer service. He is pictured here dealing with a customer, Maureen Casey, who wants to change her membership status. The change requires quite a bit of paperwork and Malcolm's shift was due to finish at 5.00pm. The customer complained to the manager later that evening about Malcolm's attitude.

   The next day the manager sent a letter to the customer making a formal apology on behalf of the club and offering the customer a £20 voucher to spend in the club shop.

1. Why is body language so important when communicating face-to-face? *(2 marks)*
2. Give three tips on appropriate language when communicating. *(3 marks)*
3. Use this case as an example to explain the difference between open and closed body language. *(4 marks)*
4. Write a letter to the customer apologising on behalf of the club. *(7 marks)*

Getting started...

When working in customer services, it is important to look presentable. Appearance is important because one of the first things that customers see when they go into any organisation is the 'front line' staff. Appropriate dress does not always involve wearing a suit and tie so, for example, a diving instructor teaching a class how to scuba dive might wear specialised diving clothing. Look at the staff in the cases below.

Simone Dupont

Simone works on the reception desk for a large hotel in London. Her job involves:

- ✪ dealing with telephone enquiries
- ✪ taking bookings
- ✪ assisting guests when they check-in
- ✪ settling accounts when guests leave.

Bert Moss

Bert works for an adventure centre in Wales. He takes groups of youths trekking and camping in the Welsh Mountains.

Andrea Miles

Andrea Miles is an experienced member of the customer service team at a large airport. She has worked at the airport for 15 years and enjoys giving good customer service to passengers. Andrea is particularly good at dealing with children who have got lost from their parents.

Susan Blanchflower

Susan is a swimming instructor at a large leisure centre in Birmingham. Most of her work involves teaching people how to swim. When she does not have any classes, she sometimes helps out on reception.

(a) Which of the above employees are likely to dress smartly? Explain why.
(b) Which of the above staff are likely to be issued with a uniform?

Dress

Organisations in the leisure and tourism industries want to impress customers and one way of doing this is to ensure that their employees look good. Customers make judgments about organisations when they see their staff, so employees have to dress in a way that fits in with the image of the organisation. Some organisations such as airlines, travel agents and leisure centres, issue their staff with corporate uniforms. This helps:

British Midland cabin crew

- ✪ customers to recognise employees in an organisation

- ✪ the organisation to present a professional image

- ✪ to give staff a sense of belonging

- ✪ to encourage staff to look smart

- ✪ to meet the cost of work clothes.

If an organisation does not issue staff with a uniform, it might have a **dress code**. This is a set of guidelines about what staff should and should not wear. If there is no dress code, employees should look smart and tidy.

Finally, some people have to wear specialised clothing. This may be to help them do their job properly or it may be required for health and safety reasons. For example, staff in leisure centres usually wear tracksuits or shorts. Or a supervisor taking a group of people white-water rafting will wear a life-jacket.

Personal hygiene

In addition to the clothes that are worn at work, an employee's appearance can depend on personal hygiene and cleanliness. What does this mean? Before going to work it is important to ensure that:

- ✪ a bath or shower is taken

- ✪ anti-perspirant deodorant is used

- ✪ teeth are cleaned (and perhaps carry some mints to freshen the breath later)

- ✪ clothes are clean and ironed

- ✪ hair is clean, neat and tidy

- ✪ fingernails are clean

- ✪ make-up is not applied too heavily.

These points are important because when giving customer service, it is possible that customers will be physically close. For example, cabin crew work in a confined space and often have to lean over people. When working in the catering industry, personal hygiene is even more important. A stricter set of guidelines is shown here.

Guidelines for food handlers

- ✪ Wash hands regularly, especially:
  - on starting work
  - after using the toilet
  - between handling raw and cooked foods
  - after breaks for eating, drinking and smoking
  - after coughing, sneezing or blowing your nose
  - after touching hair
  - after handling refuse or waste materials
  - after handling cleaning chemicals.

- ✪ Cover cuts, sores and burns with clean waterproof dressings.

- ✪ Wear clean and, where appropriate, protective clothing.

- ✪ Keep fingernails short and clean and remove all nail polish.

- ✪ Do not wear jewellery other than a plain wedding ring.

- ✪ Do not wear strong-smelling perfumes or aftershaves.

Personality

Everyone has a different personality. This means that a person has their own distinctive character traits, attitudes and habits that make them different from everyone else. If someone has a good personality, it usually means that they are fun to be with because they are friendly, outgoing, humorous, considerate and generally pleasant. Having a good personality will help an employee to provide good customer service.

Not all jobs in leisure and tourism require the same type of personality. For example, working as a tour guide in a large museum will require a different type of personality to someone working with children in a crèche.

It is important to think about the type of personality you have when deciding what job you want. There is little point in applying for a job which involves talking to groups of people if you are shy, quiet, reserved, introverted, good with IT and a creative thinker. You may be better suited to other types of work such as problem solving, office work or design.

A tour guide working with young children

Attitude and behaviour

A person's attitude and the way they behave will affect the quality of customer service given. It is a very important part of personal presentation. There is little point in an employee being smart in appearance if he is not interested in the customer. Customers are very sensitive to the attitude of staff and the way they behave.

Examples of positive behaviour

- ✪ Attending to customers immediately.
- ✪ Greeting customers with a smile.
- ✪ Showing interest in what customers say.
- ✪ Treating customers as individuals and making them feel important.
- ✪ Being patient with difficult, awkward or demanding customers.
- ✪ Making every effort to give customers exactly what they want.
- ✪ Supporting colleagues at work.

Customers can make a judgment about an employee's attitude and behaviour within seconds. Employees with a bad attitude who behave in a negative way will lose customers. An employee's own negative thoughts, feelings and troubles must not be expressed at work when dealing with customers.

Positive behaviour   Negative behaviour

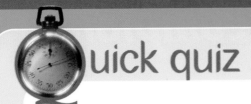

Quick quiz

1 **True or false?**
- Personality is the distinctive character traits, attitudes or habits which make a person different from everyone else.
- Customers can make a judgment about an employee's attitude and behaviour within seconds.
- A tour operator is likely to issue staff with a corporate uniform.

2 Which of these is **not** an example of positive behaviour?
(a) Greeting customers with a smile.
(b) Treating customers as individuals and making them feel important.
(c) Asking difficult or awkward customers to wait while others are served first.
(d) Making every effort to give customers exactly what they want.

3 State three things that you should do to improve your personal appearance before going to work.

4 State three reasons why an organisation might issue a corporate uniform.

5 Explain briefly why personal hygiene is important when providing customer service.

Portfolio practice

The Chiltern Animal Park

The Chiltern Animal Park is located in the Chilterns, Buckinghamshire. It is expanding and attracting an increasing number of visitors. It has a range of animals on show and visitors can interact with them under the supervision of the Park Ranger and park assistants. The Park also has a café, nature walks in the woods, a large lake for anglers and an adventure playground for young children.

The Chiltern Animal Park
Park Assistant

- Due to the expansion of this popular visitor attraction, we require another assistant.

- You should be well presented, enthusiastic, keen to learn and enjoy working with other people to provide excellent customer service.

- You will also need to enjoy working with animals. Your duties will include the cleaning and maintenance of animal areas, feeding animals and handling them in front of visitors.

- No previous experience is necessary because full training will be given. A qualification in leisure and tourism would be an advantage.

- Salary £12,000 pa.

1. Explain why no previous experience is necessary for the job advertised. *(2 marks)*
2. State three examples of positive behaviour that a park assistant might show. *(3 marks)*
3. Describe the sort of personality that might be suitable for the job advertised. *(4 marks)*
4. Explain what is meant by a dress code and suggest one for the job advertised. *(7 marks)*

54 Handling complaints

Getting started...

One of the most difficult jobs in the leisure and tourism industries is handling complaints from customers. Unfortunately, even when an organisation is totally committed to providing excellent customer service, things can go wrong. For example, bad weather might prevent ferries from crossing the English Channel. This might result in complaints from passengers whose journeys are delayed. Look at the complaints below.

Jason Dodds

Jason bought a squash racquet from a sports shop. After using it three times, some of the strings snapped. This meant that it was totally useless.

Kelly Jones

Kelly's train from Southport to Liverpool stopped at Formby and passengers were asked to get off. She needed to get  a connection at Liverpool to take her on to Birmingham but there was no information about what was going to happen next. To make sure that she caught her connection, she had to take a taxi from Formby to Liverpool which cost her £20. When she got home, she filled in a complaints form.

Mr and Mrs Jakamarra

Mr Jakamarra had promised his wife that they would celebrate their 25th wedding anniversary in a posh hotel in London. When they were shown to their room, it was obvious  that the previous occupants were smokers. The room reeked of stale cigarette smoke.

The Wheeler family

The Wheeler family went on the holiday of a lifetime to New Zealand. They spent £250 on a helicopter trip for the four of them to see whales off the coast of  Kaikoura. Unfortunately, much to the disappointment of the two children, there were no whales to be seen. Mr and Mrs Wheeler wanted their money back!

How might the organisations in the above cases have dealt with the complaints?

Complaints

Generally, working with customers in the leisure and tourism industries is a pleasant and rewarding experience. This is because customers are out to have a good time and will be in a happy and positive frame of mind. But when things go wrong employees have to be prepared. What might customers complain about?

- **Queueing** This is a common problem. People get irritated when they have to queue for rides at a theme park, getting into sports stadiums and buying tickets for a train, for example.

- **Faulty goods** If products such as sports equipment, electrical goods and sportswear are faulty or do not live up to expectations, customers may wish to return them.

- **Poor customer service** If people feel that an organisation's employees have a poor attitude, behave badly or take no interest in them, they are likely to be upset. Waiting to be served when an employee has already noticed you waiting, is particularly irritating.

- **Delays** Unfortunately delays are quite common particularly when waiting for flights or trains. Some flights can be delayed for many hours, or even days.

- **Broken promises** When a service does not live up to expectations, customers get annoyed. This is especially so when promotional materials have built up the customer's expectations.

- **Overbooking** This is where there are not enough places for all the people that have booked. For example, on an aircraft or at an hotel.

Handling complaints

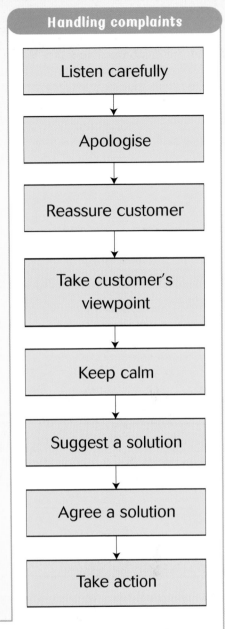

Listen carefully

Apologise

Reassure customer

Take customer's viewpoint

Keep calm

Suggest a solution

Agree a solution

Take action

Handling complaints requires staff to be composed and sympathetic. Handling face-to-face complaints can be particularly difficult if customers become angry or abusive. Staff are likely to get training in handling complaints. Organisations may also have a set of guidelines or procedures for handling complaints. One approach might be to follow the procedure shown in the diagram above.

Listen carefully to the customer

It is important to get an accurate account of the complaint. All the information relating to a complaint must be understood clearly. Staff must use their body language and other communication skills to show that they are concerned and sympathetic. It is important to be positive and attentive.

Apologise for any inconvenience caused

One way to diffuse the situation when a customer complains is to apologise. However, it is not a good idea to accept liability immediately. This means that an employee should not accept blame for the problem. It is still possible to apologise by saying something fairly general like, 'I'm very sorry that you have been inconvenienced'.

Handling complaints

Let the customer know that the matter will be dealt with
Customers will be reassured if they are told that a complaint will be dealt with. Customers often think that they will face a battle when they complain but if they are told that something will be done straight away, it will reduce their anxiety or anger.

Try to see the problem from the customer's point of view
It may be easier to deal with a complaint if employees can put themselves in the customer's place. How would you feel if you had been waiting in a sticky, humid airport for 12 hours for a flight with very little information about when it would leave? Doing this will help to deal with the customer more sympathetically.

Keep calm and do not argue with the customer
Keeping calm is crucial when dealing with customer complaints. Arguing with dissatisfied and angry customers is a negative way of dealing with the problem. It is important for an employee not to raise their voice or annoy the customer. From a customer services point of view,

THE CUSTOMER IS ALWAYS RIGHT.

Find a solution to the problem
Ideally, a member of staff should find a solution to a complaint. For example, if a customer complains to a waiter that a meal is cold, the waiter can apologise and replace the meal. However, an employee may not have the authority to find a solution. In this case, the complaint may have to be referred to a senior member of staff. It is not a weakness to get help from a colleague.

Agree a solution with the customer
To deal with a complaint satisfactorily, the customer must agree to the proposed solution. The customer must go away feeling satisfied or they will not return. They may also tell their friends and relatives about the poor service they have experienced.

Make sure that what you promised to do actually gets done
Handling a complaint is not complete until the action agreed with the customer has been taken. If a promise is made to do something at a later date, it must be done. If complaints are dealt with effectively, customers will often be impressed and tell their friends.

Recording and evaluating complaints

Many organisations keep a record of complaints. Staff might enter them in a book, for example. These records can be used to identify the causes of problems and help to improve the quality of customer service in future. Organisations that do not evaluate complaints are unlikely to improve their service to customers. Travelcare is one of a minority of organisations that publishes details of complaints.

How Travelcare performed

During 2003, Travelcare received complaints affecting 1,671 passengers (0.23% of its passengers). Travelcare believes that staff training is the best way to reduce the number of complaints. It also carries out regular quality checks at its branches and has an award scheme that rewards staff for providing exceptional customer service.

Table 1 *Main causes of complaint against Travelcare*

Quality of information	24%
Branch administration	24%
Insurance	13%
Staff service	8%
Co-op dividend/Tesco Clubcard points	4%
Travel money	3%
Meeting customer needs	2%
Low deposit schemes	1%

Source: adapted from the Holiday Report 2004

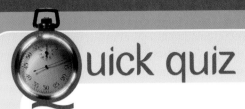

Quick quiz

1 **True or false?**
  - Complaints will not occur if organisations are committed to providing excellent customer service.
  - Complaints are only dealt with by senior employees.
  - Staff should never argue with customers who complain.

2 According to Travelcare, what is the best way to reduce complaints?
  (a) Higher compensation **(b)** Better brochures **(c)** Better staff training
  (d) Improved communications

3 Which of these is **not** a common complaint? **(a)** Overbooking **(b)** Faulty goods
  (c) Poor communications **(d)** Poor customer service

4 What is the first step when handling a complaint? **(a)** Defend the organisation
  (b) Keep calm **(c)** Listen carefully **(d)** Agree a solution

5 What are the main causes of complaint at Travelcare?

Portfolio practice

The White Hart Hotel

Wayne Tomlinson works on reception at the White Hart Hotel. One Saturday night, 45 of the hotel's 50 rooms were booked by guests who were attending a big wedding party. At 12.30 am, Wayne received an internal telephone call from a customer who was not one of the wedding party guests. The details are shown here.

Wayne:	Good morning. Reception. Wayne speaking. How can I help you?
Guest:	I've been kept awake by loud music since 11.00pm. This is the third time I've rung and its getting louder. I'm sick to death of it.
Wayne:	Oh, I'm sorry to hear that Mr Roberts. I spoke to you earlier. The problem is that the wedding party isn't due to finish until 2.00am.
Guest:	That's no good to me. I'm here for a quiet night before going to work tomorrow.
Wayne:	Well I'm not sure I can do anything. The party is booked until 2.00am.
Guest:	I want to speak to the manager.
Wayne:	She won't be in until 7.30am, Sir.
Guest:	Well what are YOU going to do about it then?
Wayne:	Well I can hardly tell the wedding party to stop can I?
Guest:	Well you can *** **?//**??

1. State two advantages of dealing with customer complaints effectively. *(2 marks)*
3. How might the manager deal with the complaint the next day? *(3 marks)*
3. How might the hotel avoid this sort of problem in the future? *(3 marks)*
4. Evaluate Wayne's performance when dealing with the complaint. *(7 marks)*

Getting started...

Many organisations keep information about their customers. Some of the information is very basic. For example, an online travel agent selling a flight may require the name, address, telephone number, credit card details and email address of a customer. This helps them to provide better customer service. Look at the records kept by the organisations below.

The Glades Hotel

The Glades Hotel is in Dorset. Most of its guests are holiday-makers who come to enjoy the attractive coastline, which is a Natural World Heritage site, and other visitor attractions such as Corfe Castle. When guests arrive, information is collected using the form shown here. It is used mainly for security reasons.

The Glades Hotel – Registration Form

Surname: .... Forename: ....

Address: .... Passport No ....

.... Car Reg: ....

.... Arrival date: ....

Post Code: .... Departure date: ....

Tel. No: .... Room No: ....

Method of payment: (please circle)

1	2	3	4	5	6
Cheque	Cash	Visa	Mastercard	Debit card	Other

Signed: ....

Cannon Green Golf Club

Cannon Green Golf Club keeps records of its membership on a computer database. The information is fairly basic. It is used mainly as a mailing list to send out information about golf tournaments, social functions and other club information.

Surname	Forename	DOB	Address	Postcode	M'ship No.	M'ship status
Adams	Patricia	12.4.78	34 Weston Avenue	BR4 6HH	AP 2377	FULL
Berry	Robert	31.3.64	The Hollows, Denworth	BR9 3DT	BR 2110	FULL
Berry	Janet	2.3.66	The Hollows, Denworth	BR9 3DT	BR 2111	SOCIAL
Collier	Adam	12.3.54	23 Brent Street	BR2 4RT	CA 4199	MID-WEEK
Crawford	Robert	23.7.71	111 Carlton Close	BR4 8HP	CR 2390	FULL
Court	Ellen	12.6.48	87 Bristol Rd	BR3 8GT	CE 1446	FULL

(a) Describe briefly why the Glades Hotel uses a Registration Form.
(b) Why does the Cannon Green Golf Club only keep basic records of its members?

Administration

Like all organisations, those in the leisure and tourism industries have to carry out administrative tasks. Administration is concerned with the paperwork in an organisation. Administrative tasks might include:

- Sorting incoming and outgoing mail, fax and email.
- Filing documents such as invoices or letters from customers.
- Updating records when new information is obtained.
- Sending letters – for example, responding to enquiries.
- Processing information such as bookings.

Some organisations might have a separate office or department where administrative staff all work together. However, many organisations will expect staff to carry out their own administrative work. For example, a travel consultant may have to process information, update records, send out letters and deal with enquiries.

Why are customer records kept?

Generally, organisations keep customer records to help them provide a better customer service. Records may be kept to:

- **Improve communications** If their telephone number is held on record, customers can be notified immediately if there is a change to their holiday itinerary.

- **Help provide the right product** A fitness club can design the appropriate fitness programme if it has information about a client's health, diet and physical condition.

- **Arrange payment for services** A tennis club might keep a member's bank details so that funds can be taken each year to pay the membership fees.

- **Send out marketing information** An hotel might send out details of a special offer to previous guests.

- **Meet health & safety regulations** A ferry operator must keep a record of all the passengers in case there is an accident.

- **Help an organisation plan ahead** An hotel will need to know how long its guests are staying so that it can take future bookings.

- **Evaluate performance** Details of visitor numbers, complaints or accidents can help evaluate performance.

Organisations also keep records on their employees – internal customers. Contact details, employment history, appraisal sheets, bank details, National Insurance Number and attendance record, are some examples.

What records might be kept?

Nearly all organisations will keep basic information such as the customer's:

- full name
- address
- postcode
- home telephone number
- email address.

This information allows an organisation to communicate with its customers.

Depending on the type of organisation, other information might be required such as:

- bank details
- credit card details
- occupation
- name of employer
- work telephone number
- medical history
- criminal record (when applying for visas)
- passport number
- car registration number
- driving licence number
- National Insurance Number
- customer's signature.

Some of this information is very personal and should only be collected if absolutely necessary. Sometimes, organisations ask customers to volunteer other information which might be used for marketing purposes.

Creating customer records

Organisations will have their own systems for keeping customer records. Staff will be trained how to create customer records using the system.

Paper-based records Many organisations keep customer records in an envelope file, for example. This file is likely to include copies of booking forms containing customer details, correspondence and payment records and invoices.

Computer databases Increasingly, customer records are kept on a computer, perhaps on a database using a spreadsheet. It is much easier and quicker to process, store, retrieve and change data on a computer. Customers may well get a better service when data is held on a computer.

Using a customer database

Accuracy and confidentiality

The customer records kept by organisations must be accurate. Inaccurate records could lead to mistakes and loss of customers. For example, if a customer's telephone number is wrong, there could be a breakdown in communication and the organisation may not be able to notify a customer of an important change.

Customer records are confidential. This means that personal information should not be passed on to anyone else. Customers are likely to be offended if they discover that, for example, junior members of staff are aware of their personal details. Customer records should be kept in a secure place to help protect confidentiality.

Data protection

Organisations that keep records of customer information must comply with the DATA PROTECTION ACT 1998 which is designed to protect customers from the misuse of their personal data. Under the Act, organisations keeping personal data must:

- obtain and process it fairly and lawfully
- hold it for specified and lawful purposes
- not disclose it to others or misuse it
- not hold more data than necessary
- keep it accurate and up to date
- not keep it longer than needed
- allow customers access to it
- correct and erase it when appropriate
- take security measures to keep it safe.

Finding and changing existing records

Customer records need to be updated when their circumstances change. For example, they may move house, change credit cards, get married, or change email addresses. Staff have to keep customer records up to date to avoid mistakes being made. For example, communications could break down or a customer could be addressed in an inappropriate way. It is much easier to make changes on computer-based records.

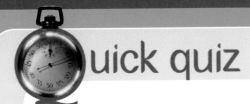

Quick quiz

1 **True or false?**

◉ Filing documents is an administrative task.

◉ Only large organisations carry out administration.

◉ Increasingly, customer records are kept on a computer.

2 Which of these personal details would **not** be required by a hotel?
(a) Medical history **(b)** Name **(c)** Address **(d)** Car registration number

3 Which of these personal details would **not** be kept by a fitness centre?
(a) Name **(b)** Passport number **(c)** Address **(d)** Telephone number

4 Which of these is **not** a requirement under the Data Protection Act 1998?
(a) Data must be kept secure **(b)** Data must be accurate and up to date
(c) Large amounts of data must not be held
(d) Customers must be sent copies of all data held

5 Why is it important to keep accurate customer records?

Portfolio practice

Latin Adventure

Marco works for Latin Adventure, a small tour operator which organises adventure holidays in Venezuela, Ecuador, Peru and Mexico. The company has built a reputation for responsible travel with an emphasis on natural history, environmental and cultural issues. It offers hiking, rafting, horseback riding, sea kayaking and snorkeling. Marco works in the office and has recently been given the job of dealing with complaints. One of the problems in his new job is that information is not collected in an organised way. He has decided to design a form to collect information from customers when they complain.

Angel Falls, Venezuela

1. State two pieces of information that Latin Adventure would need from customers when they book a holiday. *(2 marks)*

2. Latin Adventure is thinking of holding customer records on a computer database. State three advantages of this method. *(3 marks)*

3. Explain two reasons why Latin Adventure would keep customer records. *(4 marks)*

4. Design a form that Marco could use to record customer complaints. *(8 marks)*

key terms Data Protection Act 1998 – a law that organsiations must comply with when holding customer data.